D0461485

RED FLAG
OVER AFGHANISTAN

Also of Interest

Afghanistan: A Profile, Ralph H. Magnus

A Bibliography of Afghanistan, Keith McLachlan and William Whittaker

Local Politics and Development in the Middle East, edited by Louis J. Cantori and Ilya Harik

The Gulf and the Search for Strategic Stability, Anthony H. Cordesman

Oil Strategy and Politics, 1941–1981, Walter J. Levy, edited by Melvin A. Conant

†*A Concise History of the Middle East,* Second Edition, Revised and Updated, Arthur Goldschmidt, Jr.

Middle East Politics: The Military Dimension, J. C. Hurewitz

†*The Soviet Union in the Third World: Successes and Failures,* edited by Robert H. Donaldson

Afghanistan: Key to a Continent, John C. Griffiths

Soviet Involvement in the Middle East: Policy Formulation, 1966–1973, Ilana Kass

†*The Domestic Context of Soviet Foreign Policy,* edited by Seweryn Bialer

†*The Soviet Union in World Politics,* edited by Kurt London

†*The Soviet Art of War: Doctrine, Strategy, and Tactics,* edited by Harriet Fast Scott and William F. Scott

†*The Armed Forces of the USSR,* Second Edition, Revised and Updated, Harriet Fast Scott and William F. Scott

†*Red Navy at Sea: Soviet Naval Operations on the High Seas, 1956–1980,* Bruce W. Watson

†Available in hardcover and paperback.

About the Book and Author

Red Flag Over Afghanistan: The Communist Coup, the Soviet Invasion, and the Consequences
Thomas T. Hammond

How did it happen that Afghanistan, a country populated almost entirely by devout Muslims, became Communist? How did a state that had guarded its independence for centuries come to be dominated by the Soviet Union? Were the Soviets responsible for the Communist coup of April 1978, or was it a purely internal affair? Why did the Kremlin decide to invade Afghanistan: Was it one step in a master plan to gain control of Gulf oil or a defensive move to secure the USSR's southern flank against Muslim nationalism? What mistakes did the Carter administration make in its policies toward Afghanistan, and what policies should the United States follow? Will the Soviets agree to a peaceful settlement and withdraw their troops from Afghanistan?

Professor Hammond discusses these and related issues, focusing on the Communist seizure of power in Afghanistan, the disastrous policies of the various Communist leaders (Taraki, Amin, and Babrak), Soviet tactics and strategy in Afghanistan, the Afghan resistance, and possible Soviet moves in the direction of the Gulf. He makes extensive use of previously classified documents he obtained from the State Department under the Freedom of Information Act, documents that not only cast light on events in Afghanistan, but also trace the development of U.S. policy toward that country. One important document, the constitution of the People's Democratic (Communist) party, is included as an appendix.

The book benefits from Professor Hammond's interviews with former U.S. officials who helped formulate policy toward Afghanistan and the Soviet Union, including Secretary of State Cyrus R. Vance, Under Secretary of State Warren Christopher, National Security Adviser Zbigniew Brzezinski, Ambassadors Robert Neumann and Theodore L. Eliot, Jr., and Marshall Shulman, Vance's special adviser on Soviet affairs.

An authority on Communist coups, Professor Hammond edited and contributed to one of the seminal works on that subject, *The Anatomy of Communist Takeovers* (1975). He is also a recognized specialist on Soviet foreign policy and as a professor of history has taught this subject at the University of Virginia for many years. He is president of the Conference on Slavic and East European History of the American Historical Association.

My spirit will remain in Afghanistan, though my soul will go to God. My last words to you, my son and successor, are: Never trust the Russians.

—Abdur Rahman Khan
Amir of Afghanistan, 1880–1901

Turkestan, Afghanistan, Transcaucasia, Persia—to many these words breathe only a sense of utter remoteness or a memory of strange vicissitudes and of moribund romance. To me, I confess, they are the pieces on a chessboard upon which is being played out a game for the domination of the world.

—George Lord Curzon
Viceroy of India

RED FLAG OVER AFGHANISTAN

The Communist Coup,
the Soviet Invasion,
and the Consequences

Thomas T. Hammond

Westview Press / Boulder, Colorado

Copyright © 1984 by Westview Press, Inc.

Published in 1984 in the United States of America by
  Westview Press, Inc.
  5500 Central Avenue
  Boulder, Colorado 80301
  Frederick A. Praeger, President and Publisher

Library of Congress Cataloging in Publication Data
Hammond, Thomas Taylor.
  Red flag over Afghanistan
  Bibliography: p.
  Includes index.
  1. Afghanistan—History—Soviet occupation, 1979-   I.Title
DS371.2.H35   1983   958'.1044   83-10370
ISBN 0-86531-444-6
ISBN 0-86531-445-4 (pbk.)

Printed and bound in the United States of America

10   9   8   7   6   5   4   3   2

This book is dedicated to four kind professors
who treated me like a son and gave me wise counsel:

Philip E. Mosley
Dumas Malone
Joseph J. Mathews
Roland B. Parker

Contents

Figures

Preface

Two special features of this book should be noted: first, the use of previously classified documents; second, interviews with important U.S. government officials. The documents were obtained under the Freedom of Information Act—mostly from the State Department. Consisting mainly of cables and aerograms from the American Embassy in Kabul, these documents evaluate day-to-day events in Afghanistan, report interviews with Afghan officials, and make policy recommendations to Washington. They cast considerable light on developments in Afghanistan and on relations between the U.S. and Afghan governments, both before and after the communist coup of April 1978. One document of particular interest is the constitution of the People's Democratic (Communist) party, which I believe has never before been published outside of Afghanistan. (It is included as an appendix.) The Freedom of Information Office of the State Department for a long time seemed quite uninterested in supplying me with any materials at all, but patience and persistence finally paid off, and after more than a year of delay, the office cleared many items formerly marked "confidential" or "secret." Assistance in getting these documents came from Frank Machak, Thomas W. Ainsworth, Charles Mills, Benjamin Zook, Sharon Kotok, Lynn C. Dubose, Carolyn Croak, and U. Alexis Johnson, former under secretary of state for political affairs.

I was also fortunate in being able to arrange interviews with a number of important U.S. officials, past and present. Former officials whom I interviewed include Cyrus R. Vance, secretary of state in the Carter administration; Warren Christopher, his deputy secretary of state; Marshall Shulman, Vance's chief adviser on Soviet affairs (and an old friend); and Zbigniew Brzezinski, Carter's national security adviser (another old friend). Interviews were also granted by Robert G. Neumann, American ambassador in Kabul from 1966 to 1973; Theodore L. Eliot, Jr., who succeeded Neumann and served until 1978; Bruce Flatin, Eliot's political counselor; Archer K. Blood, chargé d'affaires in Kabul in 1979; and Paul Henze, a Middle Eastern expert on the National

Security Council under Brzezinski. Other interviews were with Alan Hetmanek, an expert on Central Asia formerly with the Library of Congress; Colonel James Edgar, military attaché in Kabul from 1977 to 1979; and John M. Maury, who was chief of Soviet operations at the Central Intelligence Agency (CIA) for eight years.

Officials serving in the Reagan administration were also helpful in one way or another. These include Walter J. Stoessel, Jr., former deputy secretary of state; Richard Baker, his assistant; Richard Pipes, the Soviet expert on the National Security Council (still another old friend); Gary Crocker, a specialist on Soviet military affairs at the State Department; Francis Fukuyama, a member of the State Department's Policy Planning Staff; Paul Cook, also of the State Department; Melvin Goodman of the CIA; Rear Admiral Robert P. Hilton, vice director of operations, U.S. Joint Chiefs of Staff; Robert Weinland of the Center for Naval Analyses; and Wendy Hilton of the CIA. Ernestine Heck, the Afghan desk officer at the State Department, let me examine her file of the newspaper, *Kabul Times,* and Eliza Van Hollen, a specialist on Afghanistan for the State Department's Bureau of Intelligence and Research, patiently answered my many requests for information.

I like to think that this book benefits not only from the use of previously classified documents and from interviews with government officials but also from my many years of studying and teaching Russian history, Soviet foreign policy, and Communist takeovers. This volume is, after all, as much about the USSR as it is about Afghanistan, and the United States is concerned less with what Afghans do than with what the Soviets do. To understand the Soviet invasion of Afghanistan and Soviet policies there since then, as well as to anticipate future Soviet moves in that area, one needs to be familiar with past Soviet actions in Outer Mongolia, Eastern Europe, and elsewhere. I hope that teaching courses at the University of Virginia on the history of Soviet foreign policy and preparing my book, *The Anatomy of Communist Takeovers,* have given me a broad perspective on recent events in Afghanistan.

In addition to the assistance of government officials, I received the help and encouragement of many scholars with expert knowledge of Afghanistan. Professor Leon B. Poullada of Hamline University, who served in the U.S. Embassy in Kabul in the 1950s and returned as a Fulbright scholar in the 1960s and 1970s, was kind enough to read and criticize the entire manuscript and to supply me with rare documents on the reign of King Amanullah. Professor Louis Dupree, one of the world's leading Afghanists, discussed various issues with me and gave me a copy of *On the Saur Revolution.* Professor Gaston Sigur, director of the Institute for Sino-Soviet Studies at George Washington University, shared the knowledge of Afghanistan he acquired during several years of residence in Kabul, read my manuscript, provided me with an office at his institute, and helped in other ways. Professor Richard Newell of the University of Northern Iowa took the time to look at my manuscript even though he was on his way to Asia. He and his wife, Nancy Peabody Newell, also sent me page proofs of their book, *The Struggle for Afghanistan*. Dr. Alvin J. Cottrell of the Center for Strategic and International Studies at Georgetown University explained his views on the implications of Afghan events for the Gulf area. Professor Malcolm Yapp of the School of Oriental and African Studies of the University of London spent several hours sharing his knowledge of Afghanistan and gave me a copy of a chapter he had written on recent events in that country. Henry Bradsher, who covered Afghanistan for several years for the *Washington Star,* exchanged information with me on many occasions during my year and a half in Washington. Other scholars specializing on Afghanistan who talked with me included Eden Naby of the Center for Middle Eastern Studies at Harvard and Professor Zalmay Kalilzad of Columbia University.

Interviews were granted by Habibullah Karzai, an Afghan emigré leader; Malcolm Mackintosh of the British Cabinet Office in London; and Dana Adams Schmidt, who served as a foreign correspondent in the Middle East for many years.

A number of people read and criticized all or part of the manuscript: Cyrus R. Vance, Warren Christopher, Zbigniew Brzezinski, Marshall Shulman, Richard Pipes, Gary Crocker, Bruce Flatin, Francis Fukuyama, Ernestine Heck, John L. Gaddis, Rouhollah Ramazani, Richard Parker, Vladimir Reisky de Dubnic, John A. Armitage, Wendy Hilton, Theodore L. Eliot, Jr., and Robert P. Hilton. David Powell of the Russian Research Center at Harvard spent many, many hours on a meticulous, word-by-word reading and critique of an early draft.

Former President Jimmy Carter was too busy writing his memoirs to read my chapter criticizing his administration, but he did at least respond briefly to one of the many questions I sent him. For arranging this I am grateful to his assistant, Stephen Hochman.

Very special thanks are due to the Sarah Scaife Foundation and in particular to Richard M. Scaife, chairman, and R. Daniel McMichael, secretary, for providing the financial assistance that made it possible to write this book. The preliminary research was facilitated by summer grants from the Earhart Foundation, and I am happy to express my gratitude to the trustees and to President Richard A. Ware for their support. I am also grateful to both foundations for giving me complete freedom to pursue my research and writing as I saw fit. The Center for Advanced Study of the University of Virginia did its part by naming me a sesquicentennial associate for the fall semester of 1981.

Others who helped in various ways are James Billington, director of the Woodrow Wilson International Center for Scholars; Ray S. Cline of the Center for Strategic and International Studies, Georgetown University; Abbot Gleason of the Kennan Institute for Advanced Russian Studies; Professor R. Lincoln

Keiser of Wesleyan University; James Arnold Miller, president of Interaction Systems Inc.; William Quant of the Brookings Institution; John H. Moore of the Hoover Institution; S. Enders Wimbush of the Rand Corporation; Ambassador Adam Watson, formerly of the British Foreign Service; and Samuel Wells of the Woodrow Wilson International Center for Scholars.

My wife, Nancy Bigelow Hammond, not only did everything conceivable to keep my morale high but also edited the entire manuscript several times, checked the footnotes, and helped in countless other ways.

Mr. Paul McNamara kindly allowed me to use the copying facilities at the Nantucket Cottage Hospital.

The Rockefeller Foundation extended me the privilege of spending a month writing at their delightful Bellagio Conference Center.

The highly efficient secretaries of the History Department at the University of Virginia—Lottie McCauley, Ella Wood, Kathleen Miller, and Bonnie Rittenhouse—typed large parts of the manuscript, and Ella Wood also kept my financial accounts in order. Other typists who helped were Anna Hall, Deborah Menard, Beverley Whipple, and Naomi Rich.

During the three years spent on this book I had a succession of part-time research assistants who looked up sources in libraries, made photocopies, checked footnotes, and performed other chores. They were all highly competent and deserve much thanks: Daniel Mandell, Daniel Mudd, Daniel Russell, Gennady Shkliarevsky, and Kerry O'Hara.

Thomas T. Hammond
University of Virginia
Charlottesville, Virginia

FIGURE 1. This map of Afghanistan originally appeared in Zalmay Kalilzad, "Soviet-Occupied Afghanistan," *Problems of Communism,* vol. 29, no. 6 (November–December 1980), p. 25. Prepared for *Problems of Communism* by

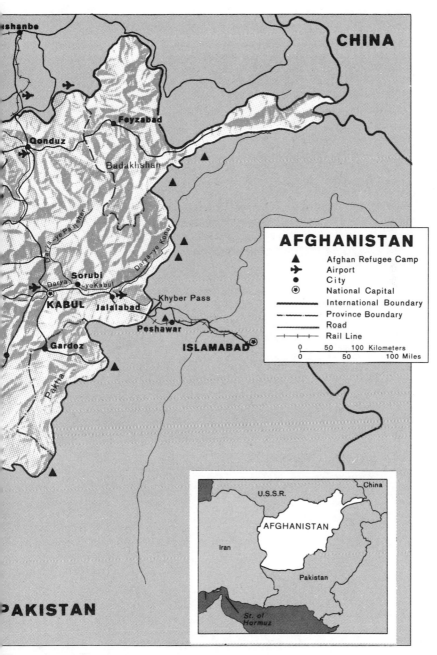

the Cartographic Services Laboratory of the University of Maryland. Reprinted by permission of *Problems of Communism*.

PART 1

Afghanistan Before
the Communist Coup

CHAPTER 1

Introduction

In July 1973 Prince Mohammad Daoud, supported by leftist officers of the Afghan army and air force, ousted King Zahir and proclaimed himself the first president of the Republic of Afghanistan.

Almost five years later, in April 1978, tanks commanded by some of the same leftist officers surrounded the palace of President Daoud. Daoud, his wife, and many of his children, grandchildren, and other relatives were killed on the spot. He was replaced by Nur Mohammad Taraki, secretary general of the People's Democratic (Communist) party.

Seventeen months later, in September 1979, Taraki was ousted (and later executed) by his "faithful student," Hafizullah Amin, who assumed all of Taraki's offices and powers.

Three months later, in December 1979, Soviet armed forces invaded Afghanistan, killed Amin, and replaced him with Babrak Karmal, a communist more subservient to their wishes. With this move the USSR gained air bases within easy striking distance of the Strait of Hormuz, acquired—in effect—a common frontier with Pakistan, and placed its troops on the eastern flank of Iran. Coming so soon after the rise to power of anti-American elements in Iran, the Soviet invasion aroused fears in the United States and allied countries that Afghanistan might be used by the Soviets as a stepping-stone to the Gulf, thereby threatening vital supplies of petroleum.

How did it happen that Afghanistan became communist, even though the population was (and is) almost 100 percent Muslim? Why did a country that had managed for centuries to maintain its independence finally fall under Russian domination? Did the Soviets give the order for the communists to overthrow Daoud, despite the fact that for years he had maintained good relations with Moscow? Or was that coup a purely internal affair? Why did the Kremlin later decide to invade the country? Was this one step in a "master plan" designed to gain control of Gulf oil? Or was it a defensive

4

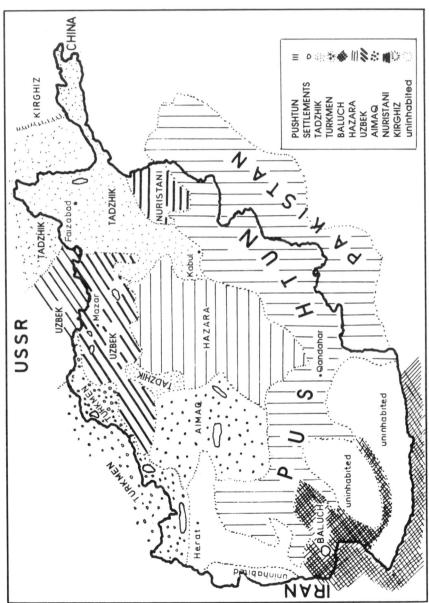

FIGURE 2. Main Ethnic Groups of Afghanistan. From John C. Griffiths, *Afghanistan: Key to a Continent* (Boulder, Colo.: Westview Press, 1981), p. 79. Reprinted by permission.

move to secure Russia's southern flank and prevent Islamic fanaticism from spreading to Soviet Central Asia?

THE LAND AND THE PEOPLE

To answer the preceding questions with any sophistication, one must first understand the history of the country and its people. Afghanistan, which is about the size of Texas, is in many respects an artificial, accidental country. Its boundaries were drawn not in order to form a united, homogeneous state, but rather to suit the whims of its neighbors. Over the centuries Afghanistan has been a "highway of conquest" for invaders—Persians, Greeks, Scythians, Huns, Mongols, Arabs, Turks, Englishmen, and Russians—and the boundaries of what today is called Afghanistan (see Figure 1) have fluctuated back and forth with the rise and fall of various Central Asian empires.[1]

As a result of this capricious history, Afghanistan today is not a national state in the modern sense of the term. For one thing, the population is very mixed ethnically and culturally. Out of a total population in 1979 of about 15,500,000, the main ethnic groups numbered approximately as follows:[2]

Pushtun (Pathan)	6,500,000
Tadzhik	3,500,000
Uzbek	1,000,000
Hazara	870,000
Aimaq	800,000
Farsiwan	600,000
Brahui	200,000
Turkmen	125,000
Baluch	100,000
Nuristani	100,000

The Pushtuns, although the leading nationality both in numbers and in political influence, constitute less than half of the population, and their dominance is resented by most of the other peoples. The cultural diversity of the country is accentuated by the fact that the various nationalities speak different languages and dialects, have different phsyical features, and practice different customs. As a result there is very little of an Afghan national consciousness. If a poll taker traveled around the country asking "What is your nationality?" or simply "What are you?" it is doubtful that many outside of the cities would answer "I am an Afghan." Instead they would identify themselves as Pushtuns, Hazaras, Nuristanis, or the like, or might describe themselves as members of a particular tribe or family or as residents of a certain village or valley.[3]

Not only is Afghanistan ethnically mixed, but most of its peoples spill over the boundaries into neighboring countries (see Figure 2). Members of almost every ethnic group in Afghanistan have brothers and sisters living across the borders. In northern Afghanistan there are Tadzhiks, Uzbeks, and Turkmen who are indistinguishable from the people living in the Tadzhik, Uzbek, and Turkmen republics of the USSR; indeed many of those in Afghanistan, or their parents, fled from the USSR after the Bolshevik Revolution. Approximately half of all Pushtuns live in Pakistan. Baluch live not only in Afghanistan, but also in Pakistan, Iran, and the USSR, while Turkmen and Tadzhiks reside in Afghanistan, the USSR, and Iran.[4]

Besides being ethnically diverse, Afghanistan also is extremely backward. Only about 10 percent of the population is literate, the annual per capita income is estimated at US$168, and life expectancy is a mere forty years.[5] There are no railroads at all in the country and few paved roads. Because communications and transportation are poor, the government offices in Kabul seem very far away to peasants in the remote valleys and mountains.

Under these conditions, most of the people in the country have little sense of national identity as Afghans, little feeling of Afghan patriotism, and little loyalty to the state. There used to be some vague sense of fealty to the king, but the monarchy was abolished in 1973. There is, above all, devotion to one's family, one's tribe, and one's religion.

Afghanistan is an underdeveloped country also in the sense that it never has had a strong, centralized government with an efficient administration. Ministers and bureaucrats have held sway in Kabul, but local chieftains and landlords have run things pretty much as they pleased in the provinces. Any regime—communist or not—that tried to infringe upon this tradition of local rule was bound to encounter resistance.

BRITISH-RUSSIAN RIVALRY

Afghanistan gained importance on the world stage in the nineteenth century because of its geographical location, just as it is important today for the same reason. The Russian tsars down through the centuries had gradually pushed their borders eastward across Siberia and southward into the broad steppes of Central Asia, while the British conquered more and more of India, extending the area under their control steadily northward. Thus both empires expanded in the direction of Afghanistan, and they inevitably clashed over which one was to dominate, or annex, this otherwise insignificant state. After many years of intrigues and maneuvers against one another, the two powers finally decided that instead of seizing parts of Afghanistan or competing for control of it, both would benefit by using it as a buffer between them. Consequently, in the Anglo-Russian Convention of 1907, Russia promised to consider Afghanistan as outside her sphere of influence and agreed to conduct relations with

Afghanistan through the British. Britain, in return, promised not to occupy or annex any Afghan territory or to interfere in the country's internal affairs.[6]

When the Bolsheviks seized power in 1917, however, they repudiated the treaties of the tsarist regime and proclaimed their goal of fomenting revolution throughout the world. They announced their intention to aid colonial peoples struggling against imperialism and sent agents to Asian countries to spread revolutionary propaganda. Lenin and his cohorts were particularly eager to incite revolutions in British colonies, since Britain was the chief instigator of Allied military intervention against the Bolshevik regime. The Bolsheviks believed that their capitalist enemies in Europe could be weakened and eventually destroyed by inciting revolutions in their rich Asian colonies. As Leon Trotsky put it, "the road to Paris and London lies through the towns of Afghanistan, the Punjab, and Bengal." Lenin made many statements along the same line, declaring, for example, that "the outcome of the struggle" between capitalism and communism "will be determined by the fact that Russia, India, China, etc., constitute the overwhelming majority of the population of the globe."[7]

During the first months of their rule, however, the Bolsheviks were busy trying to retain power and paid little attention to Afghanistan. When it did come to their notice, they were interested in it primarily for two reasons, one defensive and the other offensive. Defensively, they wanted to keep Britain out of Afghanistan for fear that Britain would use the country as a route to invade Russia and overthrow the Soviet government or seize Soviet territory. Offensively, the Bolsheviks looked upon Afghanistan as a stepping-stone to India—a base from which they could incite the Indian people to rise up and throw out the British.

Soviet and Afghan interests coincided in part because both were afraid of the British. Britain had exercised strong influence in Afghanistan for many years and, after a series of wars, had forced the Afghans to let Britain conduct their foreign relations. The Afghans wanted to get out from under British control and achieve complete independence, and they hoped that Soviet Russia would help them achieve this goal. Eventually, of course, the British got out, and Afghanistan gained its independence. Later, however—as we shall see—it fell under foreign domination once more, this time by Soviet Russia.

NOTES

1. A brief summary of the history of Afghanistan is contained in Chapters 13 through 17 of Louis Dupree, *Afghanistan* (Princeton, N.J.: Princeton University Press, 1980), pp. 255–413.

2. Ibid., pp. 59–62. The total population figure is from U.S. Department of State, Bureau of Public Affairs, *Background Notes: Afghanistan* (Washington, D.C.: Government Printing Office, April 1980), p. 1. Population figures for Afghanistan

are little more than guesses. For an excellent discussion of the ethnic situation, see Eden Naby, "The Ethnic Factor in Soviet-Afghan Relations," *Asian Survey,* vol. 20, no. 3 (March 1980), pp. 237–256.

3. This paragraph and much of this section was inspired by an interview with Professor Gaston Sigur, who lived in Afghanistan for several years and is now director of the Institute for Sino-Soviet Studies at George Washington University.

4. Naby, "The Ethnic Factor," pp. 238–240; Alexandre Bennigsen, "Soviet Muslims and the World of Islam," *Problems of Communism,* vol. 29, no. 2 (March-April 1980), p. 40, says that there were 13,000 Baluch in the USSR in 1970.

5. U.S. Department of State, *Background Notes,* p. 1.

6. Dupree, *Afghanistan,* p. 433. On page 342 there is a map of "Russian Advances in Central Asia; British Advances in India."

7. Both quotations are cited by Professor Albert L. Weeks in the *New York Times Book Review,* June 21, 1981, p. 13.

CHAPTER 2

King Amanullah and the First Soviet Invasions of Afghanistan

> *The position of Russia in Central Asia is that of all civilized states which are brought into contact with half savage, nomad populations possessing no fixed social organization. In such cases it always happens that the more civilized state is forced, in the interests of security of its frontiers and its commercial relations, to exercise a certain ascendancy over those whom their turbulent and unsettled character makes undesirable neighbors.*
> —Prince Alexander M. Gorchakov
> Russian foreign minister, 1864[1]

When the Soviet armies marched into Afghanistan in December 1979, few people realized that this was nothing new, that the Soviet Union had invaded its southern neighbor at least three times previously—in 1925, 1929, and 1930. Although two of these invasions were rather small-scale affairs, with limited objectives, and none of them came close to matching the massive assault of 1979, one of the invasions—in 1929—involved thousands of troops and thousands of casualties and had as its aim nothing less than the overthrow of the Kabul government.

AMANULLAH'S INITIAL RELATIONS WITH SOVIET RUSSIA

The amir (later king) of Afghanistan during the first two invasions was Amanullah Khan, a reformer who tried to modernize his backward country in a manner similar to what Kemal Ataturk had done in Turkey and Reza Shah had done in Iran. Amanullah called himself a revolutionary, and he regarded Lenin as a brotherly spirit. In 1919, soon after seizing power,

Amanullah sent a friendly letter addressed to Lenin, the "High-Born President of the Great Russian Republic."[2] Lenin replied and did two things that greatly pleased Amanullah—recognized his accession to the throne and recognized the independence of Afghanistan.[3]

At about the same time, Amanullah demanded that the British grant similar recognition to him and his country, and he added emphasis to his demand by attacking India. Although his army was defeated, the British acceded to his demands anyhow. Britain was exhausted from World War I and India was in rebellion, so London signed a treaty giving Afghanistan full independence. This concession may have been granted in part because the British feared that otherwise Amanullah would become friendly with Russia.[4]

Later Amanullah sent a second cordial letter to Lenin, and on November 27, 1919, Lenin answered, calling Amanullah the leader of "the only independent Muslim state in the world" and declaring that Afghanistan was preordained for "the greatest historic task of uniting around itself all the enslaved Muslim peoples and leading them on the road to freedom and independence." Soviet Russia and Afghanistan, he said, should "continue the joint struggle against the most rapacious imperialistic government on earth— Great Britain." Lenin also suggested that the two countries sign a treaty of friendship and offered to give Afghanistan military aid against England.[5]

Soviet Mistreatment of Its Muslims

The prospect for friendly relations between Amanullah and Moscow was soon clouded over, however, by Soviet mistreatment of the Muslims in Russia. Before the Bolshevik Revolution, Lenin and his trusted lieutenant Stalin (who later became commissar of nationalities) promised that all of the peoples of the Russian Empire would be granted the right of self-determination, even including secession. Both men, after they seized power, continued to preach "self-determination," but in practice they ruthlessly suppressed movements for independence and autonomy wherever possible, using armed force when necessary.

Amanullah was naturally interested in how the new Soviet government treated its Muslim nationalities, particularly those in the Emirate of Bokhara and Khanate of Khiva, located just north of Afghanistan. These two Muslim states had been protectorates of tsarist Russia, retaining sovereignty over their internal affairs but allowing Russia to control their foreign relations. When the tsar was overthrown and the Bolsheviks proclaimed the right of national self-determination, Bokhara and Khiva asserted their independence and established close ties with Afghanistan. Amanullah was delighted; he began to dream of founding a Central Asian confederation under his leadership.

Bokhara and Khiva did not remain independent for long, however. As soon as the Bolsheviks finished fighting against the White Russians and foreign interventionists in other parts of Russia, they sent elements of the

Red Army to reconquer Bokhara, Khiva, and other Muslim-populated areas. This outraged Amanullah, who dispatched Afghan soldiers and artillery to the aid of his coreligionists. In 1920 Soviet troops nevertheless captured the two Muslim states, forcing their rulers to flee into exile in Afghanistan. Amanullah gave them refuge and sent aid to the Basmachi, the Moslem rebels in Central Asia who continued to fight against Soviet domination.[6]

The Basmachi freedom fighters of Soviet Central Asia were remarkably similar to the freedom fighters of Afghanistan half a century later, and Afghanistan in the earlier period served as a haven for anticommunist rebels in much the same way that Pakistan does today. Basmachi guerrillas who were hard pressed by the Bolsheviks would flee across the frontier into Afghanistan, where they could rest, regroup, and obtain weapons for further fighting. When the Basmachi were finally defeated, many of them settled permanently in Afghanistan, and those who were still alive in 1980 (or their descendants) took up arms against the Soviets once more.

Afghan-Soviet Treaty of 1921

Although Amanullah was very angry at the Soviet Union because of its policies in Central Asia, he was also fundamentally, consistently anti-British (he had inherited this bias from his mother). If he was to get aid from any major power in that area, therefore, he had no place to turn to but Russia. The Soviets, for their part, were eager to have friendly relations with Amanullah, so they made him several attractive promises: (1) to respect the independence of Bokhara and Khiva (a promise they never kept); (2) to return two districts, Terek and Kerki, that had been seized by Russia in the nineteenth century (another promise that was not kept); and (3) to give Amanullah a subsidy of 1 million rubles a year (a promise that was only partly kept). Amanullah did not know that the Soviets would be so duplicitous, however, and in February 1921 he agreed to a treaty of friendship.[7]

One of the advantages of this treaty from the Soviet point of view was the prospect that Afghanistan could be used as a base for fomenting revolution in India. The Bolsheviks sent some Indian revolutionaries to Kabul, where they were allowed to establish a "Provisional Government of the People of India," and plans were made to train and equip an "Indian Liberation Army" in Afghanistan. The Soviet ambassador in Kabul, Joseph Surits, also dispatched secret agents among the Pushtun tribes along the Indian frontier in an effort to get them to commit acts of violence against the British. Surits even dreamed of using Soviet planes with Afghan pilots for air attacks in support of the Indian revolutionary movement. According to Amanullah's chief of intelligence, the king knew about these anti-British activities and approved of them.[8]

In 1924 Amanullah was faced by a rebellion of Afghans opposed to his internal reforms, and the Soviets came to his rescue with warplanes, which bombarded the rebels into submission. The Soviets also helped him in other ways: they erected telephone and telegraph lines, built a radio station, established an airline connecting Kabul with Tashkent and Moscow, and gave him a dozen airplanes, along with the pilots and mechanics to service them.[9]

THE FIRST SOVIET INVASION

The following year, however, Afghan and Russian interests came into conflict once more, leading to the first small-scale Soviet invasion of Afghanistan. The Amu Darya (Oxus River), which had marked the boundary between Russia and Afghanistan since 1872, shifted its course at the end of the nineteenth century so that the island of Urta Tagai—which previously had been north of the main channel—now lay south of it. Over the years Afghans had gradually settled on the 160-square-mile island, and Kabul considered it Afghan territory. After the Bolshevik Revolution, about 1,000 Uzbek refugees from Soviet Central Asia moved to the island, including some Basmachi, who used it as a base for raids into Soviet territory. Suddenly, in 1925, Soviet troops invaded Afghanistan and declared the island annexed to the USSR.[10] Thus the first Soviet invasion of Afghanistan occurred not in 1979, but more than fifty years earlier.

Grigorii Agabekov, who served as a Soviet secret police (OGPU) agent in Afghanistan and later became chief of the OGPU's Eastern Section, arrived on the scene shortly after the invasion. He gives this account in his memoirs, written after he defected:

When I reached Tashkent [in December 1925], the Red Army had just taken possession of a certain island in the River Amu Daria. . . .

The general representative of OGPU at Tashkent explained to me, not without a smile, that never, no, never, would the Red Army violate the Afghan frontier.

"But," he exclaimed, "the population of that island, very discontented with the Afghan authorities, have effected a social revolution and have demanded annexation of the island as an independent district of the U.S.S.R."

Still smiling, he begged me to spread that interpretation in the course of my journey through Afghanistan.

I protested that the business might have disastrous consequences, whereupon he became serious and told me the truth as follows: The island in question had served as a base for insurrectionary bands which thence invaded Soviet territory. For strategic reasons it was therefore decided to seize it. One night Red soldiers, natives of the neighboring region, in civilian clothes, invaded the island, arrested the authorities, and proclaimed its annexation to the U.S.S.R. . . .

The Turkestan authorities had acted on their own initiative and without consulting Moscow, and they hoped that the Moscow Government would ratify the *fait accompli*. However, to fortify their position, they proceeded to

a referendum. The world should know that "the population as one man
expressed the wish to be annexed to the U.S.S.R."[11]

This story sounds believable. On many occasions, both before and after
1925, Soviet forces have moved into an area, taken control of it by force,
and then held a "referendum" in which the local people supposedly voted
to be annexed to the Soviet Union. They did this in the districts of Terek
and Kerki, which the Soviets had promised to return to Afghanistan in the
treaty of February 1921, and they used similar tactics in the Baltic States
in 1940 and Carpatho-Ukraine in 1945.[12] The only thing surprising about
Agabekov's story is the statement that the Turkestan authorities acted on
their own, without first consulting Moscow, but this part of his account seems
to have been substantiated by subsequent events.

The Afghan government was greatly alarmed by the annexation of the
island. According to Agabekov, the Afghan army "openly demonstrated"
against Russia, public opinion in Afghanistan was "violently aroused," and
the members of the Soviet mission in Kabul did not dare to show their faces
in public.[13] King Amanullah sent additional troops to the northern part of
the country and hinted that war might break out momentarily.[14] England
also was alarmed by the invasion: the British minister in Kabul warned
London that this might be the first step in a gradual infiltration of northern
Afghanistan, until all the country north of the Hindu Kush would become
a Russian province.[15]

Moscow apparently decided that the island was not worth the price of
antagonizing both the Afghans and the British; so in 1926 it withdrew all
of its troops, signed a protocol recognizing Afghan ownership of the disputed
area, and followed this up with a treaty of neutrality and nonaggression.[16]

THE REBELLION AGAINST AMANULLAH

In the years that followed, Amanullah encountered no more serious problems
with the Soviets, but he aroused dangerous opposition from his own subjects
by his Western ways and his radical reforms. Many Afghans were upset when
King Amanullah and Queen Soraya went on a grand tour of Europe and
the Middle East in 1927–1928. Photographs reached Afghanistan showing
the queen in public wearing European clothes and without a veil. The king,
said his enemies, "had turned against Allah and Islam!"[17]

When Amanullah returned to Kabul, after seeing the many wonders of
the outside world, he was more determined than ever to westernize his country,
and he announced a program of reforms that aimed "to alter completely the
structure and nature of Afghan society."[18] He reduced the autonomy of the
tribes and the influence of the religious leaders, opposed polygamy and the
veil, established schools for girls, required the delegates to the Loya Jirgah

(a national assembly) to wear Western clothes, and extended the military draft to the whole country. Behaving as if he were deliberately trying to antagonize his subjects, Amanullah also increased the customs duties and introduced a new monetary system, which caused economic hardship for many. As a result of all these unpopular measures, another revolt broke out. In January 1929 Amanullah, forced out of Kabul, fled to Qandahar in his Rolls-Royce. The leader of the rebellion was an illiterate Tadzhik bandit called Bacha-i-Saqao ("Son of a Water Carrier"), who proclaimed himself king and formed a ministry consisting partly of peasants like himself, some of whom could not even sign their own names.[19]

The Soviet Reaction

The Soviet government now faced an unexpected situation—a revolt by the "poor, oppressed masses" of Afghanistan against an autocratic king who was friendly toward the USSR. How should Moscow react to this situation? Should it rally behind the popular revolution, or should it save the monarchy? From an ideological point of view the Soviets obviously belonged on the side of "Son of a Water Carrier," but, as always, Russian national interests had to be considered, and a debate ensued among top officials in Moscow.

Fortunately, we have an inside source of information about these secret debates—Agabekov, the former OGPU official. He said the OGPU argued in favor of aiding Bacha in the hope that he would carry out a radical revolution in Afghanistan and that, through him, the country would gradually be sovietized. The commissariat of foreign affairs, on the other hand, pointed out that most of Bacha's supporters were Tadzhiks, Uzbeks, Turkmen, and other nationalities who lived in northern Afghanistan, just across the frontier from their fellow ethnics in Soviet Central Asia. This being the case, Bacha would probably adopt a hostile attitude toward the USSR and would support the Basmachi, the anticommunist rebels who had fled in large numbers from the USSR to Afghanistan. Amanullah, by contrast, was a Pushtun and got most of his support from the Pushtuns, who resented British rule over their fellow tribesmen in India. So it seemed that the king was more likely than Bacha to follow pro-Soviet and anti-British policies. In addition, Moscow claimed that the British minister in Kabul had negotiated the surrender of Kabul to Bacha, and it suspected (probably unjustly) that the British had supplied him with arms. Besides, there was considerable doubt in Moscow that Bacha and his fellow peasants could hold power very long in a country that traditionally had been ruled by Pushtun monarchs and tribal chieftains. According to Agabekov, the Politburo took the advice of the commissariat of foreign affairs and decided to aid the king.[20]

This decision is not surprising when viewed from the perspective of earlier Soviet actions in similar situations. In the case of Turkey, for example, the newborn Soviet government at first encouraged the Turkish communist party and tried to foment revolution. But it soon decided that the prospects for communizing Turkey were not very good and that Russian national interests would be better served by cooperating with the anti-British government of Kemal Ataturk. So the Soviet government concluded a treaty of friendship with Kemal in March 1921 and issued no more appeals for the Turkish workers and peasants to revolt against his government.[21]

Similarly, the Bolsheviks initially tried to overthrow the government of Iran, in 1920 even going so far as to send troops to support Kuchik Khan's revolutionary "Soviet Republic of Gilan." But before long the Bolsheviks realized that it would be more advantageous for them to have friendly relations with the government in Teheran. So they signed a treaty of friendship with Iran in February 1921 and, some months later, withdrew their troops from Iran. The Soviets abandoned Kuchik Khan, telling him that they favored a "strong central government" in Iran because it would be "dependent on Soviet Russia" and would oppose the "imperialist" activities of the British in Iran.[22]

The Soviet decision to aid Amanullah in 1929 can be compared with these earlier actions in Turkey and Iran. In all three countries the communist movements were either weak or nonexistent and the prospects for communist revolutions were correspondingly poor. All three were ruled by men who wished to reduce British influence in the area, an aim the Bolsheviks shared. So the Soviets postponed their goal of communizing their neighbors and made peace with the existing regimes. The cause of world revolution was subordinated to the national interests of the Russian state.

The Politburo's decision to aid Amanullah was probably due also to the influence of the four Charkhi brothers, all of whom held important positions in Amanullah's government: Ghulam Nabi, minister to Moscow; Ghulam Siddiq, foreign minister; Ghulam Jilani, who had been governor of Mazar-e-Sharif but was now minister to Turkey; and Abdul Aziz, who succeeded Ghulam Jilani as governor of Mazar.[23] Ghulam Nabi, the minister in Moscow, "pleaded earnestly with the Soviet Government to give energetic support" to Amanullah.[24] Soon his pleas were reinforced by those of Ghulam Siddiq, the foreign minister, whom Amanullah had sent to Moscow, and Ghulam Jilani, who arrived from Turkey.[25]

Agabekov says that Ghulam Jilani met one night with Stalin and Vitalii Primakov, an experienced military commander who had been a hero in the Russian civil war, a military adviser to the Nationalist Army in China in 1925–1926, and military attaché in Kabul since 1927.[26] "It was decided," according to Agabekov, "to form an expeditionary force of Red soldiers disguised as Afghans," who would "secretly cross the frontier and march against Kabul." "The nominal leader" would be Ghulam Nabi, but the real leader would be Primakov.[27]

THE SECOND SOVIET INVASION

Specialists on Afghanistan generally write about this second invasion as if it were entirely an Afghan affair and Ghulam Nabi was its sole leader, without even mentioning Primakov. Agabekov and another former Soviet official, Alexander Barmine, on the other hand, describe the invasion as primarily a Soviet operation, with Ghulam Nabi serving largely as a front man. This difference in point of view is reflected, for example, in conflicting statements on the nationality of the troops who invaded Afghanistan. Agabekov and Barmine say they were Red Army soldiers disguised as Afghans, but Professor Ludwig Adamec, Ali Ahmed Mohmand (Amanullah's private secretary), and a British General Staff report all say the troops were Afghan subjects who had been living in the Soviet Union.[28] As we have seen, the Soviets had used the device of camouflaging Red Army soldiers as Afghans earlier, in the invasion of 1925. There have been other occasions where Moscow used its ethnic minorities for military operations in neighboring countries. In 1921, for example, it launched an invasion of Outer Mongolia with a combined army of native Mongols, Soviet Mongols, and other Soviet soldiers.[29] All things considered, it seems most likely that the 1929 invasion of Afghanistan also was carried out by a mixed army of natives and Soviet citizens who looked like natives. Finding Soviet subjects who could pass as Afghans would not have been difficult since several of the ethnic groups living in Soviet Central Asia were the same as those living in northern Afghanistan. Perhaps in some cases the men didn't know what their citizenship was— Soviet or Afghan—but simply looked upon themselves as Turkmen or Uzbeks or whatever.[30]

The sources also disagree as to the size of the army that invaded Afghanistan. Agabekov says 800 men, one British report says 1,000, Ali Ahmed Mohmand says 1,500, and another British report puts the figure at 6,000. All agree, however, that Russia supplied the rifles and other military equipment. According to a British attaché reporting from Peshawar, the Soviets provided forty airplanes, as well as horsemen specially equipped with machine guns.[31]

In any event, the small army, with its arms and ammunition, was assembled at the Soviet town of Termez, just north of the Afghan frontier—the same place where, fifty years later, another Soviet expeditionary force would gather. After Soviet airplanes machine-gunned the Afghan frontier guards, the soldiers crossed the Amu Darya. Ghulam Nabi, once he reached Afghan territory, was able to recruit more soldiers, increasing the size of his army to about 8,000 men.[32] Then they marched south and, after considerable fighting, captured the town of Mazar-e-Sharif on April 30, 1929. Agabekov says that about 2,000 Afghans were killed in this part of the expedition.[33]

Since two of Ghulam Nabi's brothers had been governors of Mazar-e-Sharif and Ghulam Nabi himself had served as commandant there, he had good connections in this area and was able to get additional troops to join his force.[34] This enlarged army then marched east, took the town of Khulm, killed around 3,000 of Bacha-i-Saqao's supporters, and prepared to push on toward Kabul.[35] At this point it looked as though the invasion force, with its superiority in weapons and Soviet air support, might defeat Bacha, take Kabul, and restore Amanullah to his throne. The British War Office received unconfirmed reports that the Soviet Union had decided to send "volunteers" from Central Asia to help in the fighting.[36] Bacha was fearful, and he issued the following proclamation: "My dear brethren! I again remind you and inform you that Amanullah has been cursed by God, the Prophet. He is a loser in this as well as in the world to come. . . . Rest assured from this direction, and exert for the arrest of Ghulam Nabi the infidel drunkard."[37]

Bacha apparently retaliated against the Soviets by encouraging two Basmachi leaders to make raids into the Soviet Union from Afghanistan. Whether due to Bacha's instigation or not, Ibrahim Beg and Faizullah Khan, prominent Basmachi commanders, did make successful incursions into Soviet territory at this time, and the Soviet press claimed that either Bacha or the British had instigated these attacks.[38]

At this critical moment, with Ghulam Nabi, Primakov, and their army marching toward Kabul, word came that Amanullah had abdicated and fled with his family to India. The whole *raison d'être* for the campaign disappeared, and most of the forces recruited by Ghulam Nabi deserted.[39] The Soviets promptly withdrew their troops, the last of them leaving Afghanistan in June 1929.[40] Moscow perhaps decided that without Amanullah it would be difficult to set up a pro-Soviet regime in Kabul. Agabekov says that the Bolshevik leaders also were influenced by the hostile reaction the invasion had provoked in several European states, as well as in Turkey and Persia.[41] Georgii Chicherin, the Soviet commissar of foreign affairs, later confirmed this: "Our adversaries spread the rumor that a red army detachment was on the way to Kabul. Teheran was immediately on its feet in utmost wrath. Soviet soldiers in Kabul!!! Immediately we assured Persia it was untrue. Russian soldiers or artillery in Kabul would have meant war with England: so near India!!!"[42]

The Soviets were eager not to alarm the British at that particular moment, because the Kremlin was hoping to restore diplomatic relations, which had been broken off by the Conservatives in 1927. Ramsay MacDonald, the leader of the Labour party, had promised during his election campaign that he would grant recognition to the Soviet government, and when he came to power on June 7, 1929, the Soviets expected that normal relations would be reestablished promptly and trade would grow rapidly.[43] Arousing British fears about India might prevent the USSR from achieving these important objectives.

Another factor that may have influenced Stalin to abandon the Afghan invasion was the First Five Year Plan. In 1929 he was deeply involved in trying to carry out his "revolution from above," designed to expand Soviet industry and collectivize agriculture, and perhaps he didn't want to expend any more of his manpower and resources on Afghanistan at that time.

The Soviet regime had demonstrated, nonetheless, that, like its tsarist predecessor, it had ambitions regarding Afghanistan and was willing to use military force to back them up. As Agabekov said, "the result was definitely to compromise Red prestige and Communist influence in Afghanistan. He [Stalin] confirmed in the most outrageous manner the accusations of imperialism against the Soviet regime.[44]

Bacha-i-Saqao, the illiterate adventurer, ruled for nine months, until October 1929, when he was driven out by Mohammad Nadir Khan, a member of one branch of the Afghan royal family. Nadir Khan reigned as king until 1933. He reversed all of Amanullah's unpopular reforms, and—most important—largely eliminated Russian influence in Afghanistan.[45]

THE THIRD INVASION

During the reign of Nadir Khan the Soviets staged their third small invasion of Afghan territory. This came about as a result of the Soviet campaign against the Basmachi. One of the Basmachi leaders, an Uzbek named Ibrahim Beg, made repeated raids against the Soviets, fleeing each time for refuge into Afghanistan. Finally, in June 1930, the exasperated Soviet forces crossed the Amu Darya and pursued Ibrahim Beg for about forty miles into Afghanistan. They failed to capture him, but the invasion naturally alarmed the Afghan government. The following year Afghan forces drove Ibrahim Beg across the border into the Soviet Union, where he was captured and killed.[46]

Nadir Khan was assassinated in 1933 and was succeeded by his young son, Mohammad Zahir, who reigned, but did not rule, for forty years. Real power lay in the hands of relatives, including three uncles, who ran Afghanistan as if it were a family enterprise. Zahir was not an energetic or ambitious man, and the first two decades of his rule were a period of stagnation.[47] During this period, Afghanistan lived largely detached from the rest of the world. Stalinist Russia, meanwhile, was busy building "socialism in one country," and efforts to foment revolutions in other lands were given low priority for the time being.

NOTES

1. Quoted in Firuz Kazemzadeh, "Afghanistan: The Imperial Dream," *New York Review of Books,* vol. 27 (February 21, 1980), p. 11. The statement comes from Gorchakov's circular memorandum to the Russian foreign service, November

9, 1864. The author is extremely grateful to Professor Leon B. Poullada of Hamline University for reading and criticizing this chapter.

2. Fred Halliday, "Revolution in Afghanistan," *New Left Review*, no. 112 (November-December 1978), p. 11. For good scholarly accounts of Amanullah and his reign, see: Leon B. Poullada, *Reform and Rebellion in Afghanistan, 1919–1929; King Amanullah's Failure to Modernize a Tribal Society* (Ithaca, N.Y.: Cornell University Press, 1973), and Ludwig W. Adamec, *Afghanistan's Foreign Affairs to the Mid-Twentieth Century; Relations with the USSR, Germany, and Britain* (Tucson: University of Arizona Press, 1974).

3. Harish Kapur, *Soviet Russia and Asia, 1917–1927: A Study of Soviet Policy Towards Turkey, Iran and Afghanistan* (Geneva: Michael Joseph, 1966), pp. 217–219.

4. Ibid., pp. 218–220; letter to the author from Leon B. Poullada, August 3, 1982.

5. Louis Fischer, *The Soviets in World Affairs* (London: Jonathan Cape, 1930), vol. 1, p. 286.

6. Kapur, *Soviet Russia and Asia*, pp. 222–225. See also Seymour Becker, *Russia's Protectorates in Central Asia: Bukhara and Khiva, 1865–1924* (Cambridge: Harvard University Press, 1968); Richard Pipes, *The Formation of the Soviet Union; Communism and Nationalism, 1917–1923*, rev. ed. (Cambridge: Harvard University Press, 1954); and Alexander Park, *Bolshevism in Turkestan, 1917–1927* (New York: Columbia University Press, 1957).

7. Kapur, *Soviet Russia and Asia*, pp. 227–229; Adamec, *Afghanistan's Foreign Affairs*, p. 61; letter to the author from Professor Poullada, August 3, 1982.

8. Notes of an interview conducted by Leon Poullada with Mahmood Khan Yawar, Amanullah's chief of intelligence, March 31, 1968, supplied to the author by Professor Poullada; Kapur, *Soviet Russia and Asia*, pp. 230–233.

9. Louis Dupree, *Afghanistan* (Princeton, N.J.: Princeton University Press, 1980), p. 451; Kapur, *Soviet Russia and Asia*, pp. 238–239; Xenia Joukoff Eudin and Robert C. North, *Soviet Russia and the East, 1920–1927* (Stanford, Calif.: Stanford University Press, 1957), pp. 262–263.

10. Adamec, *Afghanistan's Foreign Affairs*, p. 109.

11. Georges [Grigorii] Agabekov, *OGPU: The Russian Secret Terror* (New York: Brentano's, 1931), pp. 69–70. Agabekov worked for the OGPU in Afghanistan from 1924 to 1926.

12. According to Leon Poullada in his letter of August 3, 1982, the Soviets held a fake plebiscite in Terek and Kerki, and everyone supposedly voted to stay in the USSR. On the Baltic States see Edgar Thomson, "The Annexation of the Baltic States," in *The Anatomy of Communist Takeovers*, ed. by Thomas T. Hammond (New Haven, Conn.: Yale University Press, 1975), pp. 225–228. On Carpatho-Ukraine see F. Nemec and V. Moudry, *The Soviet Seizure of Subcarpathian Ruthenia* (Toronto: W. B. Anderson, 1955). In 1945 the Chinese government promised Moscow that it would recognize the independence of Outer Mongolia if the people indicated that this was their wish. Later it was announced that 100 percent of the Mongolians had voted for independence, which meant, in effect, that Outer Mongolia remained a protectorate of the USSR.

13. Agabekov, *OGPU*, p. 71.

14. Adamec, *Afghanistan's Foreign Affairs,* p. 110.

15. Ibid.

16. Ibid., pp. 111–112.

17. Dupree, *Afghanistan,* p. 450.

18. Poullada, *Reform and Rebellion,* pp. 79–80. The reforms are described by him in great detail on pages 66–142.

19. Nancy Peabody Newell and Richard S. Newell, *The Struggle for Afghanistan* (Ithaca, N.Y.: Cornell University Press, 1981), pp. 37–38; Adamec, *Afthanistan's Foreign Affairs,* pp. 139–144; Poullada, *Reform and Rebellion,* pp. 170–172, 177; Vartan Gregorian, *The Emergence of Modern Afghanistan* (Stanford, Calif.: Stanford University Press, 1969), pp. 264–265, 276.

20. Agabekov, *OGPU,* pp. 164–165. The negotiations for the surrender were described by Sir Francis Humphrys, the British minister, in a letter to the foreign secretary that is quoted in Adamec, *Afghanistan's Foreign Affairs,* pp. 144–145. According to Adamec, pp. 150–151, the British government did not support Bacha, but adopted a policy of neutrality and nonintervention. By refusing to let arms for Amanullah pass through India, however, it helped Bacha's cause.

21. Kapur, *Soviet Russia and Asia,* pp. 91–103; Walter Z. Laqueur, *The Soviet Union and the Middle East* (New York: Praeger, 1959), pp. 26–29.

22. Rouhollah K. Ramazani, *The Foreign Policy of Iran, a Developing Nation in World Affairs, 1500–1941* (Charlottesville: University Press of Virginia, 1966), pp. 151–154, 190–191. The Soviet message to Kuchik Khan, which is quoted by Ramazani on p. 191, was from the Soviet ambassador to Iran, Theodore Rothstein. It might be pointed out that 1921 marked an important turning point in Soviet foreign policies not only in Turkey and Iran, but elsewhere; the Soviet leaders realized that their early optimism about world revolution was premature and that it was essential for them to come to terms with existing governments. As a consequence, between 1921 and 1939 the Soviets made only one major effort to spread communism to another country—the ill-fated adventure in China. Stalin's next big push to spread communism came, of course, during and after World War II.

23. Adamec, *Afghanistan's Foreign Affairs,* p. 192; Poullada, *Reform and Rebellion,* p. 185.

24. Agabekov, *OGPU,* p. 166.

25. Ali Ahmed Mohmand, "The Fall of Amanullah," pp. 41–42. These are unpublished memoirs written by Amanullah's private secretary and translated by Major R. N. Scott of the British Army. Portions were copied for the author by Leon Poullada.

26. Agabekov, *OGPU,* p. 166; Ilia V. Dubinskii, *Primakov* (Moscow: "Molodaia Gvardiia," 1968), p. 173; *Who Was Who in the USSR* (Metuchen, N.J.: Scarecrow Press, 1972), p. 462. The commander's full name was Vitalii Maksimovich Primakov.

27. Agabekov, *OGPU,* pp. 166–167. Agabekov says that he was in Moscow at the time, and thus he was presumably in a position to know about these decisions. Most books and articles by Afghan specialists on this period do not mention Primakov, Agabekov, or Agabekov's book. Soviet sources, of course, have good reasons not to reveal anything about the role of the USSR in the invasion.

28. Ibid. Barmine, a Soviet diplomat who defected, says in his memoirs: "The Politburo decided to send the crack troops of the Red army to his [Amanullah's] assistance. Two divisions entrained for Afghanistan to fight for Amanullah." Barmine, *One Who Survived; The Life Story of a Russian Under the Soviets* (New York: Putnam's, 1945), pp. 230–231. Adamec, *Afghanistan's Foreign Affairs*, p. 160, says: "According to unconfirmed British intelligence reports, Ghulam Nabi was able to raise about one thousand Afghans in Soviet territory, including some Soviet Kirgiz soldiers who could easily be taken for Afghan Hazaras. They were officered by some twenty Afghans who had come with Ghulam Nabi from Europe." The British account referred to is in *Military Report; Afghanistan, Part I, History, General Staff, India, 1940* (Simla: Government of India Press, 1941), p. 192. It says: "Ghulam Nabi's force was composed of Afghan subjects living in Soviet territory." However, it also reports (p. 193) that Russian casualties were found on the field of battle after a clash between the troops of Ghulam Nabi and those of Bacha-i-Saqao.

29. Thomas T. Hammond, "The Communist Takeover of Outer Mongolia: Model for Eastern Europe?" in *The Anatomy of Communist Takeovers,* ed. by Thomas T. Hammond, pp. 12–21.

30. See the ethnic maps in Dupree, *Afghanistan*, p. 58, and Poullada, *Reform and Rebellion*, p. 294.

31. Telegram to the Government of India from the Oriental Attaché, Peshawar, no. 25, dated June 9, 1929, in Archives of the India Office Library, London, LPS/10/1203, p. 135/1927. Professor Poullada kindly supplied the author with a copy of this document.

32. Ali Ahmed Mohmand, "The Fall of Amanullah," p. 42.

33. Agabekov, *OGPU,* p. 167. The date is from Adamec, *Afghanistan's Foreign Affairs,* p. 160.

34. Poullada, *Reform and Rebellion,* p. 185; Ali Ahmed Mohmand, "The Fall of Amanullah," p. 43.

35. Agabekov, *OGPU,* p. 168.

36. Adamec, *Afghanistan's Foreign Affairs,* p. 161.

37. Ibid.

38. Ibid., p. 162.

39. Poullada, *Reform and Rebellion,* p. 186.

40. Agabekov, *OGPU,* p. 168.

41. Ibid., pp. 168–169.

42. Louis Fischer, *Men and Politics; An Autobiography* (New York: Duell, Sloan and Pearce, 1941), pp. 144–145.

43. Fischer, *The Soviets in World Affairs,* vol. 2, p. 817; K.W.B. Middleton, *Britain and Russia: An Historical Essay* (London: Hutchinson, 1947), pp. 144–145. There is an interesting parallel between "linkage" then and now. The Soviets withdrew from Afghanistan in 1929 partly because they wanted to have good relations with Britain, whereas the Soviet refusal to withdraw from Afghanistan today has hindered good relations with the United States and other countries. (Suggested by Leon Poullada.)

44. Agabekov, *OGPU,* p. 170.

45. Halliday, "Revolution in Afghanistan," p. 14.

46. Dupree, *Afghanistan,* pp. 460–461; Adamec, *Afghanistan's Foreign Affairs,* p. 202.

47. Halliday, "Revolution in Afghanistan," p. 14.

CHAPTER 3

Afghanistan and the Great Powers After World War II

I went there [to Afghanistan] with Bulganin . . . on our way back from India [in 1955]. We were invited by the king of Afghanistan to stop over in Kabul. . . .

It was . . . clear that America was courting Afghanistan. . . . The Americans were undertaking all kinds of projects at their own expense—building roads, giving credit loans, and so on. But . . . the Americans . . . hardly bother to put a fig leaf over their self-centered, militaristic motives. . . .

It's my strong feeling that the capital which we've invested in Afghanistan hasn't been wasted. We have earned the Afghans' trust and friendship, and it hasn't fallen into the Americans' trap; it hasn't been caught on the hook baited with American money.

—Nikita Khrushchev[1]

With the establishment of the independent states of India and Pakistan in 1947, the British left South Asia. Their departure opened the way for the Soviet Union to increase its influence in Afghanistan, but Stalin was busy with postwar reconstruction and the consolidation of his hold on Eastern Europe and he paid little attention to the Third World. It was not until his death and Khrushchev's rise to power that the Soviet Union began to court the Third World actively and to compete with the United States in substantial aid programs.

When Britain left the area, the United States to some extent took its place. After World War II the United States began making small loans and grants to Afghanistan, although there was no attempt to establish dominant American influence. Successive administrations in Washington realized that, for geographic reasons, Afghanistan had to maintain good relations with the Soviet Union. Afghanistan was looked upon as "the Finland of Asia," a small state located next to the Soviet Union and therefore eager to avoid antagonizing it. In addition the United States considered Afghanistan an unimportant country, with few natural resources and relatively little strategic importance. U.S. goals were to maintain a presence in the country, assist in economic development, and encourage the Afghans to maintain their independence.[2]

THE PUSHTUNISTAN ISSUE

Soviet influence in Afghanistan increased in the 1950s partly because of the Pushtunistan issue. The Pushtuns are the largest ethnic group in Afghanistan; there are between 6 and 7 million of them in Afghanistan and almost as many in Pakistan. (All population figures for Afghanistan are estimates.) When the British moved out of India, the Afghan government hoped that the Pushtuns living in the Northwest Frontier Province would be given a chance to choose between being independent or becoming part of Afghanistan. Instead the British insisted that the Pushtuns join either India or Pakistan; the Pushtuns, being Muslim, chose Pakistan. The Afghans claim the Pushtun areas of Pakistan not only on ethnic grounds but also on historic grounds, since the Northwest Frontier Province formerly was part of Afghanistan. It is natural, therefore, for Afghanistan to demand that these Pushtuns be liberated from Pakistani rule and be allowed to rejoin their brothers and sisters in Afghanistan. Pakistan has of course refused.[3]

This issue has repeatedly poisoned relations between the two countries. When the Afghan government has actively engaged in agitation and propaganda on the Pushtunistan issue, the Pakistan government has retaliated by closing the frontier to Afghan trade, thereby blocking the natural route for most Afghan exports and imports. This has often caused Afghanistan to seek Soviet aid. The Soviets have, of course, been happy to support Afghanistan against Pakistan since Pakistan is a friend of the United States. After border clashes in 1950, Pakistan closed the frontier, and in the same year the Soviet Union signed a new trade agreement with Afghanistan; during the next five years, trade between Afghanistan and the USSR increased by 50 percent. This turn toward the Soviet Union gained further impetus when the United States refused to give arms to Afghanistan, but chose instead to send military aid to Pakistan, which joined the South East Asia Treaty Organization (SEATO) in 1954 and the Baghdad Pact (later called the Central Treaty Organization or CENTO) in 1955. To Kabul it seemed that the United States was arming the Afghans' chief enemy while rejecting their own appeals for arms. Thus on two crucial issues—Pushtunistan and military aid—the United States refused to support Afghanistan, whereas the Soviet Union was glad to do so. As a result of decisions on these issues in the 1950s, Afghanistan moved further and further into the Soviet sphere of influence, and this led eventually to the Communist coup of 1978 and the Soviet invasion of 1979.[4]

SOVIET AID TO AFGHANISTAN

In October 1954 Prime Minister Mohammad Daoud sent his brother to Washington to make another appeal to Secretary of State John Foster Dulles for military assistance. In December Dulles not only rejected the Afghan request, but did so in a manner that infuriated the Afghans. One month later, in January 1955, Daoud turned to the Soviets for military aid. Moscow responded in a big way the following December when Communist party First Secretary Khrushchev and Prime Minister Bulganin visited Kabul as part of their new policy of wooing the Third World. Whereas in January 1954 the Soviet leaders had loaned Afghanistan a mere $3.5 million,* this time they granted a $100-million line of credit, some of it for military aid, the rest economic. Among the development projects agreed to were highways, bridges, the Bagram airport north of Kabul, and the Salang Pass tunnel through the towering Hindu Kush. It was probably no accident that the roads and bridges Moscow constructed were strong enough and wide enough to carry the Soviet tanks that invaded Afghanistan two decades later. Similarly, the Salang tunnel and the chain of supply depots for grain and oil were on the main road used by the invading Soviet army, and the Soviet-built airfields at Shindand and Bagram were important landing sites for the Soviet airborne troops that were flown into Afghanistan in December 1979. Thus the Soviets used their aid program to prepare the way for their subsequent conquest of Afghanistan![5]

Daoud and the Soviets also agreed that large numbers of Afghan army and air force officers would be sent to the USSR for training. In the years that followed several thousand Afghan officers attended military schools in the USSR and Czechoslovakia, whereas those trained in the United States numbered only in the hundreds.[6] The decision to send officers to the Soviet Union for training may have been one of the most fateful choices ever made by the Afghan government. As a result, a majority of the officer corps spent some time in the USSR, where the Soviets could attempt to indoctrinate them with pro-Soviet and procommunist views or recruit them as Soviet agents.[7] Even those officers who went to the Soviet Union and did not become communists often returned home with a desire to change the existing order. In addition, the Soviet-trained officers generally were viewed with suspicion by the king and were not allowed to rise to top positions; thus, many were resentful and opposed the royal government.[8] It is not surprising, therefore,

---

*Most international trade and aid figures, including Soviet ones, are expressed in U.S. dollars. That convention is followed throughout this book.

that army officers played an essential role in the ouster of the king in 1973 and in the communist seizure of power in 1978. It is armies, after all, that usually carry out such coups.

U.S. POLICIES TOWARD AFGHANISTAN

Should the United States have given military aid to Afghanistan to prevent it from turning to Russia? Robert G. Neumann, who served as ambassador to Afghanistan from 1966 to 1973, says that Secretary of State Dulles refused the Afghan request because, in view of Afghanistan's "location and poor communications, an enormous logistics effort would have had to be undertaken by the U.S. where the risk of escalating the Cold War would have been high."[9] Theodore L. Eliot, Jr., who succeeded Neumann, agrees, adding that Dulles was probably influenced by two other factors: (1) the United States had close ties with Pakistan, which was a much more important country, and (2) Washington was afraid that sending military equipment to Afghanistan would so alarm the Soviets that they would make some kind of move against Afghanistan.[10] The decision to refuse arms was consistent with general U.S. policy toward Afghanistan. U.S. diplomacy, says Ambassador Neumann, "recognized tacitly that the Soviet Union had a legitimate interest in stability along its southern border, while the U.S. interest was of a lesser degree, that is, to help Afghans protect their independence."[11] Washington also may have felt that even huge amounts of military aid would not have made Afghanistan secure if the Soviet Union ever decided to invade the country. The United States did, however, continue to give economic aid, although not as much as the Soviet Union.

U.S. policy toward Afghanistan prior to the communist takeover was well summed up by Ambassador Neumann in a Policy Review that he prepared for the State Department in June 1971. It said in part:

> For the United States, Afghanistan has at the present limited direct interest; it is not an important trading partner; it is not an access route for U.S. trade with others; it is not presently . . . a source of oil or scarce strategic metals; . . . there are no treaty ties or defense commitments; and Afghanistan does not provide us with significant defense, intelligence, or scientific facilities. . . .
>
> However, . . . Afghanistan has important interests for us which have in large part derived from its strategic location between Central Asia and the Indian subcontinent.[12]

The United States, he continued, had certain objectives in Afghanistan:

> A. The preservation of Afghanistan's independence and territorial integrity;
> B. The creation of a viable political and economic system, responsive through evolutionary change to the needs and desires of the people;

C. The prevention of Soviet influence in the country from becoming so strong that Afghanistan would lose its freedom of action; and

D. The improvement of Afghanistan's ties with Pakistan and Iran.[13]

While recommending that the United States continue to pursue these objectives, Neumann nonetheless recognized that Washington was in no position to try to gain greater influence in Afghanistan than the Soviet Union. As he said in his Policy Review:

> The United States has long understood that Afghanistan has had little choice but to have close relations with the USSR. Among the factors are: the long border, the slowly developing desire to transform the economy and the concomitant need for massive economic assistance; the decision to have a modern military force; and the intermittent preoccupation with its quarrels with Pakistan. The Soviets responded to these opportunities and since 1953 they have assiduously exploited the situation and developed a strong position here with considerable and growing influence and leverage.[14]

Ambassador Neumann then listed additional factors that tended to produce strong Soviet influence in Afghanistan: (1) the fact that the USSR was Afghanistan's largest trading partner; (2) the large debt owed to Moscow; (3) the infiltration of the government by Soviet agents; (4) Afghanistan's dependence on Soviet arms; (5) strong Soviet influence in, and financial support for, the educational system; (6) the large exchange program for military and civilian students; and (7) the vast Soviet propaganda apparatus in Afghanistan. As a result of all this, he said, "although the RGA [Royal Government of Afghanistan] may not do everything the Soviets wish it to do, it is rare that the RGA does what the Soviets strongly wish it *not* to do."[15]

U.S. policy toward Afghanistan remained remarkably consistent, under both King Zahir and President Daoud, and under both Ambassadors Neumann and Eliot. Annual policy reviews sent from the American Embassy in Kabul to the State Department contained few modifications in the recommendations.[16] This is not surprising, however, because the underlying geographic, economic, and political situation remained basically unchanged until the communist coup in April 1978.

NOTES

1. Nikita Khrushchev, *Khrushchev Remembers* (Boston: Little, Brown, 1970), pp. 507–508.

2. Interview with Theodore L. Eliot, Jr. Eliot was the American ambassador to Afghanistan from 1973 to 1978. He is now dean of the Fletcher School of Law and Diplomacy.

3. Theodore L. Eliot, Jr., "Afghanistan After the 1978 Revolution," *Strategic Review,* vol. 7, no. 2 (Spring 1979), pp. 58–59; Fred Halliday, "Revolution in Afghanistan," *New Left Review,* no. 112 (November-December 1978), pp. 8, 15; Stephen Oren, "The Afghani Coup and the Peace of the Northern Tier," *The World Today,* vol. 30, no. 1 (January 1974), pp. 26–32.

4. Halliday, "Revolution in Afghanistan," p. 16; Eliot, "Afghanistan After the 1978 Revolution," pp. 58–59; Nancy Peabody Newell and Richard S. Newell, *The Struggle for Afghanistan* (Ithaca, N.Y.: Cornell University Press, 1981), pp. 41–42; Leon B. Poullada, "Afghanistan and the United States: The Crucial Years," *The Middle East Journal,* vol. 35, no. 2 (Spring 1981), pp. 186–189. Poullada's detailed article is very critical of American policy during these years.

5. Halliday, "Revolution in Afghanistan," pp. 15–18; Hannah Negaran [pseud.], "The Afghan Coup of April 1978: Revolution and International Security," *Orbis,* vol. 23, no. 1 (Spring 1979), pp. 97–98; Poullada, "Afghanistan and the United States," pp. 187–189; Leon B. Poullada, "Soviet Activities in Afghanistan During the First Daoud Regime, 1953–63," paper delivered at the South Asia Conference, University of Wisconsin-Madison, November 3–6, 1982, pp. 3–4. Poullada was counselor for economic affairs in the U.S. Embassy in Kabul from 1954 to 1958 when the Soviet aid program was begun.

6. Hasan Kakar, "The Fall of the Afghan Monarchy in 1973," *International Journal of Middle Eastern Studies,* vol. 9, no. 2 (May 1978), p. 212.

7. Bruce Flatin, who served as political counselor in the American Embassy in Kabul from 1978 to 1980, says flatly that "many of the Afghan officers trained in the USSR became communists." Interview, September 3, 1980.

8. Kakar, "The Fall of the Afghan Monarchy," p. 212.

9. Robert Neumann, "Afghanistan Under the Red Flag," in *The Impact of the Iranian Events Upon Persian Gulf and U.S. Security,* ed. by Z. Michael Szaz (Washington, D.C.: American Foreign Policy Institute, 1979), p. 130.

10. Interview with Ambassador Eliot, August 13, 1980, and Eliot, "Afghanistan After the 1978 Revolution," p. 58.

11. Neumann, "Afghanistan Under the Red Flag," p. 130.

12. Airgram no. A-71 from Kabul to State, June 26, 1971, p. 1 (this airgram contained the Policy Review). This is one of many classified State Department documents obtained by the author under the Freedom of Information Act.

13. Ibid., pp. 1–2.

14. Ibid., p. 4.

15. Ibid., pp. 4–5.

16. See, for example, the annual policy assessments contained in the following documents sent from Kabul to the State Department: airgram no. A-66 of June 5, 1972; cable no. 01090 of February 21, 1974; cable no. 01837 of March 26, 1975; cable no. 01765 of March 9, 1976; airgram no. A-26 of March 24, 1976; cable no. 00468 of January 19, 1977; airgram no. A-6 of January 27, 1977, and airgram no. A-13 of February 27, 1978.

CHAPTER 4

The King and the Communists

KING ZAHIR AND PRIME MINISTER DAOUD

King Mohammad Zahir, who occupied the throne from 1933 to 1973, was a rather weak, indifferent ruler, who left most of the work of governing to his relatives, including Prince Mohammad Daoud, his cousin and brother-in-law. Daoud, a bald, chubby-faced man with thick lips and black-rimmed glasses, was much more able and energetic than the king, and he dominated the government as prime minister from 1953 to 1963. Daoud was a fairly enlightened, forward-looking administrator who built up the economy and expanded education. After a decade as prime minister, he wrote a series of letters to the king in which he proposed a sweeping program of reforms, including the granting of a constitution. The king failed to respond; perhaps he and his advisers decided that Daoud was becoming too bossy. It may be that the two cousins also disagreed on the Pushtunistan issue and relations with the USSR. In any event, Daoud left the government and for ten years remained on the sidelines, watching with a disapproving eye as the king ruled without him.[1]

There is disagreement as to whether Daoud or the king took the initiative in Daoud's departure from office, but since Daoud loved power it is unlikely that he left on his own initiative. The king probably would not have had the courage to fire Daoud if he had not been encouraged to do so by leading members of the royal family. There is an interesting story about the dismissal, which may or may not be true: When the king told Daoud he would have to step down, Daoud reportedly said in effect, "You can't run the country without me; I have the army on my side." Whereupon the king retorted, "If you think so, pick up the phone and call the army." Daoud telephoned some of the generals and, to his surprise, got no support because the king had sent a relative to the army officers in advance to make sure of their loyalty. This exchange is not documented, but troops did patrol the streets of Kabul for several days after Daoud was fired, in case there was any trouble.[2]

No sooner had Daoud left the government than the king adopted many of the reforms Daoud had recommended. In 1964 he introduced his "New Democracy" program, which included a constitution, a parliament, elections, freedom of the press, and freedom to form political parties.[3]

THE PDPA AND ITS FOUNDERS

During this period of liberalization, on January 1, 1965, the People's Democratic Party of Afghanistan (PDPA), a communist party in fact if not in name, was formed.[4] Its secretary general, later to become the first president of communist Afghanistan, was Nur Mohammad Taraki.

Nur Mohammad Taraki

The son of a Pushtun shepherd, Taraki was born in a provincial village in 1917, the year of the Bolshevik Revolution—a fact that he later pointed to with pride. While just a teenager, Taraki got a job with a fruit company, which sent him to Bombay, where he learned Marxism from Indian communists. In 1937 he returned to Afghanistan and worked in several government jobs, including that of editor-in-chief of the official news agency. In 1952 the government sent him to Washington, D.C. to serve as press attaché in the Afghan embassy. While there he decided to defect, called a press conference, criticized Prime Minister Daoud, and requested political asylum. Ironically enough, some U.S. bureaucrat made the fateful decision to refuse him asylum, so Taraki was forced to return home, where he subsequently carried out a communist revolution![5]

Taraki went back to Kabul, where, according to his official biography, he telephoned Daoud and said, "I am Nur Mohammad Taraki. I have just arrived. Shall I go home or to prison?"[6] Surprisingly, in view of Taraki's reputation as a leftist and his earlier criticism of Daoud, he was not sent to prison but was given a job at the official Afghan news agency. Later he worked as a translator and interpreter for the U.S. aid mission and the American Embassy in Kabul.[7]

A distinguished-looking—perhaps even bourgeois-looking—man with thin gray hair, bushy black eyebrows, and a neat mustache, Taraki seems to have been more an intellectual than a practical administrator. He wrote poetry, novels, and other works and became the leader of a group of radical intellectuals, some of whom he converted to Marxism. It was not surprising, therefore, that the founding meeting of the PDPA was held in his house and that he was elected secretary general.

Hafizullah Amin

Another prominent member of the PDPA was Hafizullah Amin, the man who would become the second president of communist Afghanistan. About a dozen years younger than Taraki, Amin was a husky, muscular, handsome man, with a full head of hair and a strong, rugged face. Like Taraki, Amin was a Pushtun and had spent some time in the United States but none in the Soviet Union. In 1957 he won a scholarship to Teachers College at Columbia University, where he earned an M.A. degree. When he returned to Afghanistan, he served as principal of the Kabul Teacher Training High School for several years. Then in 1963 he received another scholarship to Columbia, this time to work for a Ph.D., which he never finished. He is reputed to have become a radical as a result of attending a summer work-study camp at the University of Wisconsin.[8] He was elected president of the Associated Students of Afghanistan in the U.S.A. and tried to use the organization to radicalize his fellow students. When he returned to Afghanistan in 1965, he got a job at the University of Kabul, where he actively recruited students to the revolutionary cause.[9]

Years later, after Amin had become president of Afghanistan, an American diplomat described him as follows: "The man is impressive. His survival to date is by itself impressive, as is the air of quiet self-confidence he exudes. . . . He masks his ruthlessness and toughness quite well by his soft-spoken manner. In remarkable contrast to his turgid public speeches, his private discourse is refreshingly free from Marxist cant and cliches. His English is quite good and very easy to understand."[10] Another official from the American Embassy also found it difficult to resist Amin's attractive personality. "He was all charm and friendliness. . . . It was . . . hard to realize in talking with this friendly fellow that it was he too that [sic] has been directly responsible for the execution of probably 6,000 political opponents. In everything he said, he sounded reasonable and projected the image of a man you could reason with and reach understanding."[11]

Babrak Karmal

A third founding member of the PDPA, who eventually became the third president of communist Afghanistan, was Babrak Karmal. Babrak's most prominent physical feature was a large hook nose, which marred an otherwise pleasant face. Unlike Taraki and Amin, Babrak was a city boy and came from the upper class, his father being a general in the army. There were rumors that he adopted the name "Karmal" because it was an abbreviation for "Karl-Marx-Lenin," but this is quite unfounded.[12] Elected to parliament, Babrak established a reputation as a charismatic leader and an eloquent orator. His connections with the Soviet embassy were known to be very close; indeed, he was probably a KGB (Soviet secret police) agent.[13]

The Newspaper *Khalq*

Taking advantage of the freedom of the press that King Zahir had granted as part of his "New Democracy," the PDPA started a newspaper called *Khalq,* which published six issues between April 11 and May 16, 1966. The general line followed by *Khalq* was very similar to that of the Soviet press, as indicated by this typical quotation, "The main issue of contemporary times and the center of the class struggle on a world-wide basis, which began with the great October Revolution, is the struggle between International Socialism and International Imperialism."[14]

THE PDPA SPLITS INTO KHALQ AND PARCHAM

In 1967, only about a year and a half after its founding, the People's Democratic party split into several factions, the two most important being Khalq ("masses") headed by Taraki and Parcham ("banner") headed by Babrak. The split was in part over organizational tactics; Taraki favored a Leninist-type party based on the working class, while Babrak wanted to form a broad national-democratic front.[15] Also separating the two groups were the personal backgrounds of the members: those in Khalq were mainly Pushtuns from the country, while those in Parcham tended (with exceptions) to be non-Pushtuns who spoke Persian, came from the big cities (especially Kabul), and had benefited from better education and more prosperous backgrounds.[16]

Babrak's faction began issuing its own newspaper, *Parcham,* and managed to continue publication more than a year (from March 1968 to July 1969), much to the annoyance of the Khalq faction, whose paper had been banned. As a result, Khalq accused Parcham of having connections with the king and even referred to Parcham as the "Royal Communist Party."[17] The rivalry between the two factions, however, was less ideological or tactical than personal. Ambassador Neumann states that Taraki and Babrak hated each other so much that they even quarreled in his presence.[18] According to Neumann, "Parcham was regarded as the official communist party. Babrak told me that personally. He prided himself on his close relations with the Soviet embassy. The Parcham line was always exactly the same as the Soviet line."[19]

Still, Soviet relations with Khalq were close also. It was Taraki who later headed the united party. Apparently Moscow maintained ties with both factions, keeping its options open, and waiting to see how events would unfold.[20] This is not to say, however, that Moscow treated either Khalq or Parcham as full-fledged communist parties, worthy of ranking among the important organizations in the world communist movement. No Afghan delegate ever spoke at any of the congresses of the Communist Party of the Soviet Union during the decade prior to the 1978 revolution, and no message from Khalq or Parcham was read at any of these meetings.[21] As far as we know, neither Taraki,

Amin, Babrak, or any of the other top civilians in Khalq or Parcham had ever been invited to attend an international communist conference,[22] which would indicate that the Kremlin did not take the two parties very seriously. Perhaps it also meant that the Kremlin was not expecting them to seize power in the near future. Another indication of the limited contact between Afghan communists and the Soviet Union prior to the coup is the fact that when the first postrevolution cabinet was appointed, most of the ministers knew English, but only four (three of them military men) knew Russian. Ten of them had attended schools in the United States, but only four had been trained in the Soviet Union.[23] Nevertheless, the Afghan communists looked to the USSR as their model, mentor, and friend.

NOTES

1. Hasan Kakar, "The Fall of the Afghan Monarchy in 1973," *International Journal of Middle Eastern Studies,* vol. 9, no. 2 (May 1978), pp. 198–199.

2. Fred Halliday, Robert Neumann, and Theodore Eliot say that Daoud was dismissed, while Louis Dupree, Hannah Negaran, and Hasan Kakar say that he resigned. Professor Gaston Sigur told the story about the conversation between Zahir and Daoud, but does not vouch for its authenticity.

3. Fred Halliday, "Revolution in Afghanistan," *New Left Review,* no. 112 (November-December 1978), p. 19.

4. In countries where there is little support for communism it is common for communist parties to disguise their true nature by using some harmless-sounding name.

5. Louis Dupree, *Red Flag Over the Hindu Kush.* Part I: *Leftist Movements in Afghanistan* (Hanover, N.H.: American Universities Field Staff Reports, 1979/no. 44, Asia), pp. 6–7; Hannah Negaran [pseud.] "The Afghan Coup of April 1978: Revolution and International Security," *Orbis,* vol. 23, no. 1 (Spring 1979), p. 96.

6. *Kabul Times* (October 30, 1978), quoted in Richard S. Newell, "Revolution and Revolt in Afghanistan," *The World Today,* vol. 35, no. 11 (November 1979), p. 434.

7. Secret cable from Kabul to State Department, no. 03372, April 20, 1978, p. 2.

8. Louis Dupree, *Red Flag Over the Hindu Kush.* Part II: *The Accidental Coup, or Taraki in Blunderland* (Hanover, N.H.: American Universities Field Staff Reports, 1979/no. 45, Asia), p. 5; Nancy Peabody Newell and Richard S. Newell, *The Struggle for Afghanistan* (Ithaca, N.Y.: Cornell University Press, 1981), p. 61.

9. Newell and Newell, *The Struggle for Afghanistan,* p. 61.

10. Comments by Archer K. Blood in cable no. 07726 from Kabul to State, October 28, 1979, p. 5.

11. Observations by J. Bruce Amstutz, chargé d'affaires of the American Embassy in Kabul, in cable no. 7218 from Kabul to State, September 27, 1979, p. 1.

12. Halliday, "Revolution in Afghanistan," p. 22; Newell and Newell, *The Struggle for Afghanistan,* p. 62. Afghans usually do not have family names. According

to Louis Dupree, Babrak Karmal was given the name "Babrak" by his parents; it means "Little Tiger." Years later he added "Karmal," which means "work-loving" or "hard-working." It is not quite correct to refer to him as "Karmal," but either "Babrak" or "Babrak Karmal" is proper. His father is named Mohammad Hussein Khan.

13. Interview with Gaston Sigur. Vladimir Kuzichkin, a former KGB major, says that Babrak "had been a KGB agent for many years." *Time,* November 22, 1982, p. 33. A "reliable Afghan official" who served as minister of the interior in the 1960s told Leon Poullada that, after examining the police dossiers, he concluded that the leaders of the PDPA were "controlled, subsidized, paid, and ordered directly by KGB elements of the Soviet embassy in Kabul." Leon B. Poullada, "The Failure of American Diplomacy in Afghanistan" (mimeographed article), p. 21.

14. Negaran, "The Afghan Coup of April 1978," p. 96.

15. Halliday, "Revolution in Afghanistan," p. 25. *Tariqush Shaab,* a publication of the Communist party of Iraq, in issue no. 841 (June 23, 1974), published an article describing Babrak as "the founder of the party" and denouncing Taraki for his "bureaucratic attitude" and "divisive policies." It says further that the Khalq "splinter group" had become "the center of Maoist activities" and had "caused the interference of the American CIA" in Afghanistan. The article was translated in airgram no. A-79 from Kabul to State Department, October 15, 1978.

For a sample of Khalq views as to how the government should be organized, see the "Outline of the Proposal of the Central Committee of the Afghanistan Khalq Democratic Party, Party of the Painstaking People of Afghanistan, For Drafting the Constitution," dated April 4, 1976, which was translated in airgram no. A-41 from Kabul to State Department, May 24, 1978. This proposal apparently was prepared during the period when Daoud was writing his own constitution and the communists presumably hoped to have some influence on its contents.

Apparently Parcham was in close touch with the Communist party of Pakistan. On June 1–5, 1976, meetings took place in Kabul between the two parties. According to their "Joint Statement," the delegation of the PDPA was headed by "its General Secretary, Comrade Babrak Karmal." The Joint Statement was translated in airgram no. A-58 from Kabul to State, June 29, 1977. It took a strongly pro-Soviet line.

16. Interview with Habibullah Karzai, November 30, 1980. Karzai is a high-ranking member of the Popolzai tribe, now living in Pakistan.

17. Negaran, "The Afghan Coup of April 1978," p. 97, footnote 7; Newell, "Revolution and Revolt," p. 435; Louis Dupree, "Afghanistan under the *Khalq,*" *Problems of Communism,* vol. 28, no. 4 (July-August 1979), p. 38.

18. Interview, September 4, 1980.

19. Ibid.

20. The Soviets honored Taraki by awarding him a literary prize. Halliday, "Revolution in Afghanistan," p. 26.

21. *Events: News Magazine of the Middle East,* no. 45 (June 16, 1978), p. 28.

22. Dupree, "Afghanistan under the *Khalq,*" p. 39.

23. Ibid., p. 40; Dupree, *The Democratic Republic of Afghanistan, 1979* (Hanover, N.H.: American Universities Field Staff Reports, 1979/no. 32, Asia), p. 2.

CHAPTER 5

Daoud as President, 1973–1978

DAOUD OUSTS KING ZAHIR

Although King Zahir's "New Democracy" permitted greater freedom than before, it promised more than it delivered. Elections were held in 1965 and 1969, but only 10 percent of the electorate participated; the third election, scheduled for 1973, never took place. The parliament was dominated by conservatives who blocked progressive legislation, and when a liberal law somehow was passed, the king usually vetoed it. A third or more of the members of parliament were illiterate, and often business could not be conducted because a quorum was lacking.[1] The press was far from free, the controls being particularly severe after the elections of 1969. The Constitution of 1964 did not limit the powers of the king in any way, and he was not responsible to anyone. The king, moreover, was rather lazy, let things drift, and spent much of his time abroad.[2]

The communists also share a considerable part of the blame for the failure of King Zahir's experiment in constitutional democracy. The communists made inflammatory speeches in parliament, exploited resentments that had been accumulating during the king's years of dictatorial rule, and organized street riots that resulted in bloodshed. These tactics so alarmed the king that he refused to sign the law legalizing political parties. Meanwhile, "the new and inexperienced parliament, instead of concentrating on legislation, quickly degenerated into a forum for irresponsible criticism of the government and the royal family."[3]

Robert G. Neumann, who was the U.S. ambassador in Kabul at the time, described the king's situation in June 1972 as follows: "For the King and leadership group, survival is the first objective with all other goals considered secondary. The result is an excessively cautious governing style which invariably seeks to balance off external and internal forces perceived as threatening the regime's power. Domestically new power groups increasingly press for progress."[4] Further on in his policy review he added: "Barring progressive decisions or very good luck, the survival of the present Government for more than another year is problematical."[5] Since the king was overthrown thirteen months later, this was a remarkable prediction.

Prince Mohammad Daoud, cousin and brother-in-law of the king and former prime minister, presumably had found one feature of the 1964 Constitution very irksome—the provision that no member of the royal family could hold a top position in the government. Daoud must have suspected that this provision had been designed by the king for the precise purpose of preventing Daoud's return to high office. After running the country for ten years, Daoud probably found it frustrating to sit on the sidelines. It is not surprising, therefore, that he plotted to seize power, particularly since he knew that he had the support of many army and air force officers.

The officers had good reasons to favor Daoud. First of all, he was the man who as prime minister had obtained large supplies of modern arms from the Soviet Union. Second, Daoud had brought about closer ties with the USSR, which appealed to those officers who were pro-Soviet.[6] Third, Daoud was a former army officer himself, having been commander of the central-forces garrison, with the rank of lieutenant-general. In addition, progressive Afghans had been antagonized by the king's on-again off-again reform program. Having been promised change, many politically active Afghans were determined to have it.

Daoud discussed rebellion for more than a year with various opposition elements—both moderates and leftists, including military officers, Parchamis, and Khalqis.[7] The king made the mistake of leaving Afghanistan to visit Italy, thus making it easier for the plotters. On July 17, 1973, while the king was taking the mud baths at Ischia, army units supporting Daoud occupied strategic points in Kabul and encountered no organized opposition. The almost bloodless coup was over in a few hours.[8]

Daoud went on the radio and announced that the monarchy was being replaced by "a republican system, consistent with the true spirit of Islam." He promised to institute "basic reforms" designed to achieve "a real democracy to serve a majority of the people," in contrast with the "pseudo-democracy" of the king's "corrupt system," based "on personal and class interests, intrigues and demagogy."[9] Daoud became the founder, president, and prime minister of the Republic of Afghanistan. Abolishing the monarchy may have been a fatal mistake on Daoud's part. The masses were accustomed to having a king, and the monarchy was one of the few unifying forces in the diverse, loosely organized country. As a member of the royal family, he could easily have assumed the title of "king." By failing to do this, he undermined his own claim to legitimacy and made it easier for a commoner, a few years later, to assume his title of "president."[10]

DAOUD AND PARCHAM

The Parcham party had supported Daoud's coup, and he rewarded it by appointing several leftists to government positions, including Faiz Mohammad, who became minister of the interior. In addition, Daoud gave important positions in the armed forces to officers close to Parcham, including Major Abdul Qader and Mohammad Aslam Watanjar, both leaders in the coup that placed Daoud in power and the one that later deposed him.[11] Ambassador Eliot reported from Kabul in 1975 that it was widely believed that Parcham wielded great power: "In the first few months following the coup, there were reports that Babrak Karmal and his principal lieutenants . . . formed a kind of subcommittee of the GOA [Government of Afghanistan] Central Committee, which passed on all senior appointments in the GOA. During this same period, there were reported defections from . . . Khalq . . . to the Parchamists, who clearly appeared to be coming out on top."[12] Scores of eager young members of Parcham were sent out into the provinces to reform the rural administration, but most of them eventually became frustrated, disillusioned, or corrupt or were fired or quit.[13]

Before long Daoud began to reduce the power of the leftists in the government and moved his regime somewhat to the right. Parcham officials, one by one, were either dismissed outright or sent abroad to diplomatic posts. The left-wing minister of the interior was replaced by a rightist, and Major Qader was relieved of his command. Daoud was even reported to have threatened some of the leftists with castration![14] However, Daoud refrained from taking an openly anticommunist stance. Ambassador Eliot described the ambiguous relationship between Daoud and the Left in 1975 as follows:

> There has been no explicit voicing of anti-leftist sentiment. . . . While Daoud's domestic "platform" might be described as "populist" and includes calls for land reform and educational parity, he publicly eschews socialism and carries the banner of unreconstructed Islam during all his public speeches. Those leftist officials who have been fired have never had their ideological beliefs thrown up as a reason for dismissal, but only their corruption or inefficiency. . . .
>
> We believe it most likely that Daoud, having used the left to gain power, is now methodically and cautiously trying to whittle it down. . . . He is snipping away at some of the left's strength without leaving himself open to charges of discrimination against it. . . .
>
> In looking toward its future the Afghan left must contend with an entrenched autocrat who does not brook competition. . . .

Offsetting this disadvantage are the advantages of geographical proximity to the Soviet Union and the fact that no Afghan government can afford to antagonize the USSR by persecuting pro-Soviet communists too openly.[15]

Early in 1977 Daoud introduced a new constitution. It called for the appointment of a new cabinet, and the leftists hoped, of course, that they would be well represented. Instead Daoud chose a cabinet consisting of "friends, sons of friends, sycophants, and even collateral members of the deposed royal family."[16] The constitution permitted only one political party to operate legally, the National Revolutionary party, and Daoud took the rather undemocratic step of personally selecting the members of its central committee.[17]

DAOUD CHANGES HIS FOREIGN POLICIES

Daoud also disappointed the Left by changing his foreign policies—that is, by loosening somewhat his dependence on the Soviet Union and strengthening his relations with other countries, particularly Pakistan and Iran. This did not happen immediately, however. During the first few years of his presidency, he continued his earlier policies of hostility toward Pakistan and faithful support of the USSR. In 1974 he gave his endorsement to the Soviet Union's plan for an Asian "collective security" arrangement,[18] indicated feelings of hostility toward Iran, and supported the Pushtuns and Baluch in Pakistan. In 1975 Pakistan accused him of training 15,000 Pushtun and Baluchi guerrilla fighters to carry out rebellions in Pakistan.[19]

It was natural for Daoud to champion the Pushtunistan issue. He was a Pushtun himself, and his great-great-grandfather had been the last Afghan ruler of the Pushtun area of Pakistan.[20] Championing nationalistic claims is a good way of winning popular support, as many a ruler has discovered. During his years as prime minister, Daoud had beaten the propaganda drums on the Pushtunistan issue, and this had forced him to seek military and economic aid from the Soviet Union, as we saw earlier. When he became president, he followed the same policies at first.

Before long, however, Daoud made noticeable shifts in his foreign policies. He joined with Pakistan's President Bhutto to reduce the conflict over the Pushtunistan issue, perhaps to avoid the closing of the important trade route through Pakistan, and perhaps in part in response to American influence. Ambassador Eliot says that he urged Daoud to become truly nonaligned and to improve his relations with other states in the Middle East. Washington also asked Iran, Saudi Arabia, Kuwait, and Japan to give more economic assistance to Afghanistan. According to Eliot, the United States realized that Afghanistan had to maintain good relations with Russia, but wanted Afghanistan to be truly independent; the United States thought that the Pushtunistan conflict had made Afghanistan excessively dependent on Moscow. Since Pakistan was a friend of the United States, Washington also wanted to keep Pakistan out of unnecessary disputes and obviously did not wish to see Pakistan dismembered by Pushtuns and Baluch.[21]

Another person urging Daoud to improve his relations with Pakistan was the shah of Iran. Iran and Pakistan traditionally have been friendly, and the shah had even guaranteed the territorial integrity of Pakistan against any aggressor, whether India or Afghanistan. The shah also knew that any attempt by Afghanistan to promote the dismemberment of Pakistan would be a threat to Iran, because there was a large Baluch minority in southeast Iran, in the area where the shah was building naval and air bases—at Chah Bahar and Bandar Abbas, both near the Strait of Hormuz.[22] Thus it was in the shah's interest to patch up the long-running dispute between Afghanistan and Pakistan.

With his increased oil revenues, the shah was in a position to offer Daoud financial incentives to change his policies. In October 1974 the shah promised to provide $2 billion in economic aid over a period of ten years, which would have made Iran Afghanistan's biggest aid donor, replacing the USSR. The most important item of aid was to be the construction of a railroad form Kabul to Iran, which eventually would have provided Afghanistan with a trade route through Iranian ports, thereby decreasing Afghan dependence on Soviet trade.[23]

Selig Harrison, a former correspondent for the *Washington Post,* wrote an article after the communist takeover entitled "The Shah, Not the Kremlin, Touched Off Afghan Coup."[24] He argues as follows:

It was the shah of Iran, not Leonid Brezhnev, who triggered the chain of events culminating in the overthrow of the Mohammed Daoud regime. . . .

Beginning in 1974 . . . Iran, encouraged by the United States, made a determined effort to draw Kabul into a western-tilted, Tehran-centered regional economic and security sphere embracing Pakistan, India and the Persian Gulf states. . . .

The Communist takeover in Kabul came about when it did, and in the way that it did, because the shah disturbed the tenuous equilibrium that had existed in Afghanistan between the Soviet Union and the West for nearly three decades. . . . Given its unusually long frontier with Afghanistan, the Soviet Union would clearly go to great lengths to prevent Kabul from moving once again toward a pro-western stance.[25]

Some feel that Harrison has exaggerated the shah's role. For example, Ambassador Neumann says that the shah wanted to increase Afghanistan's independence, but knew that Afghanistan had to remain friends with the Soviets. Moscow, he says, was very tolerant about Afghanistan getting aid from other countries, because this decreased the need for Soviet aid. Besides, the Iranian aid program was to be spread over ten years and might well have stretched out over twenty years; little of it, in fact, ever got to Afghanistan. Finally, Neumann says, Afghanistan's continued dependence on the Soviet Union was still very great, since all of Afghanistan's military equipment was Soviet, much economic aid came from Russia, all of Afghanistan's natural gas was piped to the USSR, and Russia continued to be Afghanistan's chief trading partner.[26]

Whether or not the shah had anything to do with it, relations between Afghanistan and Pakistan did improve dramatically. The vitriolic propaganda war that each country had waged against the other was halted, and in March 1978, a month before his overthrow, Daoud appears to have reached an agreement with Pakistan in which he promised to expel the Pushtun and Baluchi insurgents operating on Afghan territory.[27]

In the last years of his rule Daoud made other moves that indicated his growing independence—moves that surely antagonized the communists in Afghanistan and may also have angered the communists in Moscow. First, Daoud began sending more of his military officers to Egypt and India for training and increased the number going to the United States, although the majority still went to the Soviet Union.[28] Second, Daoud took steps to strengthen his ties with the truly nonaligned members of the Nonaligned Movement. Egypt, India, and Yugoslavia were trying to prevent pro-Soviet states like Cuba from misusing the movement for Soviet purposes, and they worked hard to woo Afghanistan to their side.[29] Daoud reportedly said a few days before his downfall that Afghanistan wanted "true nonalignment," unlike Cuba, which claimed to be nonaligned but wasn't—a statement not likely to please Moscow.[30] Third, in the early spring of 1978, Daoud made trips to India, Pakistan, Egypt, Libya, Turkey, and Yugoslavia. In April he made additional visits to Saudi Arabia, Kuwait, and Egypt.[31] The shah planned a trip to Kabul in June, and Daoud announced that he would soon go to Washington to meet President Carter. The purpose of all this travel presumably was to build closer ties with these countries, which might help to make Afghanistan less dependent on the USSR. Fourth, on March 21, 1978, Daoud's minister of commerce signed a protocol with the Chinese People's Republic that provided for an increase in the exchange of goods between the two countries and a credit of 100 million yuan for the construction of several factories.[32] In view of Soviet fears of China, the prospect of an improvement in Sino-Afghan relations could hardly have been welcomed by the Kremlin. Finally, just a few days before his overthrow, President Daoud made a visit to Saudi Arabia, where, among other things, he signed a joint communique saying that the conflict between Somalia and Ethiopia should be solved "on the basis of the right of self-determination of the people of

Ogaden."[33] As the people of Ogaden are Somalis, this could only be interpreted as a slap at Ethiopia, an ally of the Soviet Union.

To sum it all up, during his last years Daoud took a number of steps to make Afghanistan's foreign policy "increasingly independent of the Soviet Union."[34]

SOVIET ATTITUDES TOWARD DAOUD

Without access to the minutes of the Politburo we cannot know what the Soviet leaders thought about Daoud's shift to the right in his domestic and foreign policies. It is difficult to believe that they were pleased, but this does not necessarily mean that they were so alarmed that they decided to oust him from office. Ambassador Neumann feels that Daoud's changes in foreign policy did *not* lead to his overthrow, because the changes did not alter the fact that Russia still had much more influence in Afghanistan than any other country.[35] Both King Zahir's government and Daoud's government, he says, "were unfailingly careful of Soviet interests." He adds, "In the United Nations, Afghanistan voted regularly either with the Soviet bloc or with the group of nonaligned countries. Inside Afghanistan, no Western activity, economic or otherwise, was permitted in the northern part. Soviet projects were not accessible to Westerners, nor were Soviet economic data revealed to them."[36]

Ambassador Eliot agrees. Daoud's shift in foreign policy, Eliot says, did make the Soviets anxious, but was not an important factor in Daoud's downfall.[37] Eliot's political counselor, Bruce Flatin, takes a similar position. All three Americans also insist that the U.S. government for years had made it clear to the Soviets that the United States understood Soviet security intersts in Afghanistan and had no thought of disturbing the peaceful relations between the USSR and Afghanistan. As Ambassador Neumann put it, "The United States never tried to weaken the Soviet-Afghan relationship. We recognized that the Soviet Union had a vital interest in Afghanistan, while the United States did not. Any attempt on our part to replace the Soviet Union would have been a no-win situation. There was no point in our picking a quarrel with the Soviets over Afghanistan. No American interest would have been served by such a policy."[38]

On the other hand, one must not forget that paranoia has long been a feature of Soviet attitudes toward the outside world. Lenin, Stalin, and their successors have all been inclined to see plots and conspiracies by "world imperialism." Even if the United States was innocent of any designs against Russia in Afghanistan, the Kremlin may have thought it guilty. And what to Daoud may have been merely an attempt to become nonaligned may have appeared to the Soviets as a shift to the American-Iranian-Pakistani camp.

One story about Daoud and the Soviets has been reported by so many well-informed people that one is inclined to accept it as true. According to this account, when Daoud made his final trip to Moscow in April 1977, Brezhnev addressed him in a rude manner and presented a long list of complaints about Daoud's policies. After taking this for a while, Daoud reportedly rose to his feet and said in effect: "I want to remind you that you are speaking to the President of an independent country, not one of your East European satellites. You are trying to interfere in the internal affairs of Afghanistan, and this I will not permit." Whereupon Daoud and his entourage marched out of the room. One associate said to Daoud, "Did you see the look on Brezhnev's face when you said that? Mr. President, you are a dead man."³⁹

Even if the story is true, this does not necessarily mean that Brezhnev decided to oust Daoud. *Pravda* reported that the talks had "exhibited an atmosphere of friendship, trust and mutual understanding." "The Soviet Union and Afghanistan," it said, "are filled with resolve to further consolidate their relations of friendship and good-neighbor cooperation."⁴⁰ The two countries signed a Treaty on Development of Economic Cooperation,⁴¹ and Brezhnev, Kosygin, and Podgorny "gratefully accepted" invitations by Daoud to visit his country. This account is typical of Soviet press coverage of Afghanistan during Daoud's presidency. In May 1977, a month after Daoud's visit, the Soviet leaders sent Daoud a telegram in which they wished him well and referred to the "traditional friendship and good-neighborly cooperation" that had been exhibited during his visit to Moscow.⁴²

Thus Soviet attitudes toward Daoud remain a mystery. It seems logical that the Politburo was displeased with some of his foreign and domestic policies. They may have looked upon these actions as minor peccadilloes that did not alter the fact that Soviet-Afghan relations were generally satisfactory,⁴³ or they may have felt these acts were so serious that Daoud ought to be ousted as soon as a favorable opportunity presented itself—alternatives that will be discussed in later chapters.

NOTES

1. Fred Halliday, "Revolution in Afghanistan," *New Left Review,* no. 112 (November-December 1978), p. 19; Hasan Kakar, "The Fall of the Afghan Monarchy in 1973," *International Journal of Middle Eastern Studies,* vol. 9, no. 2 (May 1978), p. 201.
2. Halliday, "Revolution in Afghanistan," pp. 19–20.
3. Leon B. Poullada, "The Failure of American Diplomacy in Afghanistan" (mimeographed article), p. 20.
4. "United States Mission in Afghanistan, 1972 Policy Review," contained in airgram no. A-66 from Kabul to State, June 5, 1972, p. 2.
5. Ibid., p. 9.
6. Hannah Negaran [pseud.], "The Afghan Coup of April 1978: Revolution and International Security," *Orbis,* vol. 23, no. 1 (Spring 1979), p. 99.

7. Louis Dupree, *Red Flag Over the Hindu Kush.* Part I: *Leftist Movements in Afghanistan* (Hanover, N.H.: American Universities Field Staff Reports, 1979/no. 44, Asia), p. 9.

8. Shaheen F. Dil, "The Cabal in Kabul: Great-Power Interaction in Afghanistan," *American Political Science Review,* vol. 71, no. 2 (June 1977), p. 472; Kakar, "The Fall of the Afghan Monarchy," p. 214. Some people argue that Daoud's coup was carried out with Soviet support. This may be true, but there is no solid evidence for it in open sources.

9. *Republic of Afghanistan: Statements, Messages, and Press Interviews,* no. 1, p. 2, as cited in Kakar, "The Fall of the Afghan Monarchy," p. 214.

10. Interview with Gaston Sigur. Theodore Eliot expresses the same view in "The 1978 Afghan Revolution: Some Internal Aspects," *The Fletcher Forum,* vol. 3, no. 4 (Spring 1979), p. 83.

11. Halliday, "Revolution in Afghanistan," p. 29. Dupree discusses the appointees in detail in his *Leftist Movements,* pp. 12–13. He says that the minister of the interior, Faiz Mohammad, was leftist but not a member of either Khalq or Parcham. Qader was made vice-commander of the air force. Two other key Parchami officers were Sayed Mohammad Gulabzoy and Sherjan Mazdooryar. All four officers studied in the USSR, helped place Daoud in power, later helped remove him, and eventually were appointed to Babrak's first cabinet. Their photographs adorned the January 1, 1980, issue of *Kabul News Times.*

12. Secret airgram no. A-24 from Kabul to State Department, April 30, 1975, p. 3.

13. Louis Dupree, "Afghanistan Under the *Khalq,*" *Problems of Communism,* vol. 28, no. 4 (July-August 1979), p. 39.

14. Airgram no. A-24 from Kabul to State Department, April 30, 1975, p. 4; Halliday, "Revolution in Afghanistan," p. 29.

15. Airgram no. A-24 from Kabul to State, pp. 5–7.

16. Dupree, "Afghanistan Under the *Khalq,*" p. 39. Dupree feels that this was "the crucial turning point" in Daoud's term as president.

17. Ibid. An outline of the 1977 constitution may be found in Dupree, *Towards Representative Government in Afghanistan,* Part II (Hanover, N.H.: American Universities Field Staff Reports, 1978/no. 14, Asia), p. 3.

18. *Pravda,* June 6, 1974.

19. *Pakistan Times,* August 25, 1975, as cited in Negaran, "The Afghan Coup of April 1978," p. 99.

20. Theodore L. Eliot, Jr., "Afghanistan After the 1978 Revolution," *Strategic Review,* vol. 7, no. 2 (Spring 1979), p. 59.

21. Interview with Eliot, August 13, 1980.

22. Stephen Oren, "The Afghani Coup and the Peace of the Northern Tier," *The World Today,* vol. 30, no. 1 (January 1974), pp. 30–31.

23. Louis Dupree, *Afghanistan 1977: Does Trade Plus Aid Guarantee Development?* (Hanover, N.H.: American Universities Field Staff Reports, South Asia Series, vol. 21, no. 3, August 1977), p. 4.

24. *Washington Post,* May 13, 1979, pp. C1, C5.

25. Ibid., p. C5.

26. Interview with Ambassador Robert Neumann, September 4, 1980. Eden Naby, an associate at the Center for Middle Eastern Studies at Harvard and a specialist on Afghanistan, believes that the Soviets helped plan the coup that overthrew Daoud and did so because of the change in Daoud's foreign policies. Interview with Eden Naby, August 14, 1980.

27. Selig Harrison in *Washington Post,* May 13, 1979, p. C5.

28. Eliot, "Afghanistan After the 1978 Revolution," p. 59; interview with Bruce Flatin.

29. Eliot, "Afghanistan After the 1978 Revolution," p. 59.

30. Negaran, "The Afghan Coup of 1978," p. 99.

31. Louis Dupree, *Red Flag Over the Hindu Kush.* Part II: *The Accidental Coup or Taraki in Blunderland* (Hanover, N.H.: American University Field Staff Reports, 1979/no. 45, Asia), p. 1.

32. *Kabul Times,* March 28, 1978, p. 1.

33. *Kabul Times,* April 5, 1978, p. 4.

34. Eliot, "Afghanistan After the 1978 Revolution," pp. 59–60. For a summary of why the Afghan communists were dissatisfied with Daoud, see Taraki's speech of May 9, 1978, in *Federal Broadcast Information Service* (hereafter cited as *FBIS*), Middle East and North Africa Series, May 17, 1978, pp. S1–2. All citations to *FBIS* refer to the Middle East and North Africa (later South Asia) series unless otherwise indicated.

35. Interview with Neumann.

36. Robert Neumann, "Afghanistan Under the Red Flag," in *The Impact of the Iranian Events Upon Persian Gulf and U.S. Security,* ed. by Z. Michael Szaz (Washington, D.C.: American Foreign Policy Institute, 1979), p. 131.

37. Interview with Eliot.

38. Interview with Neumann.

39. The story was first told to me by Professor Gaston Sigur, who had heard it from a former official in the Afghan Foreign Ministry who was a relative of Daoud's. Similar accounts were heard by Ambassador Eliot, Bruce Flatin, Louis Dupree, and Habibullah Karzai, a retired Afghan diplomat. Flatin says he believes the story because this is the sort of thing Daoud might do. Eliot testifies that Daoud was very sensitive about anybody, including the American ambassador, trying to tell him what to do.

40. *Pravda,* April 16, 1977, p. 1.

41. *Pravda,* April 15, 1977, p. 4.

42. *Pravda,* May 28, 1977, p. 1

43. Professor Malcolm Yapp of the University of London, writes:

There is no reason to suppose that the Soviet Union wished to get rid of Daoud. Daoud had won a special place in Soviet hearts with his policies in 1953–63 when he had drawn Afghanistan closer to the USSR. . . . If there were differences on some subjects . . . these were not in themselves reasons to upset the generally satisfactory relations. . . . Certainly the Soviet Union, which had watched with equanimity the suppression of genuine, local communist parties by many regimes allied to the USSR, was unlikely to be concerned by Daoud's rough treatment of what must have appeared as a wild and wooly bunch of radicals.

Manuscript of chapter by Yapp for a book on Soviet policy in the Middle East to be published in England, pp. 14–15.

PART 2

The Coup of April 1978 and Its Aftermath

CHAPTER 6

The Communists Seize Power

Afghanistan . . . , one of the ancient countries of Central Asia, until recently . . . remained one of the most backward. It seemed that here life had frozen along medieval lines and that the people were doomed to drag out a miserable existence. Feudal lords controlled destinies and meted out reprisals against people. In order to perpetuate this state of affairs, they propagated obscurantism, enmeshed the masses in bondage, and suppressed all attempts to bring a spark of light into the dark of lawlessness and arbitrary rule. In April 1978 the Afghan people said "no" to this rotten system. The working people of the country took its destiny into their own hands.

—*Pravda*, December 31, 1979[1]

KHALQ AND PARCHAM UNITE

After years of bitter rivalry, the two communist factions—Khalq (led by Taraki) and Parcham (led by Babrak)—finally agreed in 1977 to reunite. Because the two leaders were known to dislike each other (and subsequent events proved that they did), it is believed that the merger came about as a result of Soviet influence. Former Ambassador Eliot says that the United States had solid information from secret sources that the Soviets exerted pressure for unification.[2] This pressure was exerted in part through other communist parties in the area, including the Communist party of India.[3]

If Parcham was somewhat closer to Moscow, why was Taraki accepted as the leader of the unified party rather than Babrak? The answer, presumably, is that Khalq had more members and more support in the army at that time.[4] Did the communists unite in order to carry out a revolution? The answer seems to be yes. After all, revolution is supposed to be the *raison d'être* of communist parties. But the opportunity to seize power came sooner

than they had expected. Bruce Flatin thinks that the communists may have
planned to seize power later in 1978, but that the murder of communist
ideologue Mir Akbar Khyber accelerated their schedule.[5] Ambassador Eliot
assumed that the communists would wait until Daoud died.[6] (Daoud was
sixty-eight, which is old for an Afghan.) Louis Dupree says, "In my opinion,
the *Khalq-Parcham* coalition did not plan to seize power until President
Daoud's bodyguard (a force of 2,000 well-trained volunteers) had been
successfully penetrated and neutralized, possibly two or three years hence."[7]

Another interesting question is whether or not Moscow's motive in promoting
the reunification of Khalq and Parcham was a desire to overthrow Daoud.
Henry Bradsher, who covered Afghanistan for several years for the *Washington
Star,* observes that this was not necessarily the case, that Moscow may have
wanted the communists to become stronger so that they could exert pressure
on Daoud to behave himself.[8] Ambassador Eliot disagrees; he feels that the
Soviet objective was a communist seizure of power.[9] Eden Naby, an Iranian-
American scholar who has spent much time in Afghanistan, argues that the
Soviets had become so dissatisfied with Daoud's policies that they urged the
Afghan communists to oust him as soon as they had a good opportunity.[10]
This seems the most logical answer to the question, although we have no
real evidence one way or another.[11]

Whether the Soviets urged them to do so or not, the reunited party did
make preparations for an eventual seizure of power, and Daoud's policies
played into their hands. By 1978 Daoud had incurred the displeasure not
only of leftists, but also of Muslim fundamentalists, students, intellectuals,
army officers, and some members of the middle and upper classes. There
were also serious economic problems; unemployment was high, and several
hundred thousand Afghans were forced to go to Iran and other Gulf states
to find jobs. Daoud had trouble servicing the many loans he had made with
foreign countries and sometimes was forced to ask that the payments be
rescheduled.[12] Meanwhile, economic discontent spread as a result of severe
shortages of food and increases of taxes.

As the years passed, the Daoud regime became less and less efficient, for
a number of reasons. Daoud tried to decide everything himself and, since he
was getting rather old, he had less vigor than before. He also showed more
of an inclination to depend upon relatives and cronies, thereby excluding from
government many able people. As opposition to the regime grew, Daoud
adopted increasingly severe methods of repression. He antagonized workers
by attacking strikers in November 1977, and he offended some Muslims by
trying to suppress the Muslim Brotherhood. In February 1978 he fired the
moderate leftist members of his cabinet. Under such circumstances, it is not
surprising that there were numerous plots against him.[13]

THE COMMUNISTS PLAN TO SEIZE POWER

As opposition to Daoud increased, the leaders of the reunited PDPA made plans to overthrow him. Party organizers toured the country recruiting members, and new party cells were formed, both in the armed forces and among civilians. Amin was particularly zealous and successful in winning army and air force officers to the cause. A plan for seizing power with units of the armed forces was worked out and practiced on paper.[14]

According to Amin's history of the coup, communist army and air force personnel practiced their "revolutionary tactics" and "preparatory maneuvers" no less than ten times, so as to be ready when the day for the seizure of power arrived.[15] The official history adds: "Under the prudent guidance of Comrade Taraki, Comrade Amin, with his proletarian courage and bravery, met patriotic liaison officers, day or night, in the desert or in the mountains, in the fields or in the forests, enlightening them on the basis of principles of working class ideology."[16]

Neither Amin nor any of the other communists expected to seize power as soon as they did, however. The sequence of events leading to the communist coup began on April 19, 1978, when the PDPA organized a funeral procession in honor of one of its most prominent leaders, Mir Akbar Khyber. To the amazement of the government, about 10,000 to 15,000 people marched in military order through the streets shouting "death to the U.S. imperialists" and "down with the CIA." Daoud presumably was shocked to discover that the communists were so numerous and well organized. Frightened into action, he arrested several of the top communists, including Taraki, Amin and Babrak. The arrest of Amin was carried out very inefficiently, however. He was not locked up in prison at first, but was put under detention in his home, where party members were permitted to visit him and get instructions on how to carry out the coup! The police also allowed Amin's teenage son to come and go freely, and he carried plans for the revolt to other party members.[17] Amin appointed Colonal Aslam Watanjar commander of all rebel ground forces, while Colonel Abdul Qader was ordered to lead the revolt in the air force.[18]

That is Amin's version of how the coup came about. It is possible, however, that Amin's role was much smaller or even nonexistent and that the coup was actually carried out by military men on their own initiative. When Daoud arrested Taraki, Amin, and the other party leaders, he foolishly failed to arrest any of the left-wing army and air force officers, apparently because he suffered from the delusion that they were still loyal.[19] It may be that Watanjar, Qader, and the other officers who led the revolt decided that it made better sense to overthrow Daoud than to wait and see if he would arrest them also. Professor Malcolm Yapp of the University of London argues that the coup was "planned and executed on the spur of the moment by frightened officers."[20]

Both Watanjar and Qader had played prominent roles in Daoud's seizure of power, but had become disillusioned with Daoud. In addition, Qader had a personal grievance against Daoud: at first Daoud had appointed him deputy chief of staff of the air force, but later demoted him to the post of commandant of the military slaughterhouse.

THE COUP

As usual in such coups, the outcome was determined by which side could command the support of the most troops with the best equipment. On the morning of April 27, tanks under the command of Watanjar converged on Kabul and surrounded the Presidential Palace, which was strongly defended by the Republican Guard. Despite the fighting, life in the city went on much as usual, as Louis Dupree describes it:

> April 27 happened to be a Thursday, and at noon a half-holiday began. The Afghan government and most private firms give their employees Thursday afternoon and Friday off, Friday being *Juma,* the Muslim equivalent of Sunday. So, at noon, just as the fighting intensified, Kabul offices emptied into the streets. Despite the danger, people queued up for buses—even in the firefight zone! Taxis honked for tanks to move over, and wove in and out as the fighting continued. At some corners, traffic policemen motioned the tanks to pull over to the curb.[21]

In the afternoon, planes under the command of Colonel Qader fired rockets and 20-mm cannon shells at the Presidential Palace, killing many of the Republican Guard. Some bombs were dropped. Meanwhile, the rebels captured the ministry of the interior, the city airport, the radio station, and the prison, liberating Taraki and other communist leaders. Daoud's minister of defense rushed from one army unit to another, trying to prod loyal troops into action, but they either refused to move, took off for home, or were driven back by rebel forces. At 7:05 on the evening of the 27th the music of Radio Afghanistan stopped for an announcement read by Colonel Qader on behalf of Colonel Watanjar, leader of the Military Revolutionary Council of the Afghan Military Forces. Qader declared that "for the first time in the history of Afghanistan an end has been put to the sultanate of the Mohammadzais [the Afghan royal family]. All power has passed to the hands of the masses."[22] Finally, early in the morning of April 28, the remnants of the Republican Guard surrendered. Daoud, resisting to the end, was gunned down in his palace, along with his brother, his wife, and most of his children and grandchildren.[23] The coup was complete.

It is worth noting that in the first announcement on Kabul Radio about the coup—the announcement by Colonel Qader on the evening of April 27—

nothing was said about the PDPA, Taraki, Amin, or any of the other party leaders. Qader said that power had passed into the hands of the "Military Revolutionary Council" headed by himself. Only three days later, on April 30, was it announced that power was being exercised by a Revolutionary Council that contained civilians as well as officers and was headed by Taraki. This strengthens the impression that the initiative for the seizure of power came from the army and air force officers and that they were not simply taking orders from Amin. Professor Malcolm Yapp argues that the military men staged the coup on their own, but then turned to the PDPA leaders because they didn't know what else to do. "It seems most likely," he says, "that the rebel officers had given little thought to what was to follow their desperate attempt and had turned to the imprisoned leftists for want of any obvious alternative."[24] Yapp perhaps goes too far; many of the officers were either members of the party or sympathizers, and it was natural for them to at least share power with the top leaders of the party. But it is also reasonable to suppose that, since the coup came suddenly and unexpectedly, the officers did not have detailed plans as to what they should do after Daoud was overthrown.

BASIC FACTS ABOUT THE COUP

Several basic facts about the April coup should be emphasized.

1. *The timing of the coup was fortuitous.* Even if the leaders of the PDPA were preparing to seize power sooner or later, it was not they who determined the timing of the coup. The communists were pushed into action by Daoud's arrest of the party leaders and the fear among the military officers that he was about to arrest them also. One could theorize that the funeral demonstration was intended by the communists as the first step in a planned seizure of power, but this seems unlikely since several days passed between the funeral and the coup, and the party leaders made no attempt to hide from the police.

If Moscow gave the communists orders—or suggestions—that they overthrow Daoud, it did not pick that particular moment. And, since the rebel forces did not go into action until April 26, after the top communist leaders had been arrested, there could not have been much, if any, prior consultation with the Soviets about the timing of the coup. It is possible, however, that the Kremlin had told the PDPA weeks, months, or years earlier to take power whenever a favorable opportunity came along.

Taraki himself testifies that the arrests precipitated the coup. "The direct action of the comrades from the army was not planned a long time in advance," he said. Only when the party leaders were arrested, he added, was the army given the order to go into action.[25] Elsewhere he commented, "Daoud had seven party leaders, including myself, arrested and incarcerated.

He intended to kill us. . . . We had to act; otherwise the party would have been destroyed."[26]

2. *The Soviets probably knew about the coup in advance and gave their approval.* Ambassador Neumann writes that "Soviet foreknowledge and agreement are the very minimal assumptions that have to be made."[27] Ambassador Eliot agrees: "The Soviets may not have been involved in detailed planning, but it is doubtful that the Afghan communists would have planned the coup without contacting the Soviets and discussing it with them."[28] Since there were about 3,000 Soviet advisers in Afghanistan, since some of the Afghan officers were probably working for the KGB (the Soviet secret police) or the GRU (Soviet miliary intelligence), and since Babrak and other Parcham leaders were in regular contact with the Soviet embassy, it is difficult to imagine that the Soviets did not know a coup was being hatched. They might have received the news only a few hours in advance, however. Soviet foreknowledge of the coup is also indicated by the participation of Soviet advisers, who probably would not have dared to take part without first getting approval from Moscow. This does not mean, however, that the Soviets planned or stage-managed the coup; the initiative probably came from the Afghans.

3. *Actual Soviet participation in the coup was small.* Even if Moscow ordered or urged the communists to seize power, the coup itself was carried out almost entirely by Afghans. No Soviet combat units were present in the country or participated in the fighting. Some people have speculated that, since the jet planes attacking the Presidential Palace were flown with great skill, the pilots must have been Soviet, but we really don't know. Ambassador Eliot says that Soviet advisers accompanied the communist forces during the coup,[29] and other writers agree that Soviet personnel played an advisory role.[30] Even if no Soviet troops took part in the seizure of power, however, Soviet support and encouragement may have been crucial to its success.

4. *It was a palace coup rather than a mass revolution.* Taraki claimed many times that "this was not a putsch or a coup but a revolutionary act of the masses."[31] All the evidence is against him, however. Relatively few people took part, and almost all of them were military personnel. Even among the military, most units refused to fight on either side, but waited to see who would win. The masses did not rise up in a popular revolution, either in Kabul or in the provinces.

5. *The coup encountered little opposition at first.* Except for the Presidential Guard, who fought with loyalty and determination, not many Afghans were willing to die for Daoud. Over the years he had antagonized so many elements of the population that large numbers welcomed his downfall, even if they had doubts about his successors.[32] Although few of the military units fought for the communists, the number who fought against them was even smaller. According to Louis Dupree, out of a total of about 92,000 men in the

Afghan army, "probably fewer than 3,000 were actually engaged in the fighting, with most of the troops in the Kabul area just shuffling around."[33]

NOTES

1. A. Petrov, "K sobytiem v Afganistane," *Pravda,* December 31, 1979, p. 4.

2. Interview with Theodore Eliot. A Parcham group, "The Committee of the Afghan Communists Abroad," issued an appeal on March 18, 1976, that criticized Taraki and demanded that "the leaders of the Khalq Party . . . work for unity among the political organizations of the working class in Afghanistan." Translation in airgram no. A-79 from Kabul to State Department, October 15, 1978.

3. Fred Halliday, "Revolution in Afghanistan," *New Left Review,* no. 112 (November-December 1978), p. 31, says that mediation between the two parties was carried out by Ajmal Khattaq, a communist in Pakistan. Hannah Negaran [pseud.], "The Afghan Coup of April 1978: Revolution and International Security," *Orbis,* vol. 23, no. 1 (Spring 1979), p. 100, suggests that the merger took place with the help of the Indian Communist party. Selig Harrison, *Washington Post,* May 13, 1979, p. C5, emphasizes the role of the Iraqi Communist party. There also seems to be some uncertainty as to exactly when the merger took place, with some saying May and others saying July 1977. The Afghan communists were very secretive about the reunification. An article urging unity appeared in *Party Life,* journal of the Communist party of India, on May 22, 1976.

4. Interview with Ambassador Neumann. Henry Bradsher says that two-thirds to three-fourths of the PDPA members were Khalq. Interview with Bradsher, September 1, 1980. Bradsher covered South Asia for the *Washington Star* for several years.

5. Interview with Flatin.

6. Interview with Eliot.

7. Dupree, "Inside Afghanistan: Yesterday and Today; A Strategic Appraisal," *Strategic Studies* (Islamabad), vol. 2, no. 3 (Spring 1979), p. 74.

8. Interview with Bradsher.

9. Interview with Eliot.

10. Interview with Naby, August 14, 1980.

11. No Soviet criticisms of Daoud have come to my attention. Gaston Sigur once asked the Soviet ambassador in Kabul if Russia had designs on Afghanistan. The ambassador replied, "Look around you. Why would we want this backward, poverty-stricken country?" Interview with Sigur.

12. Louis Dupree, *Afghanistan 1977: Does Trade Plus Aid Guarantee Development?* (Hanover, N.H.: American Universities Field Staff Reports, South Asia Series, vol. 21, no. 3, August 1977), pp. 11–12; Halliday, "Revolution in Afghanistan," p. 35; David Shireff, "Afghanistan Keeps Its Plan Under Wraps," *Middle East Economic Digest,* vol. 20, no. 35 (August 27, 1976), pp. 3–5. It should be pointed out that the report by Dupree cited above presents a generally optimistic view of the state of the Afghan economy, referring, among other things, to the "remarkable improvement in Afghanistan's economic status" and its "economic vigor and diversity" (pp. 1, 2).

13. Malcolm Yapp, manuscript of chapter to be published in a book on Soviet policy in the Middle East, p. 12; Theodore L. Eliot, Jr., "The 1978 Afghan Revolution: Some Internal Aspects," *Fletcher Forum,* vol. 3, no. 4 (Spring 1979), pp. 83–84.

14. Eliot, "The 1978 Afghan Revolution," p. 85.

15. Political Department of the People's Armed Forces of Afghanistan, *On the Saur Revolution* (Kabul: Government Printing Press, May 22, 1978), p. 11. *Saur* is the Afghan word for April.

16. Ibid.

17. Louis Dupree, *Red Flag Over the Hindu Kush.* Part II: *The Accidental Coup, or Taraki in Blunderland* (Hanover, N.H.: American Universities Field Staff Reports, 1979/no. 45, Asia), pp. 4–5. Dupree says that he talked with people who testified to eyewitness knowledge of Amin's role in directing the coup and that he himself saw one of Amin's written orders. Interview with Dupree.

18. Amin's orders are contained in *Democratic Republic of Afghanistan Annual, 1979* (Kabul: Government Printing Press, 1979), pp. 44–48, and are quoted in Dupree, *The Accidental Coup,* pp. 15–16. Dupree gives an hour-by-hour account of the coup.

19. Eliot, "The 1978 Afghan Revolution," pp. 85–86.

20. Yapp, manuscript of chapter, p. 13.

21. Dupree, *The Accidental Coup,* p. 8.

22. Cable no. 03234 from Kabul to State Department, April 27, 1978, pp. 1–2.

23. Dupree, *The Accidental Coup,* p. 14, gives a list of the former members of the royal family and their fates.

24. Yapp, manuscript of chapter, p. 14.

25. *Federal Broadcast Information Service* (hereafter cited as *FBIS*), Middle East and North Africa Series, May 9, 1978, p. S2, reporting Taraki's news conference of May 6, 1978. All citations to *FBIS* refer to Middle East and North Africa (later South Asia) series unless otherwise indicated.

26. *Die Zeit* (Hamburg), June 9, 1978, p. 4, reporting an interview with Taraki; translated in *FBIS,* June 9, 1978, p. S1.

27. Robert Neumann, "Afghanistan Under the Red Flag," in *The Impact of the Iranian Events Upon Persian Gulf and U.S. Security,* ed. by Z. Michael Szaz (Washington, D.C.: American Foreign Policy Institute, 1979), p. 137.

28. Interview with Eliot.

29. Ibid. Former Secretary of State Vance, however, says in his memoirs: "We had no evidence of Soviet complicity in the coup." Cyrus Vance, *Hard Choices: Critical Years in America's Foreign Policy* (New York: Simon and Schuster, 1983), p. 384.

30. Louis Dupree, "Afghanistan under the *Khalq,*" *Problems of Communism,* vol. 28, no. 4 (July-August 1979), pp. 46–47.

31. Taraki press conference of May 6, 1978, as reported in *FBIS,* May 9, 1978, p. S1.

32. According to Louis Dupree, "Almost everyone cheered the downfall of the Mohammadzai lineage." Dupree, *Red Flag Over the Hindu Kush.* Part III: *Rhetoric*

and Reforms, or Promises! Promises! (Hanover, N.H.: American Universities Field Staff Reports, Asia, no. 23, 1980), p. 1.

33. Dupree, *The Accidental Coup,* p. 13. He estimates that about 1,000 people were killed in the coup. Others in Kabul at the time have guessed that "at the most the casualty figures could be around 1,000 killed and wounded in the fighting." Agence France Press report from Kabul dated May 4, as reported in *FBIS* May 5, 1978, p. S1. Hannah Negaran [pseud.] in "Afghanistan: A Marxist Regime in a Muslim Society," *Current History,* vol. 76, no. 446 (April 1979), p. 174, says: "Estimates of the number of people killed are as high as 10,000, although a more reasonable estimate is believed to be 2,000."

CHAPTER 7

The Communist Regime, Russia, and the United States

COMPOSITION OF THE NEW GOVERNMENT

Once they had ousted Daoud, the revolutionaries immediately set to work to establish a new government. Decree No. 1 of April 30, issued by the Revolutionary Council, announced that the council itself was "the supreme governmental power of the country." It also declared that Taraki, "the great nationalist and revolutionary of Afghanistan," would be both president of the Revolutionary Council and prime minister.[1] He also retained the post of secretary-general of the PDPA, which he had held since the very beginning of the party.

Decree No. 2 disclosed the membership of the Cabinet. Amin was named deputy prime minister and foreign minister. He was younger than Taraki, more energetic and more ruthless, and he became in practice the most important figure in the government, though the highest praise was reserved for Taraki. Taraki was usually referred to as "Beloved Leader," while Amin had to be satisfied with being called "his Noble Student."[2] Later, in March 1979, Amin became prime minister in name as well as in fact, while Taraki retained the post of president.

Babrak Karmal, as the leader of the smaller of the two factions in the party, was named vice-president of the Revolutionary Council and deputy prime minister.[3] He would not retain either post for long, however. Eleven of the members of the Cabinet were Khalq, while ten were Parcham. Both the Revolutionary Council and the Cabinet were made up entirely of party members; thus one-party dictatorship was established from the start.[4] Although military men had carried out the coup, only three of them were included in the cabinet—an indication that the party, in true Leninist fashion, would be the "vanguard" of the "Democratic Republic of Afghanistan." Both Watanjar and Qader were given high rank in the government, however, being listed fourth and fifth in the announcement of the Cabinet, after Taraki, Karmal, and Amin. Watanjar was named deputy prime minister and minister of communications, while Qader was promoted to major general and made minister of national defense.[5]

THE REGIME CLAIMS IT IS NONALIGNED AND NONCOMMUNIST

From the moment they seized power, Afghanistan's new leaders insisted over and over again that they were committed to the traditional policy of nonalignment.[6] At a news conference on May 6, President Taraki declared: "We are nonaligned and independent." He called for the friendship and aid of "all the world's nations, including the United States." At the same time, he repeatedly denied that the PDPA was communist or Marxist.[7]

One might wonder why Taraki and other leaders went to the trouble to make such statements when, in retrospect, they seem so obviously false. But their claims were received sympathetically in various quarters—in some perhaps from ignorance, in others perhaps from wishful thinking. Soon after the coup, "U.S. policymakers" (who were not identified) declared that the new government was "more nationalist than Communist."[8] The *New York Times* also took a highly optimistic view of the Khalq coup. In an editorial the *Times* declared that the Carter administration was "rightly unruffled" by the communist takeover. It continued, "A decade ago, a Communist gain anywhere would have been felt as a distinct loss for Washington. Most Americans now recognize that the world is more complicated. . . . Although the Afghan Communists historically have leaned toward Moscow rather than Peking, and will lean more decidedly that way than their predecessors, they are unlikely to become Moscow's puppets."[9]

Professor Louis Dupree said in a letter to the *New York Times* that the label "Communist" was "unjustified—as yet."[10] A British journalist named Simon Winchester cabled from Kabul: "It seems . . . probable that the democratic republic, so called, has genuine nonalignment as its aim." He continued, in a manner reminiscent of the optimistic speculations made about the Chinese communists when they first seized power, "The view . . . that Taraki and his 20 cabinet colleagues are *agrarian reformers* [emphasis added], intensely nationalistic and likely to be formidably opposed to direct Soviet intervention, is in my opinion, a correct assessment."[11]

Winchester went on to apologize for himself and other Western correspondents for their "appalling" press coverage of the Afghan revolution, which, he said, "took place with relatively little loss of life." Their biased reporting, he indicated—in a kindly tone rarely found among hard-bitten reporters—had hurt Taraki's feelings! Under such circumstances, he said, who could blame Taraki "for retiring, hurt and angry, to take counsel with the Russians and the Cubans and the Czechs?"

The State Department and the American Embassy in Kabul also seem to have been confused at first as to whether or not the new rulers were communists. For example, a cable from the State Department on April 28, 1978, said, "Fragmentary evidence suggests that they [the rebel leaders] may be leftist and/or strongly Islamic nationalists."[12] The following day the Kabul Embassy sent a cable to the State Department objecting to an article in the *Washington Post* in which a "State Department source" was quoted as saying the leaders were pro-Soviet.[13] That same day the Kabul Embassy reported that the orientation of the new regime was uncertain.[14] By April 30, however, the embassy declared that "the true political character of the coup leadership is now nakedly apparent to all."[15] The embassy did not know at first who Abdul Qader and Mohammad Watanjar were, which seems surprising since both had played prominent roles in Daoud's seizure of power.[16]

The embassy's inadequate knowledge about the communist rulers is explained in part by Professor Leon B. Poullada, who served in the embassy from 1954 to 1958 and who had two lengthy stays in Afghanistan in the 1960s and 1970s as a Fulbright professor:

> Unfortunately, it is not true that the leaders of the new government had been known to American diplomats for many years. The communist leaders worked mostly underground and it should have been the CIA's job to know about them, but for years the CIA in Kabul was under orders to concentrate its efforts on watching the Soviet bloc and ignore local politics. . . . The leftists in Afghanistan were simply not taken seriously by Americans.[17]

The Regime Shows It Is Aligned and Communist

Despite the naive and overly optimistic speculations in the Western press, the actions and statements by the leaders in Kabul soon made it clear that the new regime was definitely communist and that it had no intention of being nonaligned except in the fictitious sense that Cuba is nonaligned. Only three weeks after the coup, Foreign Minister Amin journeyed to Moscow, where he declared that Afghanistan was "linked by unbreakable ties of brotherly friendship and neighborliness with its great neighbor, the Soviet Union."[18] From Moscow, Amin traveled to Cuba, where he said that one of the main goals of his regime was the "consolidation, widening and expansion

of friendly relations with our great northern neighbor, the Soviet Union."
And the following month he described the USSR and its allies as "the real
advocates of peace," in contrast to the "imperialistic reactionaries and war-
mongers."[19]

Taraki also made statements indicating that the regime was firmly aligned
with the Soviet Union. For example, in June 1978, in an interview for *Die
Zeit,* the following exchange took place:

> ZEIT: A manisfesto of your party . . . reads: "The fight between international
> socialism and international imperialism that has been waged since the Great
> October Revolution" is "the basic conflict of contemporary history." Is this
> assessment in line with your ideology?
> TARAKI: I think this analysis is correct. That is the way it is. One camp
> represented by the Soviet Union, the other by America.[20]

There were many other indications that the new regime had aligned itself
closely with Moscow. The USSR was the first country to grant diplomatic
recognition, and it was followed in short order by other members of the
Soviet bloc. The Taraki government closed down the South Korean embassy
and welcomed a diplomatic mission from Cuba, not previously represented
in Kabul. Hundreds of additional Soviet military and civilian advisers poured
into the country. Numerous economic agreements with the USSR were signed,
and trade between the two countries increased. In December 1978 the two
governments signed a Treaty of Friendship, Good Neighborliness and Cooperation, which committed the two parties to "strengthen and broaden" their
cooperation in economic, cultural, scientific, technical, educational, health,
press, and other matters, and in "the military field." In this and other ways
the Taraki regime made it clear that it looked upon the Soviet Union as its
nearest and dearest friend.[21]

The attempts by Taraki and Amin to persuade the world that Afghanistan
was nonaligned may have reflected in part a hope that they still could get
assistance from noncommunist countries. Nonalignment under Zahir and Daoud
had made it possible for Afghanistan to get aid from all sides—to become,
in fact, one of the most-aided countries in the world on a per capita basis.
Almost immediately after the coup, Taraki asked for aid from "all the world's
nations, including the United States."[22] This was followed by specific requests
to the United States not only that aid be continued, but that it be increased.[23]
Despite Taraki's reversal of the traditional policy of nonalignment, American
aid did continue.

Just as the Taraki/Amin regime soon demonstrated that it was aligned
with the Soviet bloc, it also provided much evidence that it was communist.
Party members were referred to in the press as "Comrade" so-and-so. A red

flag, very much like the Soviet flag, was adopted. The new name for the country, "Democratic Republic of Afghanistan," was similar to the names used by several communist states. The People's Democratic party had a secretary-general, a Politburo, a Central Committee, and a Control Commission, just like the Communist Party of the Soviet Union.[24] Daoud's seven-year plan was dropped and replaced by a five-year plan, drawn up with Soviet assistance. The Afghan press was filled with references to Marx, Lenin, class struggle, "the victorious world proletarian movement," and the party as "the vanguard of the working class."[25] Speeches by party leaders were likewise full of Marxist rhetoric and praise of the Soviet Union, such as this statement by Amin: "As the Great October Revolution shook the world and commenced the downfall of imperialism and left a good example for proletariat movements in capitalist countries, so the glorious Saur [April] Revolution . . . also surprised and frightened imperialism . . . and became a shining example for the peoples in developing countries."[26]

THE MODERATE POLICY OF THE UNITED STATES TOWARD THE NEW REGIME

Despite all these indications that Afghanistan was communist and was aligned with the Soviet Union, the U.S. government gave the new regime the benefit of the doubt. Economic, cultural, educational, and Peace Corps programs were continued. Washington made no protest about the forcible seizure of power by a minority and did not accuse the Soviet Union of having encouraged the coup. Judging from its actions, the United States was unconcerned that another country apparently had joined the Soviet bloc.

This restrained, moderate response to the coup in Kabul was shared by two experts on Afghanistan, Professors Louis Dupree and Richard Frye, who went to the State Department and argued that the coup was more nationalist than communist and that the United States should follow a wait-and-see policy.[27] Theodore Eliot, who was American ambassador at the time, agreed with this moderate approach. The United States, he wrote later,

> continued to keep an open mind toward assisting Afghanistan, maintained a dialogue in Kabul on possible new AID, Peace Corps or cultural programs, and indicated a willingness to help to the extent proposals met our legislative and developmental criteria.
>
> This policy made sense because cutting off these programs unilaterally would only reduce Afghan options and drive the Afghan government deeper into the Soviet embrace.[28]

Bruce Flatin, who was Eliot's political counselor, says that the aid was continued largely for humanitarian reasons. "American policy," he says, "was to aid 'the poorest of the poor'—we wanted to help the Afghan people.''[29] Another consideration may have been information gathering. If the American mission was reduced in size, this would mean fewer American eyes and ears observing developments in the country and fewer contacts with Afghan citizens.

Zbigniew Brzezinski, who held the post of national security adviser under President Carter, approved of the restrained response to the communist coup. In an interview with me, he defended the Carter administration against charges that it should have reacted more strongly. "What could we have done?" he asked. "It was an internal coup, there was no evidence of Soviet involvement, and hence there were no grounds for an American protest. The regime was undefined and unconsolidated; there was doubt as to whether it could hold power. As long as we could have *some* influence in Kabul, why cut off aid? It was better to wait and see how things turned out."[30]

Not all Americans agreed with the policy of continuing aid to the communist regime. Former Ambassador Neumann tried to change it. He told the State Department that he had known the new leaders for years, that they were definitely communists and would follow orders from Moscow. Therefore, he argued, all aid should be stopped. He believes that the failure of the United States to respond more forcefully to the coup of 1978 led the Soviets to think that Washington would not do much when they invaded Afghanistan in 1979. Brzezinski and Marshall Shulman, Secretary of State Vance's chief adviser on Soviet affairs, admit that Neumann may be correct on this last point.[31]

Vance himself concluded later that the United States reacted too mildly to the communist seizure of power. He writes in his memoirs:

> In looking back, I think we should have expressed our concerns more sharply at the time of the April coup that brought Taraki to power. There were reasons why we did not protest more vigorously. Although there was little question that the Taraki government would make itself responsive to Moscow, there was room for doubt about whether the Soviets had planned the coup or were involved in its execution. And there was reason to think the strong Afghan nationalism of Taraki, and even more of Hafizullah Amin, might keep Afghanistan from becoming a Soviet satellite. . . . We concluded that our interests would best be served by letting Afghanistan continue its traditional balancing act between East and West. The United States had few resources in the area and historically we had held the view that our vital interests were not involved there. Moreover, our friends in the region had adopted a wait-and-see attitude. There was no disposition on their part to add to the instability by supporting opponents of the Marxists in Kabul. Although we were contacted from time to time about coup plots, my advice was that we not get involved.[32]

This is a problem for American foreign policy that has arisen before and will doubtless arise again. What should the United States do when Marxists who are not clearly subservient to the USSR seize power? Should the United States immediately adopt a posture of hostility toward such regimes or should it try to woo them away from the Soviet Union with offers of aid? Some people argue that Communist China would have broken with Moscow much sooner if Washington had not followed a policy of implacable opposition. Others claim that Castro adopted communism and allied with the Soviets because the United States took strong economic measures against him. More recently, it has been said that the late President Augustinho Neto of Angola wanted his country to be truly nonaligned, but the United States spurned his advances and drove him into the arms of the Russians. A similar problem faces our nation today in regard to Nicaragua and other Third World countries.

This is not the place to discuss China, Cuba, Angola, and Nicaragua, but some comments regarding American policy toward the Taraki regime are in order: (1) Since Taraki, Amin, Babrak, and other leaders of the new government talked and wrote and acted like communists, there should have been no doubt in Washington about their ideological leanings. (2) In view of this, and given the geographic location of Afghanistan, its poverty, and its dependence on Soviet military and economic aid, the new regime inevitably would become a satellite (perhaps a willing one) of the Soviet Union. The United States could not hope to compete for influence with a communist regime in a backward country situated on the border of the USSR, especially one whose army had been trained and equipped by the Soviets. (3) If, in spite of this, the U.S. government wished to give a modest amount of aid, such a policy would be defensible only if the United States gained some benefit, such as information gathering. (4) It is important that Washington not give the impression that it is indifferent to communist takeovers and will do nothing to try to prevent them. Carter's failure to react to the communist coup of 1978 may have given Moscow the impression that he did not care what happened in Afghanistan, thereby making it easier for the Kremlin to make the fateful decision to invade that country. (5) The United States gained very little, if anything, from continuing aid to the Khalq regime. (6) Afghanistan is definitely *not* a case where the United States, by adopting a hostile attitude, drove a leftist regime into the arms of the Soviets.

The issue of whether or not the United States should continue to have relatively cordial relations with Kabul was settled in February 1979 by the killing of U.S. Ambassador Adolph Dubs. Dubs was kidnapped by unidentified persons, said to be opponents of the regime, who held him hostage and reportedly demanded that one of their colleagues be freed from prison. American officials urged the Afghans in the strongest possible way to do nothing that might endanger the ambassador's life, but the Afghan police, under the direction of Soviet officials on the scene, disregarded their pleas and fired a barrage into the hotel room where Dubs was being held. He was killed, along with two of his captors. Foreign Minister Amin never apologized for the killing, refused to cooperate in an investigation, did not sign the book of condolences, and did not appear at the airport ceremony when Dubs's body was flown back to the United States.[33]

The callousness of the Afghan government reportedly made the Carter administration very angry. Yet aid continued, although on a smaller scale! American officials indicated that they did not want to curtail assistance completely because of humanitarian considerations and because they wanted to keep "a line open" to the Afghan authorities.[34] But in the months following Dubs's death, the size of the American Embassy staff was cut considerably and the Peace Corps was withdrawn, while Dubs was replaced not by an ambassador, but by a chargé d'affaires.[35] U.S. economic support, however, was not terminated completely until the Soviet invasion in December 1979.

NOTES

1. Cable no. 03380 from Kabul Embassy to State Department, April 30, 1978, p. 1; broadcast by Radio Kabul on April 30, 1978, as reported in *Foreign Broadcast Information Service* (hereafter cited as *FBIS*), Middle East and North Africa Series, May 1, 1978, p. S1. All citations to *FBIS* refer to the Middle East and North Africa (later South Asia) series unless otherwise indicated.

2. Louis Dupree, *Red Flag Over the Hindu Kush*. Part III: *Rhetoric and Reforms, or Promises! Promises!* (Hanover, N.H.: American Universities Field Staff Reports, Asia, no. 23, 1980), p. 4.

3. The members of the new cabinet were announced in a broadcast by Radio Kabul on May 2 and were translated in *FBIS,* May 2, 1978, p. S1.

4. Robert Neumann, "Afghanistan Under the Red Flag," in *The Impact of the Iranian Events Upon Persian Gulf and U.S. Security,* ed. by Z. Michael Szaz (Washington, D.C.: American Foreign Policy Institute, 1979), p. 137.

5. *FBIS,* May 2, 1978, p. S1; Dupree, *Rhetoric and Reforms,* p. 1.

6. See, for example, the *New York Times,* April 30, 1978, p. 10.

7. Reports of Taraki's press conference of May 6, 1978, in *FBIS,* May 9, 1978, pp. S1–2, and May 15, 1978, pp. S1–4, and in the *New York Times,* May 7, 1978, p. 1.

8. *Washington Star,* May 14, 1978; cited in Neumann, "Afghanistan Under the Red Flag," p. 142.

9. *New York Times,* May 5, 1978, p. A28.

10. *New York Times,* May 20, 1978, p. 18.

11. *Washington Post,* May 8, 1978, p. A16. In the early days of the Chinese revolution some people argued that Mao and his lieutenants were not really communists but "agrarian reformers."

12. Cable no. 108913 from State to Kabul, April 28, 1978.

13. Cable no. 03299 from Kabul to State, April 29, 1978.

14. Cable no. 03312 from Kabul to State, April 29, 1978.

15. Cable no. 03372 from Kabul to State, April 30, 1978.

16. Cable no. 03279 from Kabul to State, April 28, 1978, and cable no. 03350 from Kabul to State, April 30, 1978.

17. Letter to me from Professor Poullada, January 20, 1983.

18. *Pravda,* May 19, 1978, p. 5.

19. *New York Times,* June 16, 1978, p. A11. Further evidence that the PDPA was in fact a communist party came when the American Embassy in Kabul obtained a copy of the constitution of the PDPA. The constitution stated that the party's ideology was Marxism-Leninism and that the duty of all members was to expand and strengthen "the friendly relations between Afghans and the Soviets"; it described various party organs copied after those of the Communist Party of the Soviet Union. A translation of the constitution is reproduced in the Appendix.

20. *FBIS,* June 9, 1978, p. S3.

21. Theodore L. Eliot, Jr., "Afghanistan After the 1978 Revolution," *Strategic Review,* vol. 7, no. 2 (Spring 1979), p. 58. The text of the treaty is in *FBIS,* Soviet series, December 6, 1978, pp. J10–13. For other reports of the strengthening of Afghan-Soviet ties see the *New York Times,* June 16, 1978, pp. A1, A11, and November 18, 1978, p. 1. Commentary on the treaty may be found in *FBIS Trends in Communist Media,* December 13, 1978, pp. 5–6.

22. *New York Times,* May 7, 1978, p. 1.

23. *New York Times,* August 4, 1978, p. A4.

24. The constitution of the PDPA is very similar to the Rules of the Communist Party of the Soviet Union, the structure of the two parties being almost identical. See the Appendix.

25. Dupree, *Rhetoric and Reforms,* p. 3.

26. *Democratic Republic of Afghanistan Annual, 1979,* as cited in Dupree, ibid., p. 2.

27. Interview with Eden Naby, wife of Professor Frye.

28. Eliot, "Afghanistan After the 1978 Revolution," p. 61. Former Secretary of State Cyrus Vance indicates in his memoirs that he shared this view: "I concluded that our best chance to maintain a measure of influence in Kabul was to continue limited economic aid. To cut off all assistance or refuse recognition would almost certainly weaken our position in Kabul." Cyrus Vance, *Hard Choices: Critical Years in America's Foreign Policy* (New York: Simon and Schuster, 1983), p. 385.

29. Interview with Bruce Flatin.

30. Interview with Brzezinski.

31. Interviews with Neumann, Brzezinski, and Shulman.

32. Vance, *Hard Choices,* p. 386.

33. Eliot, "Afghanistan After the 1978 Revolution," p. 61; *Washington Post,* February 15, 1979, pp. A1, A21, and February 19, p. A29; Louis Dupree, *Red Flag Over the Hindu Kush.* Part IV: *Foreign Policy and the Economy* (Hanover, N.H.: American Universities Field Staff Reports, Asia, 1980, no. 27), pp. 2–3. Eden Naby thinks that the Soviets wanted Dubs killed because he was so good at his job. It seems more likely that the Soviet advisers simply followed their usual practice

of never negotiating with kidnappers, while the Afghan police demonstrated the common Afghan characteristic of being quick on the trigger. An eyewitness account of the murder is contained in a mimeographed article, "U.S. Ambassador Dubs Murder in Kabul," by Afzal Nasiri, former senior assistant editor of the *Kabul Times*.

34. Robert G. Kaiser in the *Washington Post,* February 16, 1979, pp. A1, A13, and February 22, 1979, p. A12. The United States also sent strong protests to the Afghan and Soviet governments; interview with Marshall Shulman.

35. *New York Times,* July 24, 1979, p. A1.

CHAPTER 8

The Communists Drive the
People to Rebellion

> *My sons and successors should not try to introduce reforms of any kind in such a hurry as to set the people against their ruler . . . they must adopt all these gradually as the people become accustomed to the idea of modern innovations.*

> —Abdur Rahman Khan
> Amir of Afghanistan (1880–1901)[1]

ARRESTS AND PURGES

The assumption of power by the communists was followed by a series of purges, imprisonments, and executions. Thousands of Daoud's civil servants, diplomats, governors, professors, army officers, police, and the like were thrown into jail, and their positions were taken over by party faithful with few qualifications and little experience.[2] Next came the turn of the Parcham leaders. As I noted earlier, Taraki and Babrak were known to dislike each other intensely, and the reunification of the party in 1977 is thought to have taken place under pressure from the Soviets. Evidently the rivalry between the two factions resumed soon after the coup, for in July 1978 most of the Parcham members of the cabinet, including Babrak, were removed from their jobs and sent abroad as ambassadors. A few months later they were relieved of their posts and ordered home, although not one was foolish enough to return.[3] Babrak, who had been ambassador to Czechoslovakia, disappeared from sight; evidently the Soviets put him in cold storage for later use. Meanwhile, lesser members of Parcham were purged, including hundreds of officers in the military.

General Abdul Qader, one of the two top leaders of the coup, had been rewarded with the post of minister of defense, but in August he was charged with engaging in a conspiracy and was locked up. With him went the chief of staff of the army, the minister of public works, the minister of planning, the minister of frontier affairs, and, in the weeks that followed, numerous other lesser figures.

One of the greatest problems in Afghanistan always had been a shortage of trained, capable administrators to run the government and the economy. With the purge—first, of the top officials from the Daoud regime, then of the Parchamis, and finally of all the others who were suspected of being anticommunist—the lack of competent personnel became acute. Young party members with no training or experience suddenly became deputy ministers, managers of state enterprises, or chairmen of state committees, much to the disgust of older bureaucrats with long years of service.[4] It is no wonder, then, that the government had difficulty in planning and carrying out its program of reforms.

THE COMMUNIST REFORM PROGRAM

There seems to be no reason to doubt that the Khalq leaders sincerely wished to institute a number of desirable and long-overdue reforms—to improve the lot of the peasants, elevate the status of women, eliminate racial discrimination, wipe out backwardness, and make Afghanistan a modern, prosperous state. But good intentions are not enough. As has happened in other communist countries, the attempt to impose rapid and arbitrary change by brute force, against the wishes of the people, produced not progress but chaos, bloodshed, and civil war.

Taraki realized that he would have to use force to carry out his program, as he indicated in an interview with *Die Zeit:*

> ZEIT: Are not you and your government running the risk of asking too much of the traditional and conservatively Islamic people of Afghanistan?
>
> TARAKI: The people will follow us out of conviction or out of fear of punishment. We do not want to overhasten our reforms; we want to implement them step by step. Yet, we will not be able to do that completely without applying some force.[5]

Taraki did use force, as he said he would. He also "overhastened" his reforms, and he failed to pay enough attention to social and economic conditions in Afghanistan. The attempt by Taraki and Amin to introduce an Afghan form of socialism, "violated practically every Afghan cultural norm, and strayed far beyond the allowable bounds of deviance in the social, economic, and political institutions. It almost appears that they systematically planned to alienate every segment of the Afghan people."[6]

Land Reform

Taraki, Amin, and many other Khalq leaders came from rural backgrounds, and one would have expected them to understand the attitudes, traditions, and customs of the peasants, but they did not. This is illustrated by the land reform decreed in November 1978. The official press gave the impression that in every village the reform was "a great success, with peasants dancing for joy, kissing the deeds of ownership, and waving aloft the red flag of the ruling Khalq party."[7]

But in fact the reform seems to have existed mostly on paper, for several reasons: First, the young, inexperienced bureaucrats (many of them city boys) who were sent into the countryside to implement the reform did not understand the complications of rural relationships and were not trusted either by the landlords or the peasants. Second, many of the peasants refused to accept the land, either because they were afraid of the landlords, were kinsmen of the landlords, or because, according to Muslim law, private property cannot be taken from another without compensation. Third, implementation of the reform was hindered by the lack of accurate statistics on landownership or population.[8] Fourth, the would-be reformers tried to apply a crude version of Marxist class relations to a society that was organized in a different way. The main divisions in Afghan society are not by class, but by "household, lineage, clan, tribe, settlement or village and ethnic group."[9] Fifth, land ownership was linked to traditions of local autonomy. "Afghan khans and other local leaders are expected to protect their clients from intrusions by the central government. Hence institutions of land control, tenancy and labour service are often linked to the performance of local leaders in maintaining local autonomy on the basis of consensus within the community."[10] As a result the communists who arrived in the villages with copies of the land decree in their hands were often looked upon as representatives of the hated central government, trying to overthrow traditional methods of local self-government. Finally, it was impossible to carry out such a complex, nationwide reform when large parts of the country were in armed rebellion.

A State Department cable described the land reform as follows: "Many landless and 'land poor' peasants had wanted to refuse to accept land because of religious scruples or fear of future retribution by the deprived landlords. The *Khalqis* forced them to accept the land, threatening them with imprisonment if they refused. . . . Several of these peasants later committed suicide."[11]

Later on, Soviet officials publicly criticized the land reform, and they may have expressed such criticisms privately to Afghan leaders at the time. Here is a sample of what they said after Amin was ousted:

> Agrarian reform, . . . as carried out during Amin's rule, did not take objective reality into consideration. . . . The peasant who acquired a piece

of land used to receive from the feudal landlord part of the harvest, seeds, agricultural machinery and water. But under Amin he was deprived of all this and therefore the agrarian reform to the peasant was a negative thing and thus a wave of indignation swept the country.[12]

After a few months, many of the government's agrarian measures, which had been introduced with much fanfare, were quietly dropped. The land distribution, combined with the civil war and the other "reforms," so disrupted Afghan agriculture that a previously self-sufficient country was faced with a large deficit of grain.[13]

Other Reforms

Another reform that was enacted without sufficient attention to existing customs and practical results was the attempt to ease the burden of peasant indebtedness. A decree of July 1978 reduced or canceled all rural debts prior to 1974 and forbade lenders to collect usury in the future. While the aim of the reform was admirable, the communists did not anticipate the consequences. Traditionally, many peasants had to borrow each year in order to buy the seed grain, farm tools, and other items needed to plant and raise a crop. When the government outlawed interest, the money lenders no longer had any incentive to make loans. The regime announced that it was going to establish a credit system for the peasants, but failed to do so in time. As a result, peasants were unable to plant their crops, and agricultural production fell.[14]

Opposition was also aroused by the decree of October 17, 1978, regarding women and marriage. It forbade "giving a woman in marriage in exchange for money in cash or commodity"—in other words, the practice of "bride price."[15] Here again the government tried to enforce an overly simple solution to a complex economic and social custom, ignoring the fact that when a girl got married, her family lost her labor and had to give a dowry, which was usually worth as much as the bride price.[16] Once more the ideologues in Kabul clashed head-on with ancient custom, thereby antagonizing the very people they were trying to help. Similarly, the attempt to impose a minimum age for marriage, prohibit arranged marriages, limit divorce payments, and send girls to school with boys inevitably aroused the opposition of Afghan men, whose male chauvinism is as massive as the mountains of the Hindu Kush.[17]

PREACHING ATHEISM

The factor that probably did most to create antagonism toward the communist regime, however, was its identification with atheism. The people of Afghanistan are almost 100 percent Muslim, and they are known to be very devout. The communist leaders repeatedly denied that they were communist, Marxist, or atheist, but few believed them because their policies and their way of talking gave them away. Many Afghans had been listening for years to radio broadcasts from the Soviet Union and were familiar with communist rhetoric.[18] In addition, there were hundreds of thousands of Tadzhiks, Uzbeks, Turkmen, and Kirghiz in Afghanistan who had fled from the USSR in the aftermath of the Bolshevik Revolution, and they were not easily fooled by communist propaganda. The Taraki/Amin regime gave itself away by making many references to Marx and Lenin, by using the term "comrade," and by replacing the country's partially green flag (representing Islam) with a red one (representing godless communism). Nor were Afghans reassured by such comments as the following one by Taraki: "We respect the principles of Islam. . . . But religion must not be used as a means for those who want to sabotage progress. . . . [The custom of] veils for women is not in line with any stipulation in the Koran. We want to clean Islam in Afghanistan of the ballast and dirt of bad traditions, superstition and erroneous belief. Therefore, we will have progressive, modern and pure Islam."[19]

On numerous occasions communist leaders made statements such as "We respect Islam. We will not prevent anybody from performing his religious rites."[20] But "respect" for Islam is a far cry from enthusiastic support for Islam, and refraining from interference in the performance of religious rites is not the same thing as encouraging them. The masses soon saw that the Taraki/Amin regime was communist and that it intended to carry out religious policies similar to those in the Soviet Union—preaching atheism and discouraging religion. This was a fatal mistake on the part of the communists since "the judicial arm of the government was intertwined with Muslim ideology, and thus in the context of civil and criminal justice the government symbolized Islam."[21] So "the introduction of communist ideology and the debunking of Muslim beliefs in the schools . . . not only aroused the emotions of the tribes people against the Taraki/Amin regime, but also destroyed the foundation of the central government's legitimacy."[22] To many Afghans, opposition to the communist regime became a religious duty.

The attitude of the common people toward the communists' religious policies is illustrated by the comment of an Afghan refugee:

> When the party workers came to our village, they . . . made jokes about us praying to Mecca five times a day and said we were backward. They said our Mullahs were backward and that we should not pay attention to what they said anymore. They said our prayer beads were like chains to tie us, and they said our daughters should go to school with the boys, which is against our custom. They ordered books on Lenin and Marx and ordered that they be read, even though our Mullahs said that they should not be read.[23]

VIOLATIONS OF HUMAN RIGHTS

The communist regime also antagonized people by its numerous executions. In a country where kinship is crucial, each execution embittered parents, brothers and sisters, aunts and uncles, cousins—indeed, all relatives and all members of the tribe. In Afghanistan there is a strong tradition that the killing of a relative must be avenged by the death of those responsible. Thus the regime created for itself a large mass of Afghans who felt that it was their familial duty to fight against the communists. The contrast between the policies of the Daoud regime and those of the communist regime regarding executions is worth noting: While many of the members of the communist government spent time in jail under Daoud, they survived, but Daoud, his family, and thousands of others are dead, the victims of communist executioners.[24]

Aside from executions, the Taraki/Amin regime incurred enmity among the people by mass arrests and torture.[25] Amnesty International issued a report in November 1979 that accused the government of holding 12,000 prisoners in Pul-i-Charkhi prison in Kabul, a facility designed for 6,000 persons.[26] Among them, the report said, were 42 women and children whose only crime was that they were relatives of political prisoners. Those incarcerated included people of all political views, from Muslim fundamentalists to Marxists. Most of the prisoners, Amnesty International reported, were held without charges and without trial, and many of them had been tortured. The torture had included "severe beatings, whippings, pulling out of prisoner's nails, burning his hair, and sleep deprivation."[27] *Time* magazine claimed in October 1979 that the regime had imprisoned 30,000 people and executed 2,000 others.[28]

To sum up the domestic program of the Taraki/Amin regime, one might say that a small elite of incompetent urban ideologues with no practical experience in governing and with little tolerance for native customs attempted by force to introduce alien and ill-conceived reforms, even though the regime had few capable administrators and little popular support. Moreover, these ideologues tried to introduce the reforms overnight, while at the same time they offended the religious beliefs and tribal traditions of the majority of the population. If the communists had set out deliberately to make themselves hated, they could hardly have done a more thorough job.[29]

THE PEOPLE RISE UP IN REBELLION

With the communist government attempting to enforce such unpopular policies, it is not surprising that opposition developed, and since Afghans have a long tradition of fighting for their rights, the opposition inevitably took the form of armed revolt. At first there was little opposition because the people didn't know much about the new regime, and the government hadn't yet had time to carry out its new policies. A cable from the American Embassy in Kabul described the situation as follows:

> For a few months, at least, following the 1978 revolution, most Afghans—rural as well as urban dwellers . . . were clearly willing to give the *Khalqis* the benefit of the doubt and see what their policies would be. Although the *Khalqis* were not universally welcomed within the country, Daoud's demise was not overly mourned, and in the Afghan tradition most were ready to tolerate any type of central government as long as that government stuck to its own turf and posed no threat to the time-honored Afghan ways of life.[30]

But already in the summer of 1978 there were uprisings in Nuristan and Badakhshan, and in the following months the revolt spread until it involved every one of the twenty-nine provinces and almost all of the ethnic groups in Afghanistan.[31] The rebellion was spurred on in part by Muslim leaders, who proclaimed a *jihad*—a holy war—against the godless communists, but the people found many things about the regime to object to besides its atheism. Chief among these was the attempt by Kabul to violate the centuries-old tradition of autonomy, of self-rule by the people themselves and by their customary local leaders. The communist bureaucrats meddled in the local affairs in numerous obnoxious ways, offensive to almost everybody. As a result, the opposition included not only mullahs, khans, landlords, merchants, and moneylenders, but all classes of the population. The revolt also cut across ethnic divisions. Indeed, some tribes that for centuries had fought each other, now united to fight against the communists.[32]

As the insurrection got into full swing, the territory under the regime's control shrank. In some areas government troops held sway during the daytime, while *mujaheddin* (holy warriors) dominated the scene at night.[33] Even major highways were subject to frequent raids, so that trucks had to be sent in convoys, guarded by tanks. In general, the rebels controlled the countryside and the villages, while the government dominated the cities. But in March 1979 Afghan soldiers in Herat, a major city, joined with rebels in a bloodbath that led to the killing of many government officials and loyal soldiers, as well as a number of Soviet advisers and their families. The Soviet citizens were beheaded, their heads stuck on pikes and paraded around the city. The government bombed and strafed Herat with jets and helicopters, but was unable to restore order until hundreds, perhaps thousands, had been killed.[34] In Kabul itself there were demonstrations, strikes, protests, bombings, assassinations, and at least two mutinies.

The Afghan army proved to be a highly unreliable tool for suppressing the rebellion because units often refused to fight, retreated under fire, or deserted, taking their weapons with them.[35] Indeed, the rebels claim that their main source of arms, particularly modern arms like rockets and antitank guns, has been from Afghan troops. In August 1979 soldiers in the Bala Hissar barracks in Kabul mutinied, and fighting continued for hours before loyal troops were able to bring them under control.[36] As rebellion spread throughout the country, the government needed more soldiers, so it increased draft quotas; this in turn led to more revolts. According to Professor R. Lincoln Keiser, the attempt to increase conscription in Darra-i-Nur was a major reason for the rebellion in that area.[37]

Faced with growing resistance, government forces retaliated with ruthless counterattacks. Since they often could not control the ground, they relied on their superiority in the air. Villages were strafed and bombed—sometimes with napalm—in an attempt to demolish completely those villages that harbored rebel forces. In addition, the communists deliberately destroyed farm crops in an attempt to starve the people into submission. These brutal methods simply drove more peasants into the ranks of the opposition.[38]

Resistance grew also because many people considered the communist leaders to be puppets of the Russians. Afghans have long looked upon the Russians with dislike. If a Russian came into an Afghan shop, it sometimes happened that the shopkeeper would refuse to wait on him or would do so in a surly manner. When the rebels seized control of Herat, they made a special point of hunting down the Soviet advisers and killed them brutally.[39] As a result, the wives and children of Soviet citizens were sent home, and Soviet men who had been living in apartments in Kabul moved for safety into the embassy compound.[40]

As the rebellion grew and the communist regime showed itself less and less able to suppress it, the Soviets were forced to increase their role in the conflict. More Soviet military personnel were sent in to advise the Afghan forces until, by the middle of November 1979, there were perhaps as many as 4,500 advisers in the country. In addition, increased supplies of modern military equipment were sent to Afghanistan, and Soviet pilots began flying helicopter gunships and jet fighters in attacks on the rebels. The Soviets also sent a special unit of airborne troops to assume control of Bagram airfield, the important military base north of Kabul.[41] Step by step, Moscow was moving in the direction of a massive invasion.

NOTES

1. Louis Dupree, *Afghanistan* (Princeton, N.J.: Princeton University Press, 1980), p. 462

2. Fred Halliday, "Revolution in Afghanistan," *New Left Review,* no. 112 (November-December 1978), pp. 37–38; Louis Dupree, *The Democratic Republic of Afghanistan, 1979* (Hanover, N.H.: American Universities Field Staff Reports, 1979/no. 32, Asia), p. 3.

3. Robert Neumann, "Afghanistan Under the Red Flag," in *The Impact of the Iranian Events Upon Persian Gulf and U.S. Security,* ed. by Z. Michael Szaz (Washington, D.C.: American Foreign Policy Institute, 1979), p. 138.

4. Anthony Hyman, "Afghanistan's Unpopular Revolution," *The Round Table,* no. 275 (July 1979), p. 225.

5. *Die Zeit,* June 9, 1978, as translated in *Federal Broadcast Information Service* (hereafter cited as *FBIS*), Middle East and North Africa Series, June 9, 1978, pp. S4–5. All citations to *FBIS* refer to the Middle East and North Africa (later South Asia) series unless otherwise indicated.

6. Louis Dupree, *Red Flag Over the Hindu Kush.* Part III: *Rhetoric and Reforms, or Promises! Promises!* (Hanover, N.H.: American Universities Field Staff Reports, Asia, no. 23, 1980), p. 4.

7. Hyman, "Afghanistan's Unpopular Revolution," pp. 223–224.

8. Dupree, *Rhetoric and Reforms,* pp. 7–9.

9. Richard S. Newell, "Revolution and Revolt in Afghanistan," *The World Today,* vol. 35, no. 11 (November 1979), p. 437.

10. Ibid.

11. Cable no. 199533 of August 11, 1979, p. 2.

12. Evgenii Primakov, director of the Oriental Institute of the Academy of Sciences, in *FBIS,* Soviet Series, January 23, 1981, p. D1.

13. "Afghan Uprisings," *Newsweek,* April 16, 1979, p. 64. Eyewitness accounts of the reaction of the peasants to the communist reformers were supplied by several papers delivered at the meeting of the American Anthropological Association in Washington, D.C., on December 5, 1980. Among them were "The Rebellion in Darra-i-Nur," by R. Lincoln Keiser of Wesleyan University, and "Effects of the Saur Revolution in the Nahrin Area of Northern Afghanistan," by Hugh Beattie of the University of London.

14. Hyman, "Afghanistan's Unpopular Revolution," p. 224; Dupree, *Rhetoric and Reforms,* p. 6; Fred Halliday, "Afghanistan—A Revolution Consumes Itself," *The Nation,* no. 229 (November 17, 1979), p. 493.

15. Hannah Negaran [pseud.], "Afghanistan: A Marxist Regime in a Muslim Society," *Current History,* vol. 76, no. 446 (April 1979), p. 174.

16. Dupree, *Rhetoric and Reforms,* p. 7.

17. This expression is adapted from one used by American Chargé d'Affaires Bruce Amstutz in cable no. 8073 from Kabul to State, November 20, 1979, p. 5.

18. Dupree, *Rhetoric and Reforms,* p. 4.

19. Taraki interview with *Die Zeit,* in *FBIS,* June 9, 1978, p. S4.

20. For one of many examples see Taraki's press conference of May 6, 1978, in *FBIS,* May 15, 1978, p. S3.

21. R. Lincoln Keiser, "The Rebellion in Darra-i-Nur," p. 8.

22. Ibid., p. 10.

23. H.D.S. Greenway, "Tales from the Land of the Pathans," *The Boston Globe Magazine,* June 28, 1981, pp. 22–23.

24. Dupree, *The Democratic Republic of Afghanistan,* p. 7; Theodore L. Eliot, Jr., "The 1978 Afghan Revolution: Some Internal Aspects," *Fletcher Forum,* vol. 3, no. 4 (Spring 1979), p. 86; interview with Bruce Flatin.

25. *New York Times,* September 16, 1979, p. 13.

26. Ibid. Afghan sources told an Associated Press reporter that the prison had more than 23,800 inmates.

27. *Violations of Human Rights and Fundamental Freedoms in the Democratic Republic of Afghanistan* (London: Amnesty International, November 1, 1979), p. 13; cited in Louis Dupree, *Red Flag Over the Hindu Kush.* Part V: *Repressions, or Security through Terror Purges,* I–IV (Hanover, N.H.: American Universities Field Staff Reports, Asia, 1980, no. 28), pp. 5–6. Amin claimed in November that "about 4,000" had been arrested; *Washington Post,* November 7, 1978, p. A17.

28. *Time,* October 1, 1979, p. 29.

29. The Soviets evidently did *not* approve of some of the domestic measures adopted by Taraki and Amin and the inept way in which they were carried out, but the Afghan people didn't know this. The people did know, however, that the Afghan communists were trying to imitate Soviet communism.

30. Cable no. 8073 from Kabul to State, November 20, 1979, p. 7.

31. Newell, "Revolution and Revolt," pp. 438–439; Dupree, *The Democratic Republic of Afghanistan,* p. 4.

32. R. Lincoln Keiser in his paper on "The Rebellion in Darra-i-Nur" tells how the Pashai tribes of the Kunar Valley region cooperated with their traditional Pushtun enemies, the Safis, as well as with other ethnic groups, in fighting against communist troops.

33. Many different terms have been used to designate those who are fighting against the communists in Afghanistan. My favorite is "freedom fighters" because it describes exactly what they are—fighters for freedom. This is longer and less convenient, however, than "rebels," so I have used the latter term most often. President Reagan, in an interview with Frank Reynolds on ABC, objected to use of the term "rebels," but they surely are rebelling against communism and Soviet domination. Other acceptable terms in common use are *mujaheddin* (holy warriors), insurgents, guerrillas, and resistance fighters. As for the movement carried on by the rebels, my preferred term is "national liberation struggle," which is not only accurate but also embarrasses the Soviets, who claim to be the world's leading supporters of national liberation struggles. Other popular designations are "resistance movement," "insurrection," and "guerrilla movement."

34. *Time,* October 1, 1979, p. 29; *Washington Post,* April 23, 1979, p. A16; *New York Times,* August 6, 1979, p. 8. According to *Time,* 20,000 were killed in Herat, but the *New York Times* says "about 1,000." For Amin's version of the Herat events, see *FBIS,* April 10, 1979, pp. S4–5.

35. *Time,* October 1, 1979, p. 29, estimated that about 8,000 soldiers out of an army of 80,000 had gone over to the rebels.

36. *New York Times,* August 6, 1979, pp. 1, 8.

37. Keiser, "The Rebellion in Darra-I-Nur," p. 10.

38. Halliday, "Afghanistan—A Revolution Consumes Itself," p. 494.

39. *New York Times,* August 6, 1979, p. 8; *Time,* October 1, 1979, p. 29.

40. *New York Times,* April 16, 1979, p. A3.

41. Testimony by Marshall Shulman in: U.S. Congress, House of Representatives, Committee on Foreign Affairs, Subcommittee on Europe and the Middle East, 96th Congress, second session, *East-West Relations in the Aftermath of Soviet Invasion of Afghanistan* (Washington, D.C.: Government Printing Office, January 30, 1980), p. 34. See also the *Washington Post,* September 18, 1979, p. A11.

CHAPTER 9

Moscow's Dissatisfaction with Amin and His Policies

THE USSR'S ROLE IN AFGHAN POLICIES

When the People's Democratic party seized power in April 1978, the Soviet Union apparently was delighted. It immediately granted diplomatic recognition to the new regime and soon promised all sorts of aid. But as the months wore on, Moscow must have looked with dismay as Taraki and Amin antagonized the population and goaded them into rebellion. Some observers have speculated that Kabul's internal policies were dictated by Soviet advisers from the very beginning, but it seems doubtful that the Kremlin would have advocated such self-defeating policies. When the Bolsheviks conquered Central Asia after the revolution, they followed moderate policies and tried not to antagonize the local Muslims. Similarly, in Eastern Europe in the 1940s, the communists trained and placed in power by Moscow initially followed mild policies—moving slowly, camouflaging their communist goals, honoring many national traditions, appearing to follow democratic procedures, respecting the church and religion, attacking opposition groups only one at a time ("salami tactics"), sponsoring measures with widespread appeal, and in general trying to get as much popular support as possible. The East European communists, under Moscow's guidance, also tried to organize and institutionalize a mass following through various front organizations such as trade unions, youth groups, and women's organizations. And when they seized power, they did so not in the name of the Communist party, but behind the facade of a broad national front—"People's Front," "National Liberation Front," or some similar organization. The object of this gradualism and camouflage was to minimize popular opposition until the communists had firm control of the country.[1]

But the Khalq regime, unlike the Soviet-sponsored governments in Eastern Europe, did little to camouflage its goals, and it certainly did not use gradualism. Although it had very little support, it attempted to revolutionize Afghan society almost overnight. The Soviet leaders must have wrung their hands in dismay as the Kabul regime made one blunder after another and created opposition throughout the country. If the rebellion grew, there was a chance that Afghanistan might fall into the hands of fanatical Muslim nationalists like the ones in Iran. In addition, it was costing the Soviets money and manpower because they were forced to send more arms and advisers to Afghanistan to bolster the shaky regime. And the Politburo probably worried that this was not enough—that eventually they would have to send Soviet combat troops to fight against the rebels.

There is considerable evidence that the Kremlin disapproved of many of the policies of the Khalq regime and urged it to broaden its base of popular support. Soviet officials in private conversations commented that they thought the Afghan government was doing too much too fast.[2] When Kabul announced that it would establish a "united national front" including all "progressive public and political forces," improve the work of local party organizations, and try to popularize the youth organizations, this news was publicized by Moscow Radio. In similar fashion, *Pravda* seemed to give its blessing to reports that Kabul was creating a "national organization for the defense of the revolution," which was to include all progressive forces "irrespective of party, religious, national, and social membership."[3] Further evidence that the Soviets were trying to get Kabul to adopt popular, conciliatory policies is provided by the fact that these were the kinds of policies instituted by their puppet, Babrak Karmal, when he took over after the Soviet invasion in December 1979.[4]

By the summer of 1979 the Kremlin apparently had become quite dissatisfied with the Afghan leadership. Instead of suppressing the insurrection, the Khalq regime seemed to be losing more areas to the rebels, even in the provinces around Kabul.[5] There were rumors that Soviet officials, in desperation, had contacted the chairman of the Afghan Islamic League to see if his group would support a move to dismiss the Khalq regime and replace it with a government of national unity.[6] There were also persistent rumors that the Soviets were planning to form a new, broadly based government that included ministers who had served under King Zahir.[7]

THE SOVIETS BLAME AMIN

It appears that the Soviets—quite correctly—placed the main blame for Kabul's unpopular policies on Amin. Amin was more able and energetic than Taraki, and as the months passed Taraki was pushed increasingly into the role of a figurehead—the "Grand Old Man" of the revolution, who held the highest titles but did not wield as much power as Amin. Some of the criticisms that the Soviets made of Amin after he was ousted probably give an accurate indication of their attitudes toward him when he was in power. For example, two Soviet officials wrote in April 1980: "The revolutionary transformations [in Afghanistan were] . . . accompanied by gross errors and extremist exaggerations on the left which failed to give due consideration to religious and tribal traditions. . . . The mass repressions unleashed by Amin further complicated the situation. Antigovernment feelings in the country were further strengthened. The military capacities of the Afghan Army were further weakened."[8]

A secret State Department cable dated August 11, 1979, reported that the Soviets were actively scheming against Amin and were supported by "members of the anti-Amin alignment" in the cabinet, all of whom, the cable pointed out, were non-Pushtuns—the finance minister, justice minister, public works minister, and the minister of information and culture. Amin, it was said, was "very alert to developments, but probably not aware of everything that has occurred."[9]

At the end of August 1979 the residents of Kabul woke up one morning to find copies of a "night letter" (an underground document distributed clandestinely) in which a group of "*Khalqis* who favor unity" denounced Amin for his many misdeeds, including the following:

1. Excess of selfishness and personality cult. . . .
3. Establishing a centralized leadership instead of a democratic leadership.
4. Separation of the Party and revolution for personal and family benefits.
5. Displacing and dismissing loyal revolutionary personalities. . . .
7. Ignoring what was promised to the people and lack of democratic freedom and personal security. Putting thousands of *Khalqis* in jail who did not come to terms with the "Loyal Student" [Amin].
8. . . . Attacking religion and tradition. . . .
12. Violent acts and the use of military force.
13. Collusion with foreign enemies. . . .
14. Collusion with domestic enemies, and assigning them to important positions.

. . . By assigning his brother as chief security officer of the northern provinces, once again Amin showed that he and only he is in charge of everything and brooks no competition. He assigned all of his relatives, tribe and close friends to important positions. His nephew and son-in-law is deputy foreign minister. Another of his close relatives is in charge of the traffic department and is busy robbing people's pockets. . . .

Amin's behavior and tyranny are an embarrassment to the democratic *Khalq* Party of Afghanistan. This has caused the oppositionist elements to unite to threaten the security and safety of the country. . . .

> Although we informed the General Secretary of the Party [Taraki] of Amin's acts and behavior many times, he told us with much regret that Amin is in charge of everything and he (the General Secretary) cannot do anything. . . .
> Therefore it is evident that all *Khalqis* should join hands against Amin and disarm him of his power.[10]

It is possible, of course, that this "night letter" was fabricated or instigated by the Soviets, the Parchamis, or the rebels, but the American Embassy considered it genuine. In any case, it is known from other evidence that there was opposition to Amin among party members, including some who held high positions, and the "night letter" probably reflected the feelings that these communists had about him.

By the time these outraged members of Khalq were denouncing Amin, the Kremlin also apparently had decided that he should be removed. A visit by Taraki to Moscow in September 1979 provided Brezhnev with an opportunity to plot against Amin. Of course we do not know what transpired between the two men, but presumably Brezhnev criticized the unpopular policies that the Kabul regime had been carrying out and demanded that Amin—the man chiefly responsible—be ousted. If Taraki protested that Amin had so much support in the army and police that he was invulnerable, Brezhnev may have suggested assassination and perhaps counseled Taraki to seek support from the Soviet ambassador in Kabul, Alexander Puzanov. Whatever was said between the two, Brezhnev went to the Moscow airport to see Taraki off and gave him a warm bear hug—pictured in the newspapers the following day.[11] We can be sure that neither man anticipated what would happen to Taraki when he returned to Kabul.

NOTES

1. For detailed discussion of these communist tactics in Eastern Europe see: Thomas T. Hammond (ed.), *The Anatomy of Communist Takeovers* (New Haven, Conn.: Yale University Press, 1975), especially pp. 23–27.

2. A junior Soviet diplomat told an American Embassy officer that the Khalqis "should have taken four or five years to effect what they tried to accomplish in a few months." Cable no. 6936 from Kabul to State, September 17, 1979, pp. 4–5.

3. *Federal Broadcast Information Service Trends in Communist Media,* July 18, 1979, pp. 3–4; *Pravda,* July 18, 1979.

4. A report in the *New York Times,* August 2, 1979, p. A10, quotes diplomats in Kabul as saying that the Soviets were urging the government to broaden its base and slow down its reforms. See also the secret State Department briefing memorandum from William R. Crawford to David Newsom, dated May 24, 1979, entitled "Soviet-Afghan Relations: Is Moscow's Patience Wearing Thin?"

5. Amin admitted in an interview that areas near Kabul were dangerous for travel. *Federal Broadcast Information Service* (hereafter cited as *FBIS*), Middle East and North Africa Series, September 12, 1979, p. S5. All citations to *FBIS* refer to the Middle East and North Africa (later South Asia) series unless otherwise indicated. See also the report by Jean-Francois Le Mounier for Agence France Press in ibid., pp. S1–2, and the report from Islamabad by Agence France Press in *FBIS,* September 5, 1979, pp. S5–6.

6. Article in *Al-Madinah* (Jidda) in Arabic, September 3, 1979, p. 1, translated in *FBIS,* September 6, 1979, p. S1.

7. Secret State Department cable no. 199533 of August 11, 1979, p. 3, reported rumors that "the Soviets are still trying to build a new regime around former royalist Prime Minister Yusuf." The cable was referring to Dr. Mohammad Yousuf (not Yusuf), who succeeded Daoud as prime minister in 1963. According to Professor Malcolm Yapp of the University of London, the Soviets contacted Nur Ahmad Etemadi, who had been prime minister from 1967 to 1971. Etemadi was in prison at the time. Interview with Professor Yapp, November 5, 1980.

8. Evgenii Primakov and Aleksandr Bovin in *L'Unita,* April 25, 1980, p. 16, as translated in *FBIS,* Soviet series, May 2, 1980, p. D5. See also Primakov's accusation that Amin was guilty of "leftist deviations" in *FBIS,* Soviet series, January 23, 1981, p. D1.

9. State Department cable no. 199533, August 11, 1979, p. 1. Resentment within the party over Amin's "high-handed behavior" and "arbitrariness" was rumored already in 1978. See cable no. 09163 from Kabul to State, November 16, 1978, pp. 1–2.

10. Cable no. 6605 from Kabul to State, September 2, 1979, pp. 2–5.

11. Tass (the Soviet news agency) reported that the Brezhnev-Taraki discussions were carried on in a "frank, fraternal atmosphere," which usually means that there were disagreements. *FBIS Trends in Communist Media,* September 12, 1979, p. 8. Some people have speculated that while Taraki was in Moscow the Soviets had him meet with Babrak or other members of Parcham and suggested to Taraki that he add some Parchamites to the government. Selig Harrison argues that an attempt by the Soviets to compel the acceptance of Babrak in the government was what led to the shootout in Kabul in September 1979. *New York Times,* January 13, 1980, p. E23.

CHAPTER 10

The Shootout in the People's Palace; Amin Rules Alone, September–December 1979

On September 11, Taraki flew back to Kabul. His reception at the airport was described by Radio Kabul in these glowing words:

> The great leader of the people of Afghanistan, Nur Mohammad Taraki, . . . today returned to the beloved country and was warmly and unprecedentedly received by tens of thousands of our noble and patriotic people, carrying flowers and revolutionary slogans. . . .
> After the airport ceremonies our great leader Nur Mohammad Taraki was escorted by Hafizullah Amin, . . . his faithful student and the great commander of the Great Saur Revolution, up to the side of his special car. . . .
> He was given a rousing and tumultuous welcome by thousands of patriotic citizens who were carrying thousands of pictures of the great leader of the people. . . . They were shouting slogans of: Good health to Comrade Taraki![1]

A few days later Taraki disappeared, the thousands of pictures of him were taken down, and his health was reported to be not good at all.

AMIN OUSTS TARAKI

Exactly what happened between Taraki and Amin after Taraki's return from Moscow is unclear, but informed sources agree that the events unfolded something like this: Amin must have learned that Taraki was planning to remove him. Amin may have been warned by Major Sayed Daoud Taroon, who was Taraki's aide-de-camp, but Amin's secret friend. Or Amin could have learned of the plot from Foreign Minister Shah Wali, who had accompanied Taraki to Moscow. In either case, on September 14 Amin strengthened his position by firing four members of the cabinet who were close to Taraki: Colonel Mohammad Aslam Watanjar, minister of the interior; Major Sherjan Mazdooryar, minister of frontier affairs; Colonel Sayed Mohammad Gulabzoy, minister of communications; and Asadullah Sarwari, head of AGSA (the secret police).[2]

One can well understand why Amin wanted to get these four men out of the government. Not only did they hold some of the key power positions, which would be crucial in any attempt to oust him, but three of the men—Watanjar, Mazdooryar, and Gulabzoy—had considerable experience in staging coups, having been leaders in the revolts against both King Zahir and President Daoud. Watanjar also had special contacts among the military, as he not only had been an officer in the army for many years but had also served as minister of defense before Amin assumed that position. By dismissing these men and ensuring his control of the armed forces, the police, and the communications system, Amin greatly strengthened his position and made it much more difficult for Taraki or anyone else to remove him. All four men fled and apparently found refuge with the Soviets, perhaps in the Soviet embassy compound. Nothing was heard from them again until after the Soviet invasion, when all four immediately reappeared as members of Babrak's first cabinet.[3]

That same day Taraki apparently telephoned Amin and asked him to come to the People's Palace to talk things over. Fearing a plot, Amin refused at first, but agreed to come when the Soviet ambassador, Alexander M. Puzanov, guaranteed Amin's safety. When Amin arrived at the People's Palace, a "wild West"-style shootout occurred. Several people were killed, including Major Taroon, who was standing in front of Amin. Amin later credited Taroon with saving his life, gave him a martyr's funeral, and renamed the city of Jalalabad in his honor.[4] Amin escaped unhurt, returned later to the palace with some of his supporters, and took Taraki prisoner.

The next day the Revolutionary Council announced that Taraki had asked "to be relieved from Party and state posts on health grounds" and had been replaced in these positions by Amin.[5] Needless to say there was considerable skepticism regarding Taraki's "illness." Some speculated that he had been killed in the shootout; others thought he was in prison. Several months later, after Babrak took over, three minor officials (including the commander of the guards at the People's Palace) confessed that on Amin's orders, in the dark of night on October 8 they had killed Taraki and buried him.[6] Whether these confessions are accurate or not (they sound authentic), it was announced on October 9 that Taraki had died "as a result of the serious illness from which he had been suffering for some time."[7] He has not been seen again.

AMIN'S RELATIONS WITH MOSCOW

After the shootout, Amin's relations with the Soviets naturally were not very warm. He apparently was convinced that Ambassador Puzanov had plotted with Taraki to kill him, and he suspected that the four cabinet members he had dismissed were hiding in the Soviet embassy. Amin demanded that Puzanov give them up, but the ambassador denied that he knew where they were. Evidently the four former ministers were being kept by the Soviets in reserve (just as they were holding Babrak) for the day when they would oust Amin. Amin must have suspected this.

In the weeks that followed, several clues to the lack of cordiality between Amin and the Soviets were noticed. Prime Minister Alexei Kosygin flew home from India without stopping in Kabul or sending the usual message of greeting.[8] Ambassador Puzanov failed to attend a ceremony celebrating the opening of a party training institute, and he arrived conspicuously late at a meeting marking the opening of the constitutional convention.[9] More important, Shah Wali, Amin's foreign minister, called together a meeting of communist ambassadors and took the highly unusual step of accusing Puzanov not only of harboring the former ministers but also of being involved in a conspiracy to assassinate Amin. Amin reportedly demanded that Moscow recall Puzanov and, after some delay, this was done.[10] In public, however, Amin pretended that his relations with the Soviets were excellent.

The Soviets, for their part, had plenty of reasons to feel antagonistic toward Amin. Aside from the fact that he had made a mess of things in Afghanistan, he had upset Moscow's plans to remove him. More than that, he had embarrassed Brezhnev by ousting Taraki just after the whole world had seen pictures of Brezhnev embracing Taraki at the Moscow airport. And, to make matters worse, Amin's foreign minister had made serious accusations against the Soviets to communist diplomats. It also is possible that Amin was too much of a nationalist for the Kremlin's taste and was unwilling to subordinate Afghan interests to those of the Soviet Union.[11] In October 1979 Amin told an American diplomat that if asked by Brezhnev himself to make a move against Afghan independence, Amin would not hesitate to sacrifice his life in opposing such a request.[12] This remark may have been prompted by pressure from Brezhnev for Amin to invite Soviet troops into Afghanistan, which would have legitimized the Soviet invasion and made it much more palatable to world public opinion.

AMIN'S TALKS WITH U.S. OFFICIALS

The Soviets may have suspected also that Amin, in desperation, was trying to improve his relations with the United States, hoping that Washington would somehow come to his rescue. As a matter of fact, Amin did make some half-hearted efforts to improve relations, but he did *not* seek aid from the United States against Russia, as Moscow later accused him of doing. On September 11, the day Taraki returned from Moscow, Amin told the American chargé d'affaires, J. Bruce Amstutz, that he wanted to have "friendly relations" with the United States. Amstutz didn't take this statement very seriously because, as he said, "public protestations by both Amin and Taraki that they want good relations with the U.S. are fairly standard."[13] A few days later, however, Amin ousted Taraki, and the State Department became more interested in the question of Amin's attitude toward the United States. Amstutz went to see Amin again, on September 27, and found that he "was all charm and friendliness" and once more spoke in favor of better relations with the U.S. government.[14]

The State Department decided to respond and made several minor gestures of friendship. An American passenger plane for the Afghan national airline was delivered, the time limit during which the Afghan government could be reimbursed by the United States for new rural schools and health centers was extended, and arrangements were made for the shipment of 200 tons of wheat seed to meet emergency needs.[15]

These gestures brought no results, however. Archer K. Blood, who served as acting chargé d'affaires for a month while Amstutz was on leave, had an interview with Amin on October 28, but learned nothing new. Amin expressed his affection for the United States—acquired, he said, while a student at Columbia—and insisted again that he wanted better Afghan-American relations. But he made no promises to do anything about the problems that were clouding these relations, such as his siding with the USSR on all foreign-policy issues, arresting and executing hundreds of his subjects, and ordering the American Embassy to cut the size of its staff. Nor did he make any move to accept responsibility for the event that had done so much to worsen relations between the two countries—the killing of Ambassador Dubs. Diplomat Blood concluded that Amin was "content for the time being with a polite but limited relationship, which both countries would refrain from exacerbating by word or action."[16] Secretary of State Vance summed up the situation in a confidential cable: "At maximum we regard our current dialogue with the Afghans as a means of exploring the possibilities for a less contentious relationship and we are not overly sanguine that even this limited objective can be sustained."[17]

Lending an air of unreality to these American-Amin discussions is the amazing fact that apparently neither Amin nor the Americans in the Kabul Embassy considered the possibility that within a few weeks the Soviets would invade Afghanistan and murder Amin. Amin said nothing to indicate that he expected a Soviet move against him or that he wanted the Americans to protect him.

On the American side, the State Department did not bother to inform its embassy in Kabul that the Soviets were collecting troops and military equipment in Central Asia. Archer Blood says that no such information arrived at the embassy while he was in charge (from October 11 to November 13),[18] and evidently none was received by Amstutz during the first few days after he returned to Kabul. On November 20 Amstutz sent a thirteen-page cable to Washington in which he discussed several possible scenarios for the future of Afghanistan, but did not include as possibilities either a Soviet invasion or a Soviet assassination of Amin.[19] According to Blood, the embassy thought the Soviets had resigned themselves to getting along with Amin and would continue to send him more men and arms to help fight the rebels.[20] Perhaps the embassy officials could have made better judgments if Washington had told them what the Soviet army was doing north of the border.

Amin may have suspected that the Soviets were out to get him (he told Blood that he didn't expect to live long),[21] but also may have felt that, since the Americans surely would not come to his rescue, he had no choice but to try to convince Moscow that he was the best man available to rule Afghanistan. Perhaps he reasoned that appealing for U.S. support was hopeless, and any such appeal would make the Soviets even more determined to overthrow him.

American support for Amin against the Russians was indeed improbable. The United States was not inclined to come to the rescue of a communist tyrant, particularly one with so much blood on his hands, who had shown no concern over the murder of an American ambassador and who made no real effort to improve relations between the two countries. So the Amin-American talks of the fall of 1979 led to nothing. Meanwhile, the Soviets went ahead with their plans to invade Afghanistan and install Babrak Karmal.

AMIN TRIES TO STRENGTHEN HIS POSITION

For the time being, however, the Soviets had to get along with Amin. He had control of the Afghan army, the police, and the cabinet, and there was no way of overthrowing him except through military intervention, for which the Soviet leaders were not yet ready. So Brezhnev and Kosygin pretended that Amin had their full support and sent him a telegram of congratulations on the occasion of his election to the top government and party posts.[22] In addition, they offered to give him more military equipment—6.7-million-dollars worth—and to send KGB experts to help him improve the efficiency of his secret police (or, more likely, to infiltrate it and prepare for the day of his ouster).[23] On the surface, relations between the two countries continued much as before. For example, the first session of a new Afghan-Soviet Economic Commission was held in Moscow on October 27.[24] Similar meetings between Afghan and Soviet officials continued throughout the remaining days of Amin's rule, as if his relations with Moscow were perfectly cordial. And in fact the Soviets may have decided to give Amin another chance—to see whether he could strengthen his government, get more popular support, and suppress the insurrection.

Amin probably feared that Moscow would try again to get rid of him. He tried to prevent this by ensuring the loyalty of the police and the army and by changing his residence frequently, so as to lessen the danger of assassination. According to a diplomat who was in contact with him at this time, he spoke repeatedly about the possibility that he might be "killed tomorrow," but was rather philosophical about it.[25]

Amin also seems to have attempted to prove to the Soviets that he could run Afghanistan better than anyone else, that he could, indeed, carry out one of the main policies that Moscow had long been advocating—broadening the base of popular support. To achieve this goal he formed various mass organizations. The one that got the most publicity was the Organization for the Defense of the Revolution, which, Amin said, would "comprise representatives from all the strata and classes of our toiling people."[26] To publicize this organization the *Kabul Times* published photographs of Afghan men with rifles in their hands, described as "patriots who voluntarily enlisted their names in the Committee for Defense of the Revolution" in a certain village.[27] Amin also announced that professional unions were being formed of "various vocational groups such as writers, artists and journalists."[28] In early November, Amin addressed the first general assembly of the Khalqi Youth Organization— also designed to rally support for the regime.[29] In similar fashion, Amin tried to recruit more members into the ranks of the People's Democratic party, and he expanded the membership of the Politburo by adding several more army and air force officers.[30] The official press claimed great success for all these moves, but since most of the population opposed Amin's regime, it seems doubtful that "the masses" came flocking into his organizations in large numbers.

Amin made efforts to pacify his Muslim subjects by promising them religious freedom, repairing and whitewashing mosques, presenting copies of the Koran to religious groups, peppering his speeches with references to Allah, presiding at important religious events, and declaring that "the great *Khalqi* revolution is totally based on the principles of Islam." He even went so far as to bring together a group of submissive religious leaders in a Jamiat-i-Ulama (religious council) and have them proclaim him Olelamar, that is, a secular leader who rules through the authority of Allah. This, in effect, bestowed upon Amin the equivalent of the divine right of kings, which meant that failure to obey him could result in the penalty of death.[31] Most Afghans paid no attention, however, to these feeble attempts by Marxist Amin to convince them that he was a good Muslim and the representative of Allah.

Amin also promised the people a new constitution,[32] and he tried to make Taraki the scapegoat for all the unpopular policies of the past.[33] He put forward his so-called "Great Slogan" of "security, legality and justice," but many Afghans knew that Amin personally was the reason why security, legality, and justice did not exist in Afghanistan.[34] Amin released (or claimed to have released) hundreds of prisoners from jail, but for each prisoner let free there was at least one new person arrested. An American diplomat described the mood in Kabul in the fall of 1979 as follows: "[There is] an atmosphere of mortal fear and dread pervading the country, as virtually every Afghan (even some 'loyal *Khalqis*') wonders if tonight is his night to fall into the clutches of the security authorities, perhaps to disappear into one of the country's overcrowded prisons, never to be heard from again."[35]

The policies that Amin announced sounded a bit ridiculous since he declared, in effect, that the government would stop doing the many harsh and unpopular things that it had been doing all along—under his leadership. "Nobody would be sent to prison," he said, "without being charged with an offense." Furthermore "whoever may have been arrested without due cause will be released immediately." "There will not be any type of pressure or force used on any individual . . . to make him act contrary to his sacred religious beliefs." Everyone would enjoy "full liberties and inviolable democratic rights." The name of the police would be changed, and they would "not engage in any unjust acts" or "engage in any acts of repression." There would be "fraternity and equality and democratic freedom for all ethnic groups." And, finally, Amin promised to produce "food, clothes and housing" for the people.[36]

But Amin's efforts to make himself popular came to naught. Since many people held him responsible for the regime's harshest measures, it is doubtful that they were impressed when the lion claimed that he had been miraculously transformed into a lamb. It is also unlikely that Amin succeeded in his efforts to make Taraki the scapegoat for unpopular policies that Amin himself had carried out. A month after he became president a mutiny broke out in the 7th Army Division at the Rishkor base, south of Kabul,[37] and throughout the country armed opposition to the regime continued at a high level. Amin's reforms were too little and much too late.

Amin also tried to suppress the opposition by the use of military power, but with little success. At the end of October he launched a major offensive against the rebels in Paktia province and forced them to flee, sweeping perhaps as many as 40,000 people across the frontier into Pakistan.[38] But this was only a temporary victory in one province; when his troops were withdrawn from Paktia, the rebels took over agian. Amin was afraid to send his most reliable army units away from the capital for fear that he would be overthrown, either by the Soviets or by the rebels. In fact, guerrilla forces did get dangerously close to Kabul during the latter part of 1979, and they also increased their activities in Badakhshan province.

If Amin's attempts to win the support of the Afghan people failed, his efforts to secure the favor of the Soviets were equally unsuccessful. They apparently had decided already by September, if not earlier, that he was a loser, and his record since then had given them no reason to change their minds. It may be that after the September shootout they had decided to see whether Amin's new policies would gain him more support and whether he would be able to make much headway in suppressing the rebels. But he had no significant success with either goal. In addition, he failed to do something the Soviets apparently had been suggesting urgently—broadening the government by admitting members of the Parcham and Taraki factions. When Taraki was alive there had been pitifully few people who could be depended upon to support the government and help carry out its policies. Now, with the flight or expulsion of many of Taraki's followers, the base of support for the regime was further narrowed. All things considered, the Soviets found no reason to cancel their preparations to intervene with military force and oust Amin.

Amin knew that Moscow was not entirely pleased with him and his policies, and he probably was suspicious about the extensive military preparations the Soviets were making. According to the *Indian Express,* President Zia of Pakistan later said that in early December Amin sent him several desperate requests for an immediate meeting. "For obvious reasons, I could not have gone to meet him," General Zia reportedly said. "I asked [my foreign affairs adviser] Aga Shahi to go, but the day he was to go to Kabul, the airstrip was under snow, and then it was too late because the Russians had arrived."[39] Just what Amin thought Zia could do to help him remains a mystery. About the only thing Zia might have done was to grant him asylum, and one wonders whether Zia would have been willing to do even that. Amin's suspicions about the Soviets were, of course, well founded, as the next chapter will explain.

NOTES

1. Broadcast by Radio Kabul in English, September 11, 1979, *Federal Broadcast Information Service* (hereafter cited as *FBIS*), Middle East and North Africa Series, September 12, 1979, pp. S3–4. All citations to *FBIS* refer to the Middle East and North Africa (later South Asia) series unless otherwise indicated.

2. *Far Eastern Economic Review,* October 5, 1979, p. 12. Their replacements were announced in the *Kabul Times,* September 15, 1979, p. 1.

3. When Foreign Minister Shah Wali accused the Soviet embassy of harboring Watanjar, Soviet Deputy Chief of Mission Vasilii Safronchuk did not deny it, but simply asked Shah Wali how he knew this. Shah Wali replied that Watanjar had

telephoned someone from the embassy. Cable no. 07444 from Kabul to State, October 11, 1979, p. 1.

4. *Kabul Times,* September 16, 1979, p. 1; November 25, 1979, p. 2; Amin in an interview with an Indian journalist, quoted in *FBIS,* December 11, 1979, pp. S2–3; *Far Eastern Economic Review,* October 5, 1979, p. 12; *The Economist,* November 3, 1979, p. 53. Taroon, former police commandant of Kabul, was described by the American Embassy as a "brutal, psychopathic killer" who was "second only to Amin in the amount of blood on his hands." Cable no. 06914, Sept. 16, 1979, p. 2.

5. *Kabul Times,* September 16, 1979, p. 1. For more details see cable no. 07428 from Kabul to State, October 11, 1979, p. 1.

6. *Kabul New Times,* January 21, 23, 27, and 28, 1980.

7. *FBIS,* October 10, 1979, p. S1.

8. Fred Halliday, "War and Revolution in Afghanistan," *New Left Review,* no. 119 (January-February 1980), pp. 34–35.

9. Cable no. 07444 from Kabul to State, October 11, 1979, pp. 1–2. The training institute ceremony was on October 2, the constitutional ceremony on October 10.

10. Ibid., p. 1. Puzanov did not attend the meeting of ambassadors; Safronchuk represented him. *The Economist,* November 3, 1979, p. 53. The new ambassador, Fikriat Akhmedzhanovich Tabeev (a Tatar Muslim name), was approved by Amin on November 8 (*Kabul Times,* November 8, 1979, p. 1), but did not arrive in Kabul until November 28 (*Kabul Times,* December 1, 1979, p. 4). In public Amin denied that he had demanded the recall of Puzanov (*FBIS,* December 11, 1979, p. S4).

11. Some writers have described Amin as a Tito or a potential Tito. This analogy seems far-fetched for several reasons. Amin's position was infinitely weaker than Tito's had been. Tito was the unchallenged leader of a strong, united communist party; had firm control of the army, the police, and the government; and was revered by many Yugoslavs as the hero of the national resistance struggle against the Axis. Amin, by contrast, had just overthrown the recognized head of the communist party and had many enemies within the faction-ridden party organization. He had few supporters in the country and was threatened by a large-scale rebellion. Unlike Yugoslavia, Afghanistan has a common border with the Soviet Union, which made Soviet intervention easier. All things considered, Amin had no chance of imitating Tito, and there is no solid evidence that he aspired to do so.

12. Cable no. 07726 from Kabul to State, October 28, 1979, p. 4.

13. Cable no. 06789 from Kabul to State, September 11, 1979, p. 1.

14. Cable no. 07218 from Kabul to State, September 27, 1979, p. 1.

15. Cable no. 275088 from State to Kabul, October 22, 1979, p. 1; cable no. 07645 from Kabul to State, October 23, 1979, p. 1.

16. Cable no. 07726 from Kabul to State, October 28, 1979, pp. 1–6. The quotation is on p. 1. Blood confirmed all this in an interview with the author on December 16, 1981.

17. Cable no. 282436 from State to Islamabad, October 29, 1979, p. 1. That Amin did *not* seek aid from the United States against Russia was confirmed in

personal interviews with Blood on December 16, 1981 and with Brzezinski on November 3, 1981. Brzezinski also confirmed that no American aid was offered to Amin.

18. Interview with Blood, December 16, 1982.

19. Cable no. 8073 from Kabul to State, November 20, 1979. For Amstutz's views regarding the future of Amin and the regime see especially pages 1, 2, 9, and 10. Marshall Shulman says he is not surprised that as late as November 20 the Kabul Embassy had not been warned about a possible Soviet invasion, since by that date the evidence regarding Soviet intentions was not conclusive. In addition, he says, the security situation in the Kabul Embassy was so poor that Washington did not send highly sensitive information there. He says that, with the seizure of the American Embassy in Teheran and the murder of Dubs fresh on their minds, American diplomats in Kabul were afraid that their embassy might be invaded or that embassy personnel would have to be evacuated quickly. Interview with Shulman, August 6, 1981. Archer Blood, however, says that security was not a problem in the Kabul Embassy. Interview with Blood, December 16, 1981.

20. Interview with Blood, December 16, 1981.

21. Ibid.

22. *Kabul Times,* September 19, 1979, p. 1.

23. *Strategic Mid-East & Africa,* vol. 5, no. 43 (November 7, 1979), p. 6, as cited in Mark Heller, "The Soviet Invasion of Afghanistan," *Washington Quarterly,* vol. 3., no. 3 (summer 1980), p. 39.

24. *Kabul Times,* October 27, 1979, p. 1.

25. Interview with Bruce Flatin, January 12, 1981; Archer Blood in cable no. 07726 from Kabul to State, October 28, 1979, p. 5.

26. *FBIS,* October 31, 1979, p. S2, citing an interview with Amin.

27. For example, see the *Kabul Times,* November 15, 1979, p. 2. According to *FBIS Trends in Communist Media,* December 19, 1979, p. 3, Moscow had been pressing Kabul for months to form such committees.

28. *FBIS,* November 2, 1979, p. S2, citing an interview with Amin in *Neues Deutschland* (East Berlin), October 30, 1979, p. 6.

29. *FBIS,* November 6, 1979, p. S3, citing a broadcast by Radio Kabul on November 4, 1979, in English.

30. Interview with Amin in *Neues Deutschland,* translated in *FBIS,* November 2, 1979, p. S2; *Daily Telegraph* (London), November 5, 1979, cited in *FBIS,* November 7, 1979, p. S2; and *FBIS,* October 25, 1979, p. S1.

31. Cable no. 07876 from Kabul to State, November 6, 1979, pp. 1–2; *Kabul Times,* November 10, 1979, p. 1; November 15, 1979, p. 2; November 26, 1979, p. 1, and November 27, 1979, p. 2.

32. *FBIS,* September 27, 1979, p. S4, citing Amin's press conference of September 23, 1979, as broadcast by Radio Kabul.

33. *Kabul Times,* November 25, 1979, p. 2.

34. Cable no. 8073 from Kabul to State, November 20, 1979, p. 13; *FBIS,* October 31, 1979, p. S3.

35. Cable no. 8073 from Kabul to State, November 20, 1979, pp. 6–7.

36. Speech by Amin on September 17, 1979, broadcast in Dari by Radio Kabul and translated in *FBIS,* September 18, 1979, pp. S2–5.

37. Cable no 07502 from Kabul to State, October 15, 1979, p. 1; cable no. 08439 from Kabul to State, December 12, 1979, p. 1; Agence France Press report in *FBIS,* October 16, 1979, p. S1; interview with Amin by an Indian journalist, *FBIS,* December 11, 1979, p. S6. Amin admitted that there had been a plot against him.

38. Cable no. 8073 from Kabul to State, November 20, 1979, p. 10; "Soviet Military Involvement in Afghanistan," *Radio Liberty Research,* no. 365/79, December 7, 1979, p. 2; Agence France Press report in *FBIS,* October 25, 1979, p. S1.

39. *Washington Post,* February 14, 1980, p. A28.

PART 3

The Soviet Invasion and Its Consequences

CHAPTER 11

The Soviet Invasion

> *Recently the Western and especially the American media have been intentionally spreading deceptive rumors about the "interference" of the Soviet Union in the internal affairs of Afghanistan. They have even asserted that Soviet "combat troops" have been moved into Afghan territory.*
>
> *All this, of course, is pure fabrication. . . .*
>
> *It is well known that relations between the Soviet Union and Afghanistan are based on a solid foundation of good-neighborly relations [and] non-interference in the internal affairs of one another. . . .*
>
> *Speaking recently, . . . Prime Minister H. Amin . . . stated: "The Soviet Union has always demonstrated deep respect for our independence and our national sovereignty. . . . It never has, and never will, violate our sovereignty and national independence."*
>
> —*Pravda*, December 23, 1979[1]

MOSCOW MAKES ITS MOVES

The Politburo may have begun to consider the possibility of military intervention as early as the spring of 1979. Information for preliminary planning could have been collected when General Alexei A. Epishev, the head of the Main Political Administration of the Soviet armed forces, made an inspection tour of Afghanistan in April. The plans probably were further elaborated when General Ivan G. Pavlovskii surveyed the situation in Afghanistan from August to October.[2]

The arrival of Pavlovskii in Kabul was a sign that something big was afoot. He was an important man—commander-in-chief of Soviet Ground Forces and deputy minister of defense. Significantly, he had made a similar trip to Czechoslovakia in 1968 prior to the invasion and had been the commander of the Soviet troops who marched into Czechoslovakia. If there was to be a similar invasion of Afghanistan, Pavlovskii was a logical person to plan it because of his previous Czechoslovak experience and because he had no operational command. Indeed, there was no other obvious reason for him to be in Afghanistan. If the Kremlin was simply planning to send more advisers and other military assistance to help Amin, this would have been handled by a separate branch of the Soviet army, not by Pavlovskii. Because he was accompanied by sixty-three officers, including eleven generals, and they stayed in Afghanistan for two months, the visit clearly indicated that they were engaged in serious, complex matters.[3] In all likelihood this means that by August the Politburo was at least thinking seriously about invading Afghanistan. As we know, in September the Soviet ambassador in Kabul was involved in a plot to assassinate Amin. When that plot failed and Pavlovskii returned to Moscow in October, the Politburo probably made the decision to go ahead with preparations for the invasion.

The collection of personnel and equipment began in the fall; reservists living in Central Asia were mobilized, and some troops were transferred from the western USSR. Specialists such as engineers, gunners, and radar operators were called to duty; tactical aircraft were flown to Central Asian airports; airborne units were assembled, a ground satellite station was set up, and a command and control system was established.[4]

Meanwhile, the Politburo apparently tried to undermine Amin from within. Lieutenant General Viktor S. Paputin, first deputy minister of internal affairs of the USSR (that is, one of the top Soviet police officials), arrived in Kabul on November 28, ostensibly for the purpose of discussing "mutual cooperation and other issues of interest" with officials of the Afghan Ministry of the Interior.[5] It is more likely, however, that Paputin's real mission was to help prepare Kabul for the invasion by getting control of the Afghan police, pressuring Amin to step aside in favor of Babrak, persuading Amin to invite the Soviet Union to send large numbers of troops into the country, or, if all those failed, assassinating Amin. There was a shooting incident in Amin's palace in the middle of December; Amin escaped, but his intelligence chief was seriously wounded. This may have been an attempt by Paputin to get rid of Amin. In any event, Paputin seems to have failed in his mission, and he died on December 28 under mysterious circumstances. There was speculation that he had committed suicide because of his failure.[6]

While attempting to get rid of Amin, the Soviets continued their military preparations for the invasion. Special attention was given to securing control of the air and land routes that would be used by the invading forces. To accomplish this, additional troops were sent to Bagram, the important military airfield north of Kabul, and to the airport at Kabul itself. Soviet soldiers also were stationed at the crucial Salang Pass tunnel that the Soviets, with great foresight, had constructed years before.[7]

Meanwhile, the Soviet propaganda machine denied that Moscow had sent any combat troops into Afghanistan. An editorial in *Pravda* on December 23 attacked the allegedly groundless rumors about this in the Western press, and insisted that Soviet-Afghan relations were based, as always, on the principle of noninterference.[8]

By late November American intelligence had picked up a considerable amount of information about Soviet military activities in areas north of Afghanistan. According to Marshall Shulman, Secretary Vance's chief adviser on the USSR, Americans observed "puzzling signs" of Soviet military preparations. Military transport planes were flown to airfields north of Afghanistan, but then left. Pallets for military equipment appeared at airfields, and then disappeared. At first, says Shulman, American intelligence thought that perhaps the Soviets were merely carrying out a military exercise of some sort. By the time they saw elements of five and a half divisions, however, they knew the Soviets were preparing to invade Afghanistan, and they also concluded that it was not a move to help Amin, but one more like the invasions of Hungary and Czechoslovakia.[9]

By late December the Soviets were ready to dispatch combat troops to Afghanistan on a large scale. As a final step they used trickery to make sure that the Afghan armed forces would be unable to attack the Soviet transport planes when they landed to unload their troops. Soviet advisers collected the batteries from Afghan tanks, saying that they had to be winterized; tank and antitank ammunition was called in for inventory; communications equipment was sabotaged; Afghan officers were invited to a Soviet reception, plied with vodka, and then locked in; and many Afghan soldiers were disarmed and confined to their barracks.[10]

On December 24 Soviet troops began moving into Afghanistan in earnest. For two days and nights Soviet transport planes landed at Kabul airport in a steady stream, bringing thousands of soldiers, who took over the capital. Meanwhile, three motorized rifle divisions invaded by land and moved on Herat, Qandahar, and Kabul.[11] On the afternoon of December 27, President Amin received a courtesy call from the Soviet minister of communications, as if everything were perfectly normal.[12] That very night a special Soviet assault unit attacked Darulaman Palace, where Amin was living. Elements of the Afghan army loyal to Amin fought fiercely and inflicted heavy casualties on the Soviet troops, but finally succumbed. Amin and several members of his family were killed.[13]

MOSCOW'S PROPAGANDA BUNGLES

From a strictly military point of view, the Soviet invasion was efficient enough, but the political and propaganda aspects were handled in extremely clumsy fashion. First, the Afghan "request" for Soviet military "assistance" came late on December 27, *after* the invasion had already been going on for several days. Second, it seemed somewhat illogical that Amin would ask the Soviets to intervene, overthrow his government, and kill him. Third, there was the awkward fact that only a few hours after a Soviet minister paid a courtesy call on President Amin, it was announced that Amin had been executed for crimes "against the noble people of Afghanistan."[14] Fourth, Babrak Karmal, who took Amin's place, arrived from the USSR four days later as a camp follower of the Soviet army, thereby strengthening the impression that he was a Soviet stooge. He apparently was not even in Afghanistan when Amin was overthrown, and his first radio address announcing the coup was a recording transmitted by a station that claimed to be Radio Kabul, but actually was located on Soviet soil.[15]

The Soviet press, of course, gave a different version of Amin's ouster. *New Times* declared: "The fact that the removal of Amin took place concurrently with the beginning of the introduction of the Soviet contingent is a pure coincidence in time and there is no causal relationship between the two events. The Soviet units had nothing to do with the removal of Amin and his accomplices. That was the doing of the Afghans themselves."[16]

The phony appeal to the Soviet Union to intervene, issued *after* the Soviet invasion was already well under way, read as follows:

> Because of the continuation and expansion of aggression, intervention and provocations by the foreign enemies of Afghanistan and for the purpose of defending the gains of the Saur Revolution, territorial integrity, national independence and the preservation of peace and security, and on the basis of the treaty of friendship, good-neighborliness and cooperation dated 5 December 1978, the Democratic Republic of Afghanistan earnestly demands that the USSR render urgent political, moral, and economic assistance, including military aid, to Afghanistan.[17]

In other words, it was claimed that the Soviet army intervened, overthrew the government, and killed the president in order to prevent "intervention" in Afghanistan!

The Soviets also made the absurd charge that Amin had been a CIA agent. According to the line spread by *Pravda,* Tass, and other Soviet agencies, Amin, on orders from the CIA, planned to ally with the Islamic party and stage a coup in order to overturn the achievements of the 1978 revolution. Amin supposedly had received assurances from "certain circles" in Washington that he and the other conspirators would receive American military support.[18] If Amin was indeed a CIA agent, why did Brezhnev congratulate him when Amin became president of Afghanistan in September? And why would Amin, the CIA employee, have asked the Soviet Union to send thousands of troops into Afghanistan in December, as the Soviets claim he did?

A more serious question about the invasion is why the Soviets carried it out in such a blatant, massive fashion, making it obvious to all the world that this was a case of aggression. One wonders why they didn't oust Amin and replace him with Babrak first, so that the "invitation" to invade would have looked more genuine. Why didn't they fly in a smaller force of, say, 5,000 or 10,000 heavily armed commandos, which would have been sufficient to kill Amin and seize control of the radio station and other key targets? Then Babrak could have asked for more Soviet troops to assist in establishing order throughout the country, and additional units could have been sent in slowly, bit by bit, in response to his plea. Why this sudden invasion by 85,000 troops, with large numbers of tanks, armored personnel carriers, and jets?

There are several possible answers. First of all, the Soviets probably did try to get rid of Amin first. In all likelihood that was General Paputin's mission, which he was unable to carry out. Second, the Soviets may have concluded that Amin had the loyalty of most of the Afghan army and police, who would fight against any invading Soviet troops if they had half a chance. At that time the Afghan army was still a formidable force, and if it had been able and willing to fight, the Soviets would have suffered many casualties. Third, the Soviets may have remembered the lesson of their invasion of Hungary in 1956, when they initially sent only two divisions, but found that they were insufficient and had to withdraw and return with ten divisions. Fourth, they may have wished to intimidate the Afghan rebels and convince them that their cause was hopeless. Finally, it is possible that the Soviets did not want to hide the massive, overwhelming power of their invasion, but deliberately planned it that way so as to demonstrate to the world that they were powerful, determined, and ruthless whenever any ruler or state defied them.

THE ROLE OF SOVIET CENTRAL ASIANS

The political and propaganda aspects of the invasion were a failure in another way also—in the use of Soviet Central Asians. Since the people living in the adjacent republics of Soviet Central Asia are the ethnic and religious kin of many Afghans and speak the same languages, Moscow may have assumed that it would be more efficient to employ them to carry out Soviet policies in Afghanistan. After Taraki seized power, many Soviet Central Asians were sent to Afghanistan as interpreters, technicians, bureaucrats, teachers, and so on.[19] Later, during the initial Soviet invasion in December 1979, large numbers of the troops were Central Asians. Perhaps the Politburo assumed that the Afghans would welcome soldiers who looked like them, spoke their language, and came from Muslim backgrounds.[20]

If this was the Politburo's intention, the policy backfired. There is no evidence to indicate that the Afghans found the invasion any more palatable just because some of the Soviet soldiers were ethnic and religious brothers. Furthermore, the fraternization seems to have worked against the USSR, rather than for it, resulting in sympathy for the Afghans among Soviet soldiers rather than sympathy for the Soviet Union among Afghans. In addition, the invasion reportedly made some Soviet Central Asians more conscious of their ethnic and religious ties with the peoples across the frontier. Perhaps for this reason, or possibly because the reservists had finished their tours of duty, most of the Soviet Central Asians were withdrawn from Afghanistan and replaced by Slavs.[21] If the Kremlin invaded Afghanistan in part to minimize the subversive effect of Muslim nationalism on Soviet Central Asia, the results may have been the opposite of what they intended. At least some Soviet Central Asians "have sympathy for the Afghan rebels because the Afghans are defending their independence against the Russians," just as the Central Asians over the years have tried to defend their own independence against the Russians.[22]

NOTES

1. A. Maslennikov, "Naprasnye potugi" ("Futile Attempts"), *Pravda,* December 23, 1979, p. 5.

2. Professor John Erickson in Great Britain, House of Commons, Foreign Affairs Committee, *Afghanistan: The Soviet Invasion and Its Consequences for British Policy* (London: Her Majesty's Stationery Office, 1980), pp. 37–38; testimony by Marshall Shulman in U.S. Congress, House of Representatives, Committee on Foreign Affairs, Subcommittee on Europe and the Middle East, 96th Congress, second session, *East-West Relations in the Aftermath of Soviet Invasion of Afghanistan* (Washington, D.C.: Government Printing Office, January 30, 1980), p. 30.

3. Interview with former U.S. intelligence officer; Jiri Valenta, "From Prague to Kabul; the Soviet Style of Invasion," *International Security,* vol. 5, no. 2 (Fall 1980), p. 125.

4. Interview with Gary Crocker, an expert on Soviet military affairs at the State Department; John Erickson in Great Britain, House of Commons, *Afghanistan,* pp. 37–38.

5. *Kabul Times,* December 1, 1979, p. 4. On the same page there is a photograph of Paputin, hiding behind dark glasses!

6. *New York Times,* February 3, 1980, p. 10; *Washington Post,* March 14, 1980, p. A27. *Pravda* on January 2, page 6, announced that Paputin had died on December 28, but did not explain where or how. Some say he was killed in Kabul, while others speculate that he committed suicide because he had failed to complete his mission.

The American Embassy in Moscow reported:

> A plausible line of speculation is that Paputin died during the Soviet Afghan takeover and overthrow of Amin. *Pravda's* six-day delay in reporting his death may have been part of a concerted effort to blur the connection between Paputin and Afghanistan. Placement of the obituary on page six (the back page), omission of a photograph of

Paputin, . . . as well as the unusual lack of any signatures from full members of the Politburo . . . all may be part of this effort.

Cable no. 94 from Moscow to State, January 31, 1980, p. 1. There were numerous other rumors about Paputin.

7. John Erickson in Great Britain, House of Commons, *Afghanistan,* p. 249; Marshall Shulman in U.S. Congress, House of Representatives, *East-West Relations,* p. 39.

8. *Pravda,* December 23, 1979, as cited in *Kabul Times,* December 24, 1979, p. 1; and *Federal Broadcast Information Service* (hereafter cited as *FBIS*), Middle East and North Africa Series, December 27, 1979, p. S1. All citations to *FBIS* refer to the Middle East and North Africa (later South Asia) series unless otherwise indicated.

9. Interview with Marshall Shulman; Shulman's testimony in U.S. Congress, House of Representatives, *East-West Relations,* p. 39.

10. "The 'New' Afghanistan," *Newsweek,* January 21, 1980, p. 35; R.D.M. Furlong and Theodor Winkler, "The Soviet Invasion of Afghanistan," *International Defense Review,* vol. 13, no. 2 (March 1980), p. 169; Edward N. Luttwak, "After Afghanistan, What?" *Commentary,* vol. 69, no. 4 (April 1980), p. 47.

11. Interview with Gary Crocker.

12. *FBIS,* December 28, 1979, p. S1. There is a photo of them on the front page of the *Kabul Times,* December 27, 1979.

13. Eliza Van Hollen, *Afghanistan: A Year of Occupation* (Washington, D.C.: Department of State, February 1981, Special Report No. 79), p. 2; *Washington Post,* January 2, 1980, pp. A1–2, and January 7, 1980, p. A16. Kabul Radio announced that Amin had been sentenced and executed; *FBIS,* December 28, 1979, p. S2. One theory has it that the Soviets did not intend to kill Amin right away, but planned to save him for a show trial in which he would serve as the scapegoat for the sins of the previous communist regimes.

14. Announcement in Dari by Radio Kabul, December 27, 1979; translated in *FBIS,* December 28, 1979, p. S2.

15. *Washington Post,* January 2, 1980, p. A2. The full text of the speech may be found in *Kabul New Times,* January 1, 1980, and in *FBIS,* December 31, 1979, pp. S1–4. It was broadcast by Radio Kabul in Dari at 22:40 Greenwich Mean Time (GMT) on December 27, 1979.

16. *New Times* (Moscow), no. 17 (April 1980), p. 18.

17. *FBIS,* December 28, 1979, p. S2. According to *FBIS,* this "announcement by the Democratic Republic of Afghanistan" was broadcast from Kabul in Dari at 22:25 GMT on December 27, 1979.

18. Cable no. 020072 from State Department to Kabul, January 23, 1980, p. 1. The charges were made first in *Pravda* on January 19, 1980, in an article by Aleksei Petrov.

19. S. Enders Wimbush and Alex Alexiev, *Soviet Central Asian Soldiers in Afghanistan* (Santa Monica, Calif.: Rand Corporation, January 1981), p. 7.

20. Ibid., p. 16.

21. Ibid., pp. 16–17. It is possible that the Soviet military command included large numbers of Central Asian troops in the initial invasion not for political reasons

but simply because these were the units most readily available. And these troops may have been pulled out of Afghanistan after two or three months merely because they were reservists who had been mobilized for short tours of duty. Enders Wimbush offers still another possible explanation regarding the Central Asian troops: He points out that these troops probably had received little or no combat training and were sent into Afghanistan not to fight but to perform construction and other support functions. Once these functions had been completed, he says, they were withdrawn. S. Enders Wimbush, "Afghanistan and the Muslims of the USSR," a paper delivered at the annual meeting of the American Association for the Advancement of Slavic Studies, Monterey, Calif., September 20, 1981, pp. 6–7.

22. *FBIS,* Soviet series, June 20, 1980, p. R3. This *FBIS* report is based on the observations of a Soviet citizen who lived in the Tadzhik capital of Dushanbe at the time of the Soviet invasion. While he refers only to the views of Tadzhiks, there is no reason to believe that such attitudes are not shared by other Central Asian nationalities.

CHAPTER 12

The Carter Administration and the Soviet Invasion

THE SURPRISE INVASION

In December 1979, in the midst of Christmas festivities, the American public was shocked to learn that the Soviet Union had launched a massive invasion of Afghanistan. People were surprised because neither President Carter, Secretary of State Vance, National Security Adviser Brzezinski, nor any other top official had indicated that the Soviets were about to invade Afghanistan. One would have expected that before such a momentous event took place, the president would have appeared on television and warned the Kremlin of the consequences that would follow such a move, but he did nothing of the sort, either publicly or privately.

People naturally wondered what had gone wrong. Had U.S. intelligence agencies known that the Soviets were massing tens of thousands of troops on the Afghan border, along with planes, tanks, artillery, and other equipment? If so, why hadn't Carter or Vance made any public announcements to that effect? Had the president sent a private warning to Brezhnev? Or had he been taken by surprise? Why had the press and the public been kept in the dark?

It is the thesis of this chapter that the Carter administration can be faulted on three counts. First, Carter and Vance, as well as some of their highest intelligence aides, failed to realize until the last moment that the Soviet Union was preparing to launch a large-scale invasion, despite considerable evidence pointing in that direction. Second, Carter and Vance issued no credible warning

---

The Honorable Cyrus Vance, Zbigniew Brzezinski, Warren Christopher, and Marshall Shulman were kind enough to read all or part of this chapter in one draft or another and to make comments.

to Moscow not to launch an invasion, in contrast with the many such warnings they later issued about Poland. Neither Carter nor Vance issued any *public* warnings, and Carter did not send any *private* warnings either. Third, they failed until very late to inform the American people and the press about the Soviet military preparations that the intelligence community had detected.

AMERICAN POLICIES PRIOR TO THE INVASION

As we saw earlier, prior to the invasion the Carter administration had treated the Afghan situation in a restrained, low-key manner. It had reacted mildly to the communist coup in April 1978 and continued economic aid on a small scale even after the killing of Ambassador Adolph Dubs in February 1979. This moderate stance was supported not only by Carter and Vance but also initially by Brzezinski (see Chapter 7). They all hoped that the United States, by maintaining a presence in Afghanistan, could retain some influence on the Taraki/Amin regime. But as the months passed American influence dropped almost to zero. It also became quite clear that: (1) the Afghan leaders were pro-Soviet communists, (2) they were tying Afghanistan ever more closely to the Soviet bloc, (3) thousands of Afghans were resisting communist rule by armed force, and (4) Soviet involvement in Afghanistan was steadily increasing. These developments perhaps called for a change in the moderate policies that the United States had been following.

Vance and Shulman vs. Brzezinski

Reaching agreement within the Carter administration on a change in policies toward Afghanistan was complicated, however, by the differences of opinion regarding the USSR that were held by Brzezinski, on the one hand, and by Vance and Marshall Shulman, his chief Soviet expert, on the other.[1] Put simply, Vance and Shulman strongly favored détente and strove zealously to revive it. They felt that great efforts should be exerted to improve relations between the two superpowers and that there was a genuine chance of achieving this goal. They believed that over the years a network of mutually beneficial relationships could be built up through trade, scientific exchanges, cultural exchanges, and so on until the Soviets realized that more could be gained by cooperating with the United States than by trying to defeat it. Otherwise the Kremlin had nothing to lose from misbehaving, and the United States would have no leverage on Soviet policies. In other words, the carrot should be used as much as the stick. If the United States was firm, patient, and reasonable, things could be worked out, but if the United States was unremittingly hostile, there could be no chance of peace.[2]

An important part of this cooperative relationship—perhaps the most important part—would be agreements like the Strategic Arms Limitation Treaty (SALT) to limit armaments, thereby reducing the risk of worldwide destruction. As Vance put it in April 1978, "The Soviets may find it difficult to understand some of the things we do. They don't like many of the things we stand for. The future is going to depend a lot on whether or not we can begin to make progress on areas of central importance. At the heart of this lies SALT. If we can eventually reach a SALT agreement, which I believe we can, this will begin to change the whole character of the relationship, put it on the right track again."[3]

At times Vance sounded overly optimistic or even naive regarding the prospects for Soviet-American relations. For example, in an interview with *Time* in 1978 he declared that Carter and Brezhnev "have similar dreams and aspirations about the most fundamental issues."[4] Negotiating with the Russians, he said, "is a sometimes frustrating experience but at the end of the road, when you reach an agreement, they stick to their bargains."[5]

Vance was frank to admit that he and Brzezinski had conflicting attitudes toward the USSR: "We have differences of view from time to time. . . . A different perspective with respect to the Soviet Union is the biggest set of differences. I believe it is essential we try to find common ground [with the Soviets]. . . . we shouldn't be fearful of everything they do and automatically accept the thesis of the worst-case motivations."[6]

Brzezinski says that he also favored détente, but was less optimistic that it would work. He believed that for many reasons—historical, ideological, psychological, and geographical, among others—the relationship between the United States and the Soviet Union was inherently competitive, and this could not be changed. No number of agreements on trade, exchanges, arms reduction, and the like would alter Russia's determination to undermine the United States and make itself the dominant power on the globe. The Kremlin, he thought, did not want true "peaceful coexistence" with the West and could not be trusted. Vance and Shulman, in his opinion, were "accommodationists," people who were willing to go much too far in accommodating American policies to please Moscow, in the vain hope that this would buy peace. The men in the Politburo, Brzezinski felt, could not be wooed away from their policies of expansion by American concessions. They were tough communists and could be handled only by U.S. officials who were equally tough.[7]

If Brzezinski looked upon the State Department's leaders as "softies" who were willing to bend over backwards to understand the Soviet point of view, they probably looked upon him as a potential troublemaker, a man who was so profoundly and passionately anti-Soviet that he might sabotage any chances of improving relations with Moscow. The State Department apparently felt that Brzezinski had to be kept on a tight leash, lest he indulge in provocative statements and actions that would needlessly exacerbate tensions between the two states. (The State Department was not alone in its views.) Many Americans found themselves disagreeing with both Vance and Brzezinski, the former because he was too dovish and the latter because he was too hawkish. Carter himself sometimes seemed to be floundering about between the two extremes, unable to decide which of his two advisers to agree with.

The conflict between Brzezinski and Vance was also a clash of personalities. If Brzezinski was flashy and colorful, Vance was deliberately inconspicuous. If the former loved the limelight, the latter preferred to work behind the scenes. While Brzezinski was outspoken, impulsive, and assertive, Vance was reserved, cautious, self-effacing, and modest. President Carter wrote in his diary in February 1979, "Zbig is a little too competitive and incisive. Cy is too easy on his subordinates. And the news media constantly aggravate the inevitable differences and competition between the two groups."[8]

Brzezinski Says Vance Opposed Firmness

As far as Afghanistan policy was concerned, Brzezinski says that Vance and Shulman generally opposed his efforts to be firm with the Soviets prior to the invasion; on the other hand, Brzezinski was usually supported by Admiral Stansfield Turner, the head of CIA; Harold Brown, the secretary of defense; and Graham Claytor, who was secretary of the navy and then deputy secretary of defense.[9] According to Brzezinski, during the spring and summer of 1979 he became worried over the rising Soviet intervention in Afghanistan and pressed for a tougher stand by the administration. He says that as early as March he advised the president to register American concern to the Soviets.[10] Perhaps as a result of this advice, the president told Vance to warn the USSR against interfering in the internal affairs of Afghanistan. Such a warning was issued on March 23—not by Vance, however, but by State Department spokesman Hodding Carter III.[11] In May Brzezinski warned Carter that the Soviets might use Afghanistan as a stepping-stone to the Indian Ocean, and similar warnings were sent to Afghanistan's neighbors. In July he told the president that the Soviets might try to get rid of Amin, and in September he prepared options for the United States in case of a Soviet invasion.[12]

On August 2 Brzezinski made a speech in which he declared that the United States expected other nations "to abstain from intervention and from efforts to impose alien doctrines on deeply religious and nationally conscious peoples."[13] Brzezinski says that in the original draft of this speech he warned the Soviet Union against intervening in Afghanistan, naming both countries, but Deputy Secretary of State Warren Christopher deleted the names. Brzezinski told Hedrick Smith of the *New York Times* that these were the countries he was referring to, and Smith quoted "administration officials" to this effect in the *Times*. But when Christopher saw Smith's article, he reproached Brzezinski for what he had done.[14] A similar incident occurred later. Brzezinski says that in the middle of December he prepared a press "backgrounder" saying that the Soviets might invade Afghanistan, but David Newsom, undersecretary of state for political affairs, vetoed it.[15]

Public Statements on Afghanistan

These episodes help to explain why the United States never issued a strong, credible warning in public to the Soviets. Vance apparently did not like to make public statements, but preferred to leave this task to subordinates. Former President Carter commented on this in his memoirs:

> I wanted the Secretary of State second only to me to be *the* spokesman for foreign policy. Vance was quite reluctant to fill that role. Sometimes I would ask Cy specifically to make a public . . . statement. Often, I would watch the evening news to see my Secretary of State, and instead I would see his spokesman, Hodding Carter, on the screen. A lot of it was because of his [Vance's] modesty. He wanted to do the hard work. He is one Cabinet member who worked harder than I did.[16]

But while Vance did not like to make public pronouncements himself, he didn't want Brzezinski to make them either. President Carter describes the situation as follows: "Zbigniew Brzezinski was always ready and willing to explain our position on international matters . . . or comment on a current event. He and I recognized the problems generated within the State Department when he spoke out on an issue, and he did so much less frequently than would have been the case had he followed his natural inclinations. There were periods when we would agree that he refrain from making any public statements."[17] But, added Carter, "the underlying State Department objection" to Brzezinski's speaking in public was not so much what he said as "that Brzezinski had spoken at all."[18]

If Vance did not wish to make public statements and Brzezinski was prevented from doing so, what official important enough to attract attention was going to do it? When a government makes a statement, its impact is determined not only by *what* is said but also by *who* says it. This fact was recognized in principle by President Carter in his memoirs, where he wrote that "to adequately explain our nation's position" on foreign policy "only a very few people in an administration can command the attention required for this task. Except on rare occasions . . . it must be the President, the Vice President, the Secretary of State—or, if the president wishes, the National Security Adviser."[19] Yet Carter did not abide by this principle in regard to Afghanistan. During the months preceding the Soviet invasion, no substantial statements were made in public by the president, the vice president, or the secretary of state, and when the national security adviser made a speech, his words were censored by the State Department.

As a result, most of the public pronouncements were made by Hodding Carter. Since he met with newsmen regularly, almost every day, his comments did not necessarily attract great attention, either in the United States or abroad. Certainly Moscow was not automatically concerned about things he said. Nor did he say anything very dramatic until the very eve of the Soviet invasion. What he did say, over and over, was simply that the United States was opposed to Soviet intervention in the internal affairs of Afghanistan. State Department announcements on Afghanistan tended to be vague, probably reflecting vagueness in administration thinking about that country.

Later, in his memoirs, Vance admitted that the Carter administration did not do an efficient job of indicating publicly how it would respond to a Soviet invasion. He wrote: "One of the lessons to be learned from Afghanistan is the importance of giving a clear forewarning of what we viewed as unacceptable behavior, both as a deterrent to Soviet aggression and to prepare our allies and the American public for swift and firm counteractions."[20]

The administration also waited until the last minute to tell the public about Soviet military preparations for a possible invasion. It was not until December 21, three days before the start of the large-scale invasion, that the State Department finally revealed that the Soviets had assembled more than 30,000 soldiers on the Afghan border and had flown three battalions of troops to an air base near Kabul. Even at that late date, Hodding Carter declined to say anything about the likelihood of an invasion. Vance did the same. When reporters asked Vance if he thought the Soviets were going to invade, he replied, "That would be only speculation on my part."[21] Brzezinski's staff showed no such caution, however. An unnamed "White House security aide" told the *New York Times,* "Their preparations on the border show all the marks of a major military intervention. We saw the same signs before the invasion of Czechoslovakia in 1968."[22]

Secretary Vance told me in an interview that he was reluctant to issue public warnings to the Soviets because he did not have enough facts. The intelligence, he said, was "mushy." "I didn't want to get out on a limb and accuse the Soviets of planning an invasion unless I was sure; otherwise I would destroy my credibility and needlessly disturb Soviet-American relations," he said.[23] This defense sounds plausible for the months of August, September, October, and perhaps part of November, but it is hardly convincing for December. He and other State Department officials have admitted that there was much evidence of Soviet military preparations by December 4, and such evidence must have been ample by the middle of December.

Private Warnings to the Soviets

If the State Department was very slow to issue public warnings to Moscow about Afghanistan, it was also slow to issue *private* ones. Vance says that the first private protest was made by him to Soviet Ambassador Dobrynin "at the end of November," after the movement of Soviet troops had been detected. According to Vance, he warned Dobrynin that if this was a move toward Soviet military intervention, it would be seen as a very grave matter by the United States.[24] Additional information about American protests was later supplied by Shulman in a letter to Congressman Lee Hamilton, chairman of the House Subcommittee on Europe and the Middle East. Shulman apparently did not know about Vance's meeting at the end of November, but he listed four other meetings with the Soviets prior to the invasion— December 8, 11, 15, and 17. Since he did not give details as to what was said in these exchanges, it is impossible to judge them, but it may be significant that he spoke of them as "discussions," not as "warnings."[25]

Congressman Hamilton found Shulman's letter insufficiently informative, so he wrote Shulman on March 18, 1980, and asked the key question:

> I and members of my subcommittee were . . . particularly interested in the timing of the discussions with the Soviets when viewed in relationship to intelligence reports, starting in the summer of 1979, of ominous Soviet military activity toward Afghanistan. You mentioned in your testimony, for instance, that we had intelligence reports in August of Soviet military activities which indicated aggressive intentions toward Afghanistan. You also stated that there was a high-level Soviet military visit to Afghanistan in October. . . . Then *why did our government wait until December to make any official presentation or protest to the Soviet government?* [Italics added.][26]

Shulman replied, "Actual Soviet movement of troops and equipment towards Afghanistan was observed only in late November, prompting us to make the December approaches to the Soviets cited in my letter. . . . In my view, we acted as promptly and as forcefully as the evidence warranted."[27] Others would disagree with this statement. They might point out that Shulman himself stated elsewhere that "the Soviet invasion came as no surprise to the U.S., which detected a gathering of Soviet transport aircraft in October, and a mobilization of Soviet troops, mostly reserves, in Turkmenistan in late November."[28]

Interpreting Soviet Intentions

The delay in protesting to the Soviets can be explained in part by the difficulty of determining the *purpose* of the Soviet military preparations. Even if American intelligence agencies were able to provide irrefutable evidence that large numbers of Soviet troops were on the Afghan border, this did not answer the question of *why* they were there. It was possible that the troops were going in to assist the Amin regime in fighting the rebels. Shulman argues that only rather late, after the military preparations were far advanced, did it seem likely that the Kremlin had decided to overthrow Amin rather than help him.[29] Some officials also speculated that the Soviet combat units would be sent to Afghanistan to provide security for the thousands of Soviet advisers and prevent a repetition of what had happened in Herat, where many Soviet citizens and their families had been murdered and mutilated.[30]

These uncertainties were reflected in the conflicting analyses that government officials gave to a *New York Times* reporter on December 21, 1979, on the eve of the invasion: "Intelligence aides are unsure about Moscow's motives in building up forces along the Afghan border, but some officials suggested that it could be preparing for a full-scale invasion. . . . However, other officials said that they doubted that Moscow would begin a major invasion and that the buildup was part of a more gradual process of military intervention in the guerrilla war."[31]

Even when a great deal of intelligence is being collected, there is still the problem of interpreting it. In fact, sometimes the more information you have, the more difficult it is to reach a conclusion and to get that conclusion into the hands of the president, as demonstrated by Pearl Harbor. One former intelligence officer explained it as follows: "In trying to forecast what other nations will do on the basis of intelligence information, nothing is unambiguous. Everything is ambiguous because it hasn't happened yet, and some new factor can alter the situation completely. Therefore, when a President or a Secretary of State is presented with a lot of conflicting intelligence reports, he believes the one he wants to believe."[32]

This may have been a factor in the case of Afghanistan. Perhaps Carter and Vance didn't want to believe that the Soviet Union would stage a massive, blatant invasion of Afghanistan, so they rejected the idea. They wished to improve relations between Moscow and Washignton, and they were reluctant to accept the notion that the Soviets would do something that would have such a disastrous effect on those relations. They may have engaged in the common human practice of wishful thinking.

Factors Influencing the Administration

The lack of decisive action by the Carter administration may also have been due in part to the tradition of U.S. governments, whether Democratic or Republican, of looking upon Afghanistan as an insignificant country. This point was stressed in a letter to me from Leon B. Poullada, a career diplomat who served in the American Embassy in Kabul from 1954 to 1958 and returned to Afghanistan as a Fulbright scholar in the 1960s and 1970s. When the United States reacted mildly to the communist coup in 1978, he says,

> Moscow got the impression that Carter did not care what happened in Afghanistan. This was equally true for most of the political leaders and amateur diplomats of the Carter and previous administrations. The ignorance about the strategic implications of the fall of Afghanistan to the communists was almost total. When I was working on Afghan affairs in the State Department, the only high level administrator I was ever able to find who had a conception of the importance of Afghanistan was Chester Bowles when

he was Under Secretary of State in the early 1960s. I am certain that Carter was in fact "surprised" when he suddenly discovered on December 27, 1979, that the invasion of Afghanistan posed a serious threat to the Persian Gulf and the West's supplies of oil.

Afghanistan's importance to the United States increased enormously when the shah of Iran was ousted. As long as Iran was friendly toward the United States, our access to Gulf oil was secure. It was the combination of two events—the communist coup in Kabul, followed soon after by the triumph of Khomeini in Iran—that completely changed the strategic situation in Southwest Asia. The Carter administration, however, apparently failed to reevaluate the enlarged significance of Afghanistan once Iran was hostile. The president seems not to have been fully aware of how threatening it would be to the United States if Soviet army and air bases were established in Afghanistan.

Another possible reason for the failure of the Carter administration to act efficiently regarding Afghanistan was the crisis over the U.S. hostages in Iran. On November 4, 1979, Iranian revolutionaries stormed the American Embassy in Teheran and seized hostages. This immediately captured the attention of the American public and of top officials, including President Carter. Indeed, the president behaved as through his reelection depended on his ability to rescue the hostages. According to one former official, during this period it was difficult to get anyone in the government to focus on any foreign problem other than Iran.[33] With so much of the administration's time and energy devoted to Iran, it was inevitable that the Afghan situation would get less consideration than it otherwise might have.

The fiasco over the "Soviet combat brigade" in Cuba also may have been a factor in the failure of the Carter administration to issue earlier warnings about Afghanistan. In September 1979 someone in the American intelligence community suddenly "discovered" that there was a Soviet combat brigade in Cuba, and this news was passed on to the president, the secretary of state, and the Senate Committee on Foreign Relations. Senator Frank Church, who would be up for reelection, immediately made a sensational statement about it on television, presumably because he thought it would help his campaign. President Carter and Secretary Vance were embarrassed by this revelation and were pushed into making strong declarations that the situation was "unacceptable." Only later did the higher-ups check with the experts whose job was to keep track of Soviet military units and discover that the brigade had been in Cuba for many years, without any American protests! After this farcical episode, the State Department and the White House may have been suspicious of intelligence reports about Soviet troop movements, and perhaps they were reluctant to make protests until the evidence was absolutely convincing.[34]

Another element influencing the thinking of some U.S. officials was "the lesson of Vietnam." They believed Vietnam demonstrated that it is very difficult for a foreign army to impose its will on a backward country if the natives are willing to fight, the civilian population supports them, and the terrain is suitable for guerrilla warfare. Some American intelligence analysts had decided that it was foolhardy for any nation to get involved in that kind of a war, and they assumed the Kremlin had learned this lesson from the U.S. experience. They knew that Afghan men loved to fight, that the people hated Russia and communism, and that Afghanistan was mountainous. So they refused to believe that Moscow would be so stupid as to invade Afghanistan and get involved in a Vietnam-like war.[35]

Comparisons with Hungary and Czechoslovakia

Of course it is easy enough now, with the advantage of hindsight, to ask, "Why didn't the American leaders realize much earlier that the Russians were going to repeat what they had done in Hungary and Czechoslovakia?" To be fair one must admit that in the fall of 1979 the Afghan situation did not look quite like the Hungarian and Czechoslovak situations had. President Amin was not in open defiance of Moscow and had never said a critical word about the USSR in public. He had never challenged the basic principles of Soviet-style communism as the reformers in Hungary and Czechoslovakia had done. He was no Imre Nagy proclaiming neutrality and independence. And he was surely no Alexander Dubček, abolishing censorship, dissolving the political police, and introducing other liberal reforms. Far from being a liberal, Amin was a ruthless, repressive dictator. The Soviets had intervened previously to overthrow reformers, but never had they invaded a country to oust a hard-line communist. The main trouble with Amin, from the Soviet point of view, was not that he was a reformer, but that he had aroused almost the entire population against his regime. So the situation in Afghanistan prior to the invasion was not the same as it had been in Hungary and Czechoslovakia. There were two crucial similarities, however—all three countries bordered on the Soviet Union, and in all three communism was threatened with being overthrown.[36]

Why U.S. Protests Were Ineffective

Brzezinski claims that American protests to the Soviets about Afghanistan usually were initiated by him, that the State Department generally was reluctant to make the protests, and that it delivered them in such a way as to weaken their impact. Furthermore, he adds, the protests made little impression on the Soviets because Vance had no record of credibility on such matters.[37] Vance disputes this. The Soviets, he says, recognized that when he made a complaint it was serious, that it had been made after careful consideration, and that he was not bluffing.[38] But Vance's credibility with the Soviets may have been weakened by his protest over the Soviet combat brigade in Cuba. In that case he did not have time for "careful consideration," and he did appear to be "bluffing."

It was not only Vance who lacked credibility with the Soviets; it was the U.S. government and the U.S. public behind it. For many years the United States had stood by and watched helplessly while the Soviets intervened militarily in one country after another—first in its European sphere of influence (East Germany, Hungary, and Czechoslovakia) and then in the Third World (Angola, Ethiopia, and South Yemen). Whether under Carter and Vance or under earlier presidents and secretaries of state, the United States had issued warnings and protests, but had not followed them up with significant actions. When Carter became president the United States was still suffering from a severe case of "post-Vietnam paralysis," which Moscow was fully aware of. Under those circumstances, the Politburo was not likely to pay much attention to warnings unless they mentioned specific moves the United States was prepared to take. Washington would have to demonstrate that this time— unlike earlier cases—their warnings really meant something.

Vance and Shulman suggest that the private warnings about Afghanistan had little effect on the Politburo because Soviet-American relations were so bad that the Soviets had little to lose by further antagonizing Washington. "Prior to Afghanistan," says Shulman, "Carter had dismantled all of the apparatus of cooperation between the United States and the USSR. We had little leverage left."[39] The protests over Afghanistan, he points out, came soon after the furore about the Soviet brigade in Cuba, which had further torpedoed relations between the two countries.[40] This is a one-sided argument, however. Surely the "apparatus of cooperation" between the United States and the USSR" had fallen apart not just because of Carter, but because of Soviet actions, including its military intervention in Angola, Ethiopia, and South Yemen.

SALT II and Afghanistan

Brzezinski says that, prior to the invasion, Vance and Shulman were reluctant to get tough with the Soviets about Afghanistan because they were so eager to get SALT II approved.[41] Vance describes this accusation as both false and illogical. He says he wanted SALT very much; that being the case, he would have been eager to prevent the Soviets from invading Afghanistan, since such an act of aggression would be apt to sabotage SALT with Congress.[42] Shulman also disputes Brzezinski's charge. He says that he and Vance always felt that SALT should stand on its own merits, as an agreement beneficial to both countries, and that it should not be tied to Afghanistan or any other issue. When a congressman asked Shulman how much the United States should be willing to pay for SALT II, he replied, "We should not pay any price for SALT. That is, we should not make any concessions in any other field

. . . for SALT. . . . This has to be a matter of interest on their part, and on our part, of avoiding nuclear war. . . . It is not the case that we were deterred by SALT from doing what we might otherwise have done. It was not because we felt we had to be nice to them in order to sign the SALT treaty."[43]

Even if Vance and Shulman did not feel that they had to be "nice" to the Soviets to get their agreement to SALT, they may have felt that it was better not to rock the boat in public until SALT was approved by the Senate. Issuing public warnings that the Soviets were massing troops on the Afghan frontier would have alarmed the Senate, whereas the Senate would not know about private warnings. Perhaps Vance and Shulman also hoped that, since Brezhnev wanted SALT approved, he would not make any moves likely to upset the Senate. In addition, they may have been so eager to get SALT ratified and to improve Soviet-American relations that they were reluctant to believe the Russians would do such a catastrophic thing as invade Afghanistan, an act that would destroy all their hopes, all they had worked for through the years. Brzezinski, on the other hand, was always willing to believe the worst of the Soviets. Reading the same intelligence reports, he apparently concluded much earlier that an invasion was probably coming.[44]

Carter Defends Himself

If blame is to be distributed for not making strong public protests to the Soviets and for not keeping the American people informed, the ultimate blame belongs to President Carter, who was the final arbiter of American foreign policy. In order to get his side of the story I asked him to read this chapter; he declined on the grounds that he was too busy. Then I sent him eleven questions, but he replied to only one. Here is the question:

> After the Soviet invasion of Afghanistan, you went on television several times to denounce this act. You also made several public announcements about Soviet preparations for a possible invasion of Poland, and you warned Moscow not to invade Poland. Why didn't you make any public announcements about Soviet preparations for the invasion of Afghanistan or issue any public warnings to the Soviets not to invade Afghanistan?

Carter wrote out, by hand, the following response:

> We began monitoring the A. situation in May, '78. As early as 3/79 I instructed Vance to "condemn the Soviets for unwarranted influence & potential future action in Afgh." (Acc to my diary notes) "We got a lot of publicity out of our warning to them." When Taraki & then Amin took over we had complete assessments of them & their relationship to S.U. During early Spring of '79 we tried to meet SU propaganda re Afgh. Later, in May, the

CIA assessed for me the growing opposition of [to?] the Afgh regime & "whether the Soviets might intercede directly." In Sept. I instructed NSC [the National Security Council] to give me an assessment of "how to handle Afgh if Soviet involvement should escalate," & to "move on deploring the potential increase of Soviet troops in Afgh." etc., etc. It is fruitless to dwell on NSC-State post-event analyses. I was the one responsible for our nation's actions. JC

While it was kind of Carter to take the time to write out these comments, he didn't really answer the question. By his silence on the key points he seems to confirm the charges made against him in this chapter.

Further support for the charges is provided by Carter's memoirs, *Keeping Faith.* For understandable reasons this book says very little about Carter's policies regarding Afghanistan *before* the Soviet invasion. As for warnings to the Soviets, Carter makes only two vague statements. The first one says, "For several months [prior to the invasion] I had been receiving reports of increasing Soviet pressure in Afghanistan and had approved several messages of warning to Brezhnev about any direct intervention there."[45] The second statement is much like the first: "Since May 1979, we had been observing closely the increased Soviet presence in Afghanistan and admonishing the Soviets about their obvious moves toward intervention in the political affairs of the small neighboring country."[46]

Several comments on these statements are in order: (1) Carter does not claim that he anticipated the Soviet invasion; (2) he does not say that he personally sent any messages to Moscow about Afghanistan; (3) the messages that he approved for others to send warned the Soviets against "intervention," not "invasion"; and (4) he does not mention any instance where he or his administration informed Congress, the press, or the public about the military preparations the USSR was making along the Soviet-Afghan border. We must conclude, therefore, that neither Carter's memoirs nor his note to me refute any of the arguments presented in this chapter. By what he says and what he fails to say he supports these arguments.

Cautious Intelligence Chiefs

Carter, however, does not deserve all of the blame for failing to act on Afghanistan; intelligence officials must also be criticized for not anticipating the invasion and warning the president until very late. As usual, the problem was not in the collection of information, but in reaching the correct conclusions. By the end of November analysts in various intelligence agencies were convinced they had sufficient hard evidence to predict that the Soviets were about to launch a large-scale invasion, but their superiors in the intelligence community and the State Department rejected their conclusions and delayed passing on such assessments to the White House. When these intelligence analyses were finally transmitted to the president, they were rewritten in such a cautious, noncommittal form that they failed to give him a clear-cut warning. Since Admiral Stansfield Turner was the director of intelligence for the U.S. government, he bears the chief responsibility for this failure. Also sharing the blame, presumably, would be the director of the Defense Intelligence Agency, the secretary of state, and the national intelligence officer for Soviet and East European affairs, Arnold Horelick.[47]

Still, one can fault the president for not warning the Soviets publicly about the consequences that would follow an invasion.[48] In an interview with me Brzezinski argued that it would not have been appropriate to issue public warnings that the Soviets were preparing to invade Afghanistan. "What if they had not invaded?" he asked. One might reply, "Great, then the United States could have claimed credit for preventing it." Brzezinski in his memoirs admits that public warnings have more impact. He writes, "We began to publicize our concerns [about Afghanistan] in order to give greater credibility to our private admonitions." He also says in his memoirs that on September 19, 1979, he suggested to the president that "further public statements" be made by the administration. Carter, he writes, responded "with a note addressed to both Vance and me, instructing that greater publicitiy be given to the growing Soviet involvement in southwestern Asia." But despite Carter's note, says Brzezinski, the State Department was "still reluctant to press the matter."[49] Not all of the blame can be put on the State Department, however. *The president himself* could have issued a public warning about Afghanistan, as he did later about Poland. Or he could have ordered Brzezinski to do so.

What Carter Might Have Done

Aside from the matter of whether or not the Soviets should have been warned *publicly,* there is also the question of whether the *private* warnings were as strong as they should have been. For example, why didn't Carter send a private message to Brezhnev? That would have made a bigger impression than communications from Vance to the Soviet ambassador. Why didn't Carter warn Brezhnev that if the Soviets invaded Afghanistan, he would take the following steps:

1.   Withdraw the SALT II treaty from consideration by the Senate.
2.   Send arms to the Afghan rebels.
3.   Resume military and economic assistance to Pakistan.
4.   Accelerate the American military buildup; that is, create a Rapid Development Force; acquire military facilities in Oman, Kenya, and Somalia; increase U.S. naval forces in the Indian Ocean; institute draft registration; go ahead with plans to install new missiles in Western Europe; and speed up the MX missile.

5. Reduce grain shipments to the USSR, prohibit the sale of high technology, and restrict Soviet fishing in American waters.
6. Establish closer relations with China and sell China advanced military equipment.
7. Boycott the Moscow Olympics.

In addition, Carter might have pointed out to Brezhnev that an invasion would probably have other consequences:

8. The USSR would be looked upon as an aggressor by people all over the world.
9. Soviet relations with many Third World countries, especially Muslim countries, would worsen.
10. Other nations would probably join the United States in imposing economic sanctions.
11. The United Nations General Assembly would condemn the invasion.

This all adds up to a rather formidable list. All of these things happened as a result of the invasion, yet it seems likely that Brezhnev did not anticipate some of them. If he had received a message like this from President Carter, it might at least have caused him to pause and consider. Who knows, perhaps it would even have made him look for other ways of solving his problems in Afghanistan. It is difficult to see how such a message would have done any harm, while the invasion brought Soviet-American relations to their lowest point in many years. Surely one of the most important ways of avoiding clashes between the two superpowers is for each to know how the other is likely to react to a particular move by its rival.

Such a message to Brezhnev probably would have had even more impact if it had been issued publicly. A public protest by Carter or Vance would have indicated that the administration was trying to mobilize Congress and public opinion, that it really meant business. Public protests also would have made the United States look better. As it was, many people concluded that the invasion caught the American government by surprise, which meant that either our intelligence services or our leaders were incompetent. Some recalled that a few months earlier, at the signing of the SALT II treaty in Vienna, Carter had hugged Brezhnev in a warm and enthusiastic embrace, as if he were a dear friend. After the invasion, however, Carter acted almost like a betrayed lover, thereby creating the impression that he had trusted Brezhnev too much and had allowed himself to be hoodwinked. (Carter wrote me, however, that there is no truth to the rumor that at Vienna Brezhnev promised not to invade Afghanistan.)[50]

Carter's behavior in the Polish crisis was quite different. When it looked as though Russia might invade Poland, he made a big issue of it and gave

Moscow many warnings, both public and private. In his memoirs he described his actions regarding Poland as follows:

> We were monitoring Soviet military preparations very closely. Fifteen or twenty divisions were ready to move. . . . The Soviets were surveying invasion routes, had set up an elaborate communications system throughout Poland, . . . and were holding their military forces in a high state of readiness.
>
> . . . I sent Brezhnev a direct message warning of the serious consequences of a Soviet move into Poland, and let him know more indirectly that we would move to transfer advanced weaponry to China. I asked Prime Minister Gandhi to pressure Brezhnev (who was about to visit New Delhi), and warned the opposition leaders in Poland so that they would not be taken by surprise. I and other administration officials also made public statements about the growing threat to European stability.[51]

The Soviets did not invade Poland, and one cannot help but wonder if Carter's warnings helped to deter them. At the very least, it became clear to the Politburo that the United States was very much concerned over the fate of Poland. In the case of Afghanistan, unfortunately, the United States gave the opposite impression.

Of course the situation in Poland was not the same as it was in Afghanistan. General Jaruzelski managed to get the opposition movement in Poland under control without the help of Soviet military intervention, whereas Amin proved unable to suppress the rebellion in Afghanistan. If an armed revolt of that kind had erupted in Poland, the Soviets probably would have invaded that country also.

AMERICAN POLICIES AFTER THE INVASION

Carter Gets Mad

If the Carter administration can be accused of insufficient attention to Afghanistan prior to the invasion, this certainly was not the case afterwards. On December 28 President Carter told a meeting of the National Security Council that the invasion represented a turning point in Soviet-American relations. He also read aloud a message from him to Brezhnev that demanded that Russia withdraw its force from Afghanistan or face "serious consequences."[52] The *New York Times* described it as "the toughest diplomatic exchange" of the Carter presidency.[53] On the same day Carter made a televised statement from the White House: "Such gross interference in the internal affairs of Afghanistan is in blatant violation of accepted international rules of behavior. This is the third occasion since World War II that the Soviet Union has moved militarily to assert control over one of its neighbors. . . . The Soviet action is a matter of concern to the entire international community."[54]

When Brezhnev replied to Carter's message, offering ridiculous arguments in defense of the invasion, Carter became very angry and wrote critical comments on the margins of the text.[55] This anger was evident in Carter's television interview with Frank Reynolds on December 31, when the president, in effect, called Brezhnev a liar and described Brezhnev's reply as "completely inadequate and completely misleading." Carter also made the naive statement that "my opinion of the Russians has changed most drastically in the last week [more] than even in the previous two-and-a-half years before that."[56]

Vance and Brzezinski Agree

After the invasion, the differences between Brzezinski and the State Department about Afghanistan largely disappeared, since Vance and his associates were outraged by what the Soviets had done. Instead of hawks versus doves, there were now only hawks. When Carter met with his aides to decide what sanctions should be imposed on the Soviets, the State Department's list was even longer than Brzezinski's.[57] Vance and Brzezinski disagreed at this time on only two important points: Vance did not want to postpone Senate consideration of SALT II, and he did not wish to sell offensive weapons to China.[58] Since previous clashes of opinion between the two men were well known, officials made a point of telling reporters that the administration was united on Afghanistan. The *New York Times* commented, "In the past Secretary of State Cyrus R. Vance has been much more interested in preserving the fabric of what has been called 'deténte' than Zbigniew Brzezinski, the President's national security adviser. But today, Mr. Vance was described as in complete agreement because of the nature of the Soviet 'aggression.' "[59]

Shulman, in testifying to a congressional committee, indicated that he (and presumably Vance) considered the Soviet invasion a matter of great gravity:

> It is absolutely necessary to indicate to the Soviet Union that the measures that we are now taking indicate the seriousness with which we take this action, that they are not simply going to be forgotten in a month or two. . . .
> It is not only what is happening on the ground in Afghanistan, but the whole pressure on the area and the apprehensions that are created by the Soviet willingness in this instance to use force on a very large scale in a country outside the Warsaw Pact.
> . . . Their action in Afghanistan . . . raises questions about whether they feel the same lack of restraint in regard to Iran or Pakistan or other countries in the area.[60]

According to Brzezinski, President Carter also saw the broader implications of the invasion—that what was involved was not just Afghanistan, but the whole area of South Asia and the Middle East, especially the Gulf and its oil. Brzezinski says that during the days following the invasion, he gave Carter a copy of President Truman's address to Congress in March 1947 in which he enunciated the "Truman Doctrine"—one of the benchmarks in the outbreak of the Cold War—and suggested that Carter make his speech to Congress in this tradition, that he too "draw a line" beyond which Soviet expansion would not be tolerated.[61]

The Carter Doctrine

Carter did deliver that type of speech in his State of the Union address of January 23, 1980, when he enunciated the "Carter Doctrine." He started by stating that "the implications of the Soviet invasion of Afghanistan could pose the most serious threat to the peace since the Second World War." Then he added, "The region which is now threatened by Soviet troops in Afghanistan is of great strategic importance: It contains more than two-thirds of the world's exportable oil. The Soviet effort to dominate Afghanistan has brought Soviet military forces to within 300 miles of the Indian Ocean and close to the Strait of Hormuz, a waterway through which most of the world's oil must flow."[62] Finally came the key sentence of the Carter Doctrine:

> An attempt by any outside force to gain control of the Persian Gulf region will be regarded as an assault on the vital interests of the United States of America, and such an assault will be repelled by any means necessary, including military force.[63]

The president also declared, "Verbal condemnation is not enough. The Soviet Union must pay a concrete price for their aggression."[64] And he took concrete steps to punish the Soviets. These sanctions, some announced in the State of the Union address and others adopted later, added up to a rather long and varied list.

Sanctions Against the Soviets

The economic sanctions included a reduction in American grain shipments to the USSR: only 8 out of the 25 million metric tons ordered that year would be delivered.[65] The export of high technology and strategic items to the USSR was prohibited.[66] Soviet fishing in U.S. coastal waters was sharply curtailed, and the shipment of American phosphates in exchange for Soviet ammonia was suspended.[67]

A number of military measures also were carried out. The SALT II treaty that Carter and Brezhnev had signed was withdrawn from consideration by the Senate; after the invasion, it probably had no chance of passage anyhow.[68] Carter expressed his determination to push ahead with plans to strengthen U.S. military capabilities—plans such as those to boost the defense budget;

create a Rapid Deployment Force; install new missiles in Western Europe; increase U.S. naval forces in the Indian Ocean; acquire military facilities in Kenya, Somalia, and Oman; resume the canceled aid program to Pakistan; and institute draft registration.[69] In addition, joint military exercises with Egypt were held in early January, as one means of demonstrating U.S. military power in the Middle East.[70] Most, if not all, of these steps had been planned before the Soviet invasion, as a result of events in Iran and Yemen; now, however, Carter had greater resolve to see them through, and Congress was more likely to support him.

The military-related act that perhaps caused the most concern in Moscow, however, was the visit to China in January 1980 by Secretary of Defense Harold Brown. Although the trip had been planned earlier, it acquired greater significance because of the Soviet invasion. Regarding Soviet intervention in Afghanistan, Brown said that American and Chinese views "are very closely parallel about the need to strengthen other nations in the region and each side will take appropriate action on its own toward that end."[71] (This probably meant that both countries had agreed to send military and economic aid to Pakistan.) Brown also declared that if other powers (obviously the USSR) "threaten the shared interests of the United States and China, we can respond with complementary actions in the field of defense as well as diplomacy."[72] The United States was not ready to form an alliance with a communist China, but it was happy to plan cooperative moves on matters of common interest, such as Afghanistan. American officials also said that their former policy of "even-handedness" toward Russia and China had been dropped.[73] Although the Carter administration still was not willing to sell arms to China, it did agree to sales of nonlethal military equipment, including a satellite ground station that could be used for military purposes.[74] Nothing was said by Brown or the Chinese about sending arms to the Afghan rebels, but it can safely be assumed that this was a topic of discussion also. Two months after Brown's visit, in March 1980, a high-level Chinese delegation visited Washington to discuss further measures to be adopted in response to the Soviet invasion.[75]

The punitive measure that probably hurt Soviet pride the most was Carter's campaign to boycott the Moscow Olympics. The Soviet leaders had been trying for many years to get approval to hold the Olympics in Moscow, and they looked upon their final success as an indication that their regime had achieved legitimacy in the international community. A Soviet propaganda pamphlet even went so far as to claim that it was "convincing testimony to the general recognition of . . . the correctness of our country's foreign policy."[76] Brezhnev was planning to use the games as the occasion for a massive propaganda campaign, much as Hitler had done in 1936. It was a serious blow to Soviet prestige, therefore, when many states, including the United States, West Germany, Japan, and China, refused to participate. In the words of one journalist, it was a "genuine punishment" for the invasion of Afghanistan.[77]

President Carter also took a number of other steps to emphasize his anger over the Soviet invasion. He called Ambassador Thomas Watson home from Moscow, an act of protest that had not occurred when Soviet troops invaded Czechoslovakia in 1968.[78] He banned visits by top U.S. officials to the USSR.[79] He canceled an agreement whereby the Soviets would open a new consulate in New York City in exchange for an American consulate in Kiev.[80] Flights to the United States by Aeroflot, the Soviet national airline, were cut from three to two a week.[81] Scientific, technological, commercial, and cultural exchanges between the United States and the USSR were either curtailed or eliminated entirely.[82] This meant, among other things, that an art exhibit from Leningrad's famous Hermitage Museum did not tour the United States as planned.

All in all, the steps Carter took were numerous and impressive. If one adds the aid that he secretly arranged for the Afghan rebels, he did just about everything he could have done without taking direct military action. How seriously the sanctions hurt Russia is another question, and a difficult one to evaluate. They would have hurt much more if other nations had been willing to cooperate, but unfortunately some states were happy to ship grain to the Soviets or pick up contracts for advanced technology that American firms canceled. But if the sanctions accomplished nothing else, they certainly made it clear that the United States strongly disapproved of the Soviet invasion and viewed the leaders of the USSR with greater fear and suspicion than before. It is no exaggeration to say that the invasion brought about a fundamental reappraisal of American policy toward the Soviet Union.[83] The only pity is that President Carter did not tell Brezhnev in advance what he would do if Russia invaded Afghanistan. Had he done so, the Afghan people might have been saved a great deal of misery and Soviet-American relations might not have become so hostile.

NOTES

1. In a telephone interview with Vance, I commented that my own views regarding U.S. policies toward the USSR did not coincide with those of either Shulman or Brzezinski but were somewhere in between. Vance responded that the same was true of him, although his position was much closer to Shulman's than to Brzezinski's. Interview, January 6, 1982.

2. See, for example, the testimony by Shulman in: U.S. Congress, House of Representatives, Committee on Foreign Affairs, Subcommittee on Europe and the Middle East, 96th Congress, second session, *East-West Relations in the Aftermath of Soviet Invasion of Afghanistan* (Washington, D.C.: Government Printing Office, 1980), especially pages 26–29, 35, and 66.

3. *Time,* April 24, 1978, p. 20.

4. Ibid., p. 20.

5. Ibid., p. 21.

6. Ibid.

7. Interview with Brzezinski, November 12, 1981.

8. Jimmy Carter, *Keeping Faith* (New York: Bantam Books, 1982), p. 450.

9. Interview with Brzezinski, November 12, 1981.

10. Interview with Brzezinski, November 3, 1981.

11. *Washington Post,* March 24, 1979, p. A12; *New York Times,* March 24, 1979, p. 4; note from President Carter to me, January 18, 1982.

12. Interview with Brzezinski, November 3, 1981.

13. Press release, Brzezinski speech of August 2, 1979, to the American Platform Association, p. 4. Also reported in the *New York Times,* August 3, 1979, p. 1.

14. Interview with Brzezinski, November 3, 1981. Christopher said in an interview with me (April 14, 1982) that he does not remember this particular incident, but that it is not improbable. He feels that it was quite improper for Brzezinski to go behind the back of the State Department in this manner.

15. Interview with Brzezinski, November 3, 1981.

16. From an interview with Carter in *Time,* October 11, 1982, p. 64. See also Carter, *Keeping Faith,* p. 54, where he makes a similar statement. Vance admits he may have neglected this aspect of his duties. In his memoirs he says: "The secretary of state is the president's spokesman on international affairs, and there is no way that he can properly shed this responsibility. . . . On looking back, perhaps I did not spend as much time as I should have with the press, as some have suggested. I had complete confidence in the department's superb spokesman, Hodding Carter, and I felt I could devote the time saved to other important matters." Cyrus Vance, *Hard Choices: Critical Years in America's Foreign Policy* (New York: Simon and Schuster, 1983), p. 15.

17. Carter, *Keeping Faith,* p. 54.

18. Ibid., p. 53. Brzezinski makes the same point in his memoirs: "His [Vance's] reluctance to speak up publicly, to provide a broad conceptual explanation for what our Administration was trying to do, and Carter's lack of preparation for doing it himself, pushed me to the forefront. (I will not claim I resisted strongly.) That in turn fueled resentments, if not initially on Cy's part, then clearly so on the part of his subordinates." Zbigniew Brzezinski, *Power and Principle: Memoirs of the National Security Adviser, 1977–1981* (New York: Farrar, Straus, Giroux, 1983), p. 37. See also pp. 29–30.

19. Carter, *Keeping Faith,* p. 54.

20. Vance, *Hard Choices,* p. 393. For State Department statements regarding Afghanistan see: *Washington Post,* April 3, 1979, p. A12; December 16, 1979, p. A30; December 19, 1979, p. A26; December 22, 1979, p. A15; December 23, 1979, p. A8; *New York Times,* September 20, 1979, p. A10; December 22, 1979, pp. 1 and 3; and December 23, 1979, p. 11.

21. *New York Times,* December 22, 1979, pp. 1, 3.

22. Ibid.

23. Telephone interview with Vance, January 6, 1982.

24. Ibid.

25. Letter of February 12, 1980, from Shulman to Hamilton, as reproduced in U.S. Congress, House of Representatives, *East-West Relations,* p. 111. Vance, however, spoke of his meeting with Dobrynin at the end of November as a "warning." Interview with Vance, January 6, 1982.

26. U.S. Congress, House of Representatives, *East-West Relations,* p. 115.

27. Shulman letter of April 10, 1980, ibid., p. 118.

28. Interview with Shulman, "Top State Soviet Expert Sees Limited Reason for Invasion," *Defense/Space Daily,* February 12, 1980, p. 233.

29. Telephone interview with Shulman, August 6, 1981.

30. Interview with Gary Crocker of the State Department, December 18, 1981; *New York Times,* December 22, 1979, p. 3.

31. Richard Burt in the *New York Times,* December 22, 1979, pp. 1, 3.

32. Confidential interview with a former intelligence officer who prefers to remain unidentified.

33. Ibid. One need take only a quick glance at the *New York Times* or other American newspapers during November and December 1979 to see how completely the hostage crisis dominated the news and how little attention Afghanistan was getting prior to the invasion. This is also indicated by the great amount of space devoted to the hostage crisis in Carter's memoirs, *Keeping Faith.* On page 480 Carter says, "The hostages were always in my mind."

Vance's memoirs provide additional evidence on this point. He says: "In November and December [1979], both the White House and the State Department were preoccupied with the Iran hostage crisis and other issues we were pursuing with the Soviets—particularly Kampuchea and southern Africa. The accumulating intelligence on Soviet activities [in regard to Afghanistan] received less top-level attention in the U.S. government than would have otherwise been the case." Cyrus Vance, *Hard Choices,* p. 387.

34. Carter's account of the confusion regarding the Soviet troops in Cuba is in his memoirs, *Keeping Faith,* pp. 263–264. For Shulman's views, see his testimony in U.S. Congress, House of Representatives, Committee on Foreign Affairs, Subcommittee on Europe and the Middle East, 96th Congress, second session, *United States Policy and United States–Soviet Relations, 1979* (Washington, D.C.: Government Printing Office, 1979), pages 17–19 and 36. According to State Department expert Gary Crocker, American intelligence had made reports about the brigade for many years, but none of the top officials had paid attention to them. Vance commented to me that the Cuban brigade fiasco "was not a glowing chapter in the history of the American intelligence community." Interview, January 6, 1982. Senator Church gave his version of the affair in the *Washington Post,* November 19, 1982, p. A23.

35. Interview with a former intelligence officer. He says that this argument was often used against those who predicted a Soviet invasion.

36. While there was much evidence by the end of November 1979 that the Soviets were going to invade Afghanistan on a large scale, there were few, if any, clues to indicate that they were planning to kill Amin. Vance says that he did not anticipate that the Soviets would kill Amin. Interview, January 6, 1982. A

former intelligence official says that, as far as he knows, nobody in the U.S. government expected it.

37. Interview with Brzezinski, November 3, 1981.

38. Interview with Vance, January 6, 1982.

39. Interview with Shulman, August 6, 1981; interview with Vance, January 6, 1982.

40. Interview with Shulman, November 15, 1981.

41. Interview with Brzezinski, November 12, 1981; Brzezinski, *Power and Principle,* p. 426.

42. Interview with Vance, January 6, 1982.

43. Interview with Shulman, November 15, 1981; U.S. Congress, House of Representatives, *East-West Relations,* pp. 57–58.

44. If I am critical of Vance and Shulman, I nevertheless wish to make it clear that I admire them greatly as fine human beings and dedicated public servants, and I am proud to count Shulman as a personal friend.

45. Carter, *Keeping Faith,* p. 264.

46. Ibid., p. 471.

47. Interview with former intelligence officer.

48. Shulman later said, "The brazen way in which the Soviets moved to topple Amin was unexpected." U.S. Congress, House of Representatives, *East-West Relations,* p. 117.

49. Interview with Brzezinski, December 4, 1981; Brzezinski, *Power and Principle,* pp. 427–428.

50. President Carter sent the following message to me through his assistant, Steve Hochman: "Brezhnev did not promise President Carter that he would not invade Afghanistan." Letter to the author, March 19, 1982.

51. Carter, *Keeping Faith,* pp. 584–585. Brzezinski in his memoirs also describes the many warnings the administration gave to the Soviets not to invade Poland. He writes, "I was guided by the thought that the United States must avoid the mistake that it made in 1968, when it failed to communicate to the Soviets prior to their intervention in Czechoslovakia the costs of such an aggression for East-West relations." (Brzezinski, *Power and Principle,* p. 465.) It seems odd that he cites the case of Czechoslovakia when a more recent case was at hand. It would have been more appropriate, one would think, if he had written, " . . . the United States must avoid the mistake it made in 1979, when it failed to communicate to the Soviets prior to their intervention in *Afghanistan* the costs of such aggression to East-West relations."

52. Interview with Brzezinski, December 4, 1981.

53. *New York Times,* December 30, 1979, p. 1. Carter calls it "the sharpest message of my Presidency." *Keeping Faith,* p. 472.

54. *Washington Post,* December 29, 1979, p. A7.

55. Interview with Brzezinski, December 4, 1981. See also Carter, *Keeping Faith,* p. 472.

56. *Time,* January 14, 1980, p. 10.

57. Interview with Brzezinski, December 4, 1981; interview with Vance, January 6, 1982. Carter agrees in *Keeping Faith,* p. 476.

58. Interviews with Brzezinski on November 2 and December 4, 1981; interview with Vance on January 6, 1982.

59. *New York Times,* January 6, 1980, p. 15.

60. U.S. Congress, House of Representatives, *East-West Relations,* pp. 28, 42.

61. Interview with Brzezinski, December 4, 1981.

62. Press release, "The President's State of the Union Address," January 23, 1980, p. 3.

63. Ibid., p. 4. Brzezinski says that he wrote this speech, word for word. Interview, November 3, 1981. Vance, however, says: "I helped draft the president's State of the Union message," Vance, *Hard Choices,* p. 391.

64. Press release, "The President's State of the Union Address," p. 3.

65. *New York Times,* January 5, 1980, pp. 1, 6. For a detailed, comprehensive description of the sanctions and their impact see the following pamphlet: U.S. Congress, House of Representatives, Committee on Foreign Affairs, Subcommittee on Europe and the Middle East, *An Assessment of the Afghanistan Sanctions: Implications for Trade and Diplomacy in the 1980s* (Washington, D.C.: Government Printing Office, April 1981). This report was prepared by Dr. John P. Hardt of the Congressional Research Service. The grain embargo is discussed on pages 23–52. Jimmy Carter's own description of the sanctions is in *Keeping Faith,* pp. 474–482.

66. *New York Times,* January 5, 1980, p. 6; *Washington Post,* January 4, 1980, p. A12, and February 21, 1980, p. A24; U.S. Congress, House of Representatives, *An Assessment,* pp. 64–78.

67. U.S. Congress, House of Representatives, *An Assessment,* pp. 53–64 and 93–94. The phosphates/ammonia exchange was a very complicated arrangement, involving Armand Hammer's Occidental Petroleum and the Export-Import Bank. The secretary of commerce described it as "this country's largest long-term cooperative project with the Soviet Union." Ibid., p. 59.

68. *Washington Post,* January 4, 1980, p. A1.

69. Press release, "The President's State of the Union Address," pp. 4–5.

70. *New York Times,* January 9, 1980, p. 1.

71. *Washington Post,* January 10, 1980, p. A29.

72. Ibid., January 7, 1980, p. A1.

73. Ibid.; *New York Times,* March 15, 1980, p. 3.

74. *Washington Post,* January 9, 1980, p. A16.

75. *New York Times,* March 15, 1980, p. 3.

76. From a Soviet manual entitled "Little Book for the Party Activist," as cited in U.S. Congress, House of Representatives, *An Assessment,* p. 81.

77. Robert G. Kaiser, *Washington Post,* January 10, 1980, p. A19. For a description of the elaborate measures taken by the Soviet regime to impress foreign visitors see "The Potemkin Olympics," *New York Times,* July 17, 1980, p. A19. A typical Soviet commentary on the boycott can be found in the *Pravda* editorial of March 18, 1980, p. 5.

78. *Washington Post,* January 3, 1980, pp. A1, A14.

79. Ibid., January 3, 1980, p. A14, and January 8, 1980, p. A9.

80. U.S. Congress, House of Representatives, *An Assessment,* p. 98; *New York Times,* January 9, 1980, pp. A1, A7.

81. U.S. Congress, House of Representatives, *An Assessment,* p. 94.

82. U.S. Congress, House of Representatives, *An Assessment,* pp. 95–97.

83. For a typical Soviet reaction to the measures adopted by President Carter in retaliation for the invasion of Afghanistan, see the article by Leonid Zamiatin, head of the International Information Department of the Central Committee of the Soviet Communist party, in *Literaturnaia Gazeta,* February 27, 1980, p. 14. Zamiatin explains Carter's sanctions as follows: "During the election campaign, J. Carter can score points on a wave of American chauvinism and amid the din of Anti-Soviet hysteria."

CHAPTER 13

Why the Soviets Invaded Afghanistan

The Afghan government . . . made an insistent request to the Soviet Union for the provision of immediate aid and support in the struggle against outside intervention.

The Soviet Union decided to satisfy this request and to send to Afghanistan a limited Soviet military contingent, which will be used exclusively to help repel armed interference from outside. The Soviet contingent will be completely withdrawn from Afghanistan when the factors that made this action necessary are no longer present.

—Pravda, December 31, 1979[1]

WHAT'S NEW ABOUT THE INVASION?

Many foolish or inaccurate statements were made about the Soviet invasion of Afghanistan. Some commentators described it as an entirely new development, as a major turning point in the history of Soviet foreign policy. Others said that this was the first time Soviet troops had invaded a Third World country, thereby ignoring several previous invasions—northern Iran in 1920, 1941, and 1946; Outer Mongolia and Tannu Tuva in 1921; China in 1929; and three earlier (but now forgotten) invasions of Afghanistan in 1925, 1929, and 1930.[2]

Still others referred to the Soviet invasion of Afghanistan as the first time Soviet troops had marched into a country outside of the Soviet sphere of influence. This too hardly seems accurate. Afghanistan may not have been a member of the Warsaw Pact, but it surely was in the Soviet sphere of influence after the communist coup of April 1978, if not before. True enough, the Taraki/Amin regime claimed to be nonaligned and participated in the Nonaligned Movement, but it was firmly in the Soviet camp.

The only thing new about the Soviet invasion of Afghanistan was that for the first time *since 1946,* Soviet troops invaded a Third World country. But the Soviets had invaded Hungary and Czechoslovakia since 1946, and they supplied the arms for North Korea's invasion of South Korea. They supported Hanoi's invasions of South Vietnam, Laos, and Cambodia. They have stationed Soviet troops in other countries, such as Poland, East Germany, Romania, Egypt, and Cuba, as well as Hungary and Czechoslovakia. In addition, Moscow made possible the deployment of Cuban combat units that fought in such Third World countries as Angola and Ethiopia. Moreover, hundreds of Soviet military advisers were sent to Ethiopia, where they even assumed command of Ethiopian battle operations.

Some observers made much of the distinction between the Soviet invasion of Afghanistan, which was a Third World country, and the invasions of Hungary and Czechoslovakia, which were not. Others emphasized the fact that Hungary and Czechoslovakia were members of the Warsaw Pact, whereas Afghanistan was not. To the Kremlin such distinctions must have seemed much less important than two key factors all three states had in common: (1) they had common frontiers with the USSR, and (2) the survival of communist regimes was in danger.

Commentators also argued that what made the invasion of Afghanistan new and alarming was that for the first time the Soviets marched their army across the "line" of the post-World War II territorial "settlement." This, they said, distinguished the Afghan case from the invasions of Hungary and Czechoslovakia. It is true, of course, that prior to Afghanistan the Soviets themselves had not invaded a country beyond that "line," but they had aided and encouraged allies who did so—North Korea, North Vietnam, and Cuba. Whether the Soviets commit aggression with their own forces or with proxies makes little difference to the victim or to the general peace of the world. Surely there is plenty of evidence that the Soviets have been trying in many ways to alter in their favor the peace settlement after World War II.

It is difficult, therefore, to classify the invasion of Afghanistan as a major turning point in Soviet foreign policy or anything very new. It was much like Soviet invasions in Eastern Europe and was consistent with earlier Soviet policies in the Third World.

The only surprising thing about the invasion was that a number of top U.S. officials were surprised, despite intelligence reports that the Soviets were massing troops and arms along the Afghan frontier. The U.S. ambassador in Moscow at the time, Thomas J. Watson, Jr., who was an amateur at diplomacy and an amateur at analyzing the Soviet Union, admits that he did not expect the Soviets to invade. "I was surprised by Afghanistan," he says, "because I thought they had a better appreciation of the [dangers] of thermonuclear [confrontation] and didn't think they'd be willing to take that kind of risk."[3] President Carter also was surprised, as was shown by statements he made at the time. Both men would have known better if they had studied Soviet actions in Eastern Europe since World War II.

REASONS FOR THE INVASION

What were the reasons for the invasion? Like all such complex matters, the decision was probably influenced by many factors. We can believe Brezhnev when he said that it "was no simple decision."[4] Probably many Soviet officials and organizations were involved, and the decision, when finally made, contained both offensive and defensive aspects. It is conceivable that each member of the Politburo had his own reasons. In all likelihood, however, some considerations carried more weight than others.

The Inviolability of the Soviet Empire

In my opinion, the main impetus behind the invasion was a combination of two closely-related factors: (1) the Soviet Union's determination to secure its frontiers by surrounding itself with a *cordon sanitaire* of friendly, subservient, or neutral states, and (2) the "Brezhnev Doctrine," that is, the Soviet view that if any of its client communist regimes is threatened, it has the right to intervene. There can be no retreats: Once a country becomes communist, it must remain communist, whether it be Hungary, Czechoslovakia, or Afghanistan. If "reactionary" elements in some country attempt to overthrow a communist regime or to lead it away from Soviet-style communism, then other communist countries are duty bound to intervene and save it.[5]

The Soviet Union is paranoid about the security of its frontiers, a result in part of its having been invaded by hostile neighbors so often throughout its history, most recently in 1941.[6] In Moscow's view, the best way to make its frontiers secure is to annex border areas, as it did to the Baltic States and other territories in 1939–1945. The next best way is to set up obedient communist regimes in neighboring countries and guarantee their loyalty by stationing large contingents of Soviet troops in them, as they have done in Outer Mongolia, Poland, East Germany, Czechoslovakia, and Hungary. The Soviets made the mistake of withdrawing their troops from China, North Korea, Yugoslavia, and Romania, with the result that these communist states have exhibited varying degrees of independence.[7] Moscow is not likely to make a similar mistake in the case of Afghanistan.

Noncommunist rulers in nearby states, the Soviets have found, are usually unreliable—witness Pilsudski, Chiang Kai-shek, Hitler, the various rulers in Eastern Europe between the wars, and, most recently, President Daoud of Afghanistan. Even communist rulers, the Soviets have discovered, cannot be relied upon unless there are sufficient Soviet troops in the country to make these rulers behave—as shown by Mao, Tito, Nagy, Hoxha, Dubček, Ceauçescu, and, in the case of Afghanistan, Amin.

Amin was inept and insubordinate, so the Soviets killed him. The Soviets perhaps were afraid that Amin, in a desperate effort to save his life, would seek support almost anywhere, even from Peking or Washington. The Soviets also feared that if Amin were overthrown by the rebels, this would bring to power an anti-Soviet regime that would establish close ties with Pakistan, Iran, the United States, China, and other enemies of the USSR. An anti-Soviet regime might even grant military bases to the United States.

The situation in Iran also had to be taken into consideration. In view of the hostage crisis, there was a chance that the United States would invade Iran, thereby placing U.S. military power next to the southern border of the USSR. There was already a large American naval task force in the area. To Soviet military strategists, this all added up to the absolute necessity that Afghanistan not fall into hostile hands. Otherwise the Soviet army would have to defend 1,500 additional miles of frontier. As Brezhnev put it, there was

> a real threat that Afghanistan would lose its independence and be turned into an imperialist military bridgehead on our southern border. . . . The time came when we no longer could fail to respond to the request of the government of friendly Afghanistan. To have acted otherwise would have meant leaving Afghanistan a prey to imperialism, allowing the aggressive forces to repeat in that country what they had succeeded in doing, for instance, in Chile. . . . To have acted otherwise would have meant to watch passively the establishment on our southern border of a seat of serious danger to the security of the Soviet state.[8]

In Brezhnev's view, the Soviet Union already had a nightmarish problem of guarding its borders, especially the one with China, which requires the stationing of forty-six Soviet divisions and three tactical air fleets.[9] Up until 1979 it had not been necessary to defend the border with Afghanistan. But if the Afghan rebels won out, if they received aid from the United States and China, and especially if the United States obtained bases in Afghanistan, Soviet defense problems would be dramatically increased. As one Soviet official expressed it, "the introduction of a limited Soviet troop contingent into Afghanistan in December 1979 should be considered not only in the context of Soviet aid to the revolutionary regime in that country at the latter's request, but also in a broader geopolitical context, taking into account corresponding military moves by the United States and China."[10]

Soviet leaders had been worrying about the possibility of U.S. bases in Afghanistan for many years. Khrushchev in his memoirs gives this as the reason why he decided in 1955 to grant Afghanistan $100 million in aid:

> In its desire to encircle us with military bases, America threw itself all over a country like Afghanistan. . . . It was clear the Americans were

penetrating Afghanistan with the obvious intent of setting up a military base there. . . .

The amount of money we spent in gratuitous assistance to Afghanistan is a drop in the ocean compared to the price we would have had to pay in order to counter the threat of an American military base on Afghan territory. Think of the capital we would have had to lay out to finance the deployment of our own military might along our side of the border.[11]

If Khruschchev was fearful in 1955 that the United States was trying to obtain military bases in Afghanistan, it is conceivable that Brezhnev had similar fears in 1979, no matter how illogical this might seem to Americans.

Fears of Muslim Fanaticism

Brezhnev's apprehensions were compounded by his knowledge that the Afghan rebels were Muslims fighting a *jihad,* a holy war, and that they looked upon the Soviet Union as the purveyor of atheism, communism, and Russian imperialism. If the Muslims in Afghanistan succeeded in overthrowing communism and driving the Russians out of their country, the Muslims in Central Asia might try to do the same thing. Adding to this danger was the triuimph in Iran of Khomeini and his supporters, who were busily spreading the propaganda of Islamic nationalism throughout the area. If Afghanistan also came under the rule of Muslim fanatics, this would increase the danger of Islamic infection spreading into the USSR. And, since Pakistan and Turkey were Muslim too, Moscow might be faced with four hostile Islamic neighbors close to the Muslims in Soviet Central Asia and the Caucasus.[12]

Some writers have suggested that the Kremlin's fears about the effect the Afghan rebels might have on Soviet Muslims were the *chief* reason for the Soviet invasion. I disagree. Even if the majority of Soviet Muslims dislike communism and Russian rule, there is little they can do about it. Dissident movements in the Central Asian republics apparently are small, while the police and the army—both dominated by Slavs—seem to be in firm control.[13]

"Defensive Aggression"

The Soviet Union may have been concerned about Muslim fanaticism in Afghanistan and may have wished to secure its southern frontier, but it makes no sense to say that the Soviet invasion of Afghanistan was "defensive" in the normal meaning of the term. One might better describe it as "defensive aggression." The Soviet Union may feel that it has a right to invade countries on its borders and place friendly regimes in charge so as to protect itself from possible future attacks. But we can hardly accept such a position as it would be the equivalent of saying that any country has the right to attack its neighbors in order to make itself more secure. Hitler's invasion of Russia might be defended on these grounds. If the Soviet Union had to invade Afghanistan to protect its security, does this mean that it will also have to invade Poland, Yugoslavia, Romania, China, and Western Europe? Perhaps for the Soviets to feel really secure from "capitalist encirclement," the whole world, or most of it, would have to consist of subservient communist states.[14]

Averell Harriman expressed this view in 1944 when, as American ambassador to Moscow, he witnessed Soviet expansion in Eastern Europe: "What frightens me is that when a country begins to expand its influence by strong arm methods beyond its borders under the guise of security it is difficult to see how a line can be drawn. If the policy is accepted that the Soviet Union has a right to penetrate her immediate neighbors for security, penetration of the next immediate neighbors becomes at a certain time equally logical."[15]

The Brezhnev Doctrine

One manifestation of the Soviet desire for secure frontiers is the Brezhnev Doctrine, the insistence that Moscow-style communism must be maintained throughout the Soviet bloc and that the USSR has the right to intervene to preserve it. World communism, says Moscow, is indivisible, and its defense is the common cause of all communists. The men in the Kremlin realize that their hold on Eastern Europe is fragile because so many of the people in those countries hate communism and Russian domination. The Politburo fears that if one communist regime were to fall, all of them would be in jeopardy; if one part of the Soviet empire escaped from Moscow's control, other satellites might try to do the same. The Soviet bloc, therefore, must maintain an image of unity, solidity, and permanence.

The Brezhnev Doctrine has raised this long-time policy to the level of an ideological principle, making it the *duty* of the USSR to intervene whenever a communist regime is threatened with "counter-revolution." A monarchical Afghanistan under King Zahir or a republican Afghanistan under President Daoud could be tolerated as a neighbor without Moscow feeling any compulsion to invade the country and overthrow its government. But once Afghanistan became communist, it had to remain communist because Soviet prestige was involved. If the people of Afghanistan were to oust their communist leaders, this would destroy the myth that the masses everywhere desire communism. And if more states, in addition to China, Yugoslavia, and Albania, broke away from the Soviet bloc, this would further undermine another myth—that Russia's satellites are bound to it by comradely affection. Thus the Soviet Union feels compelled to prevent any communist state, and particularly one on its borders, from becoming noncommunist. Brezhnev put it in these words: "The revolutionary process in Afghanistan is irreversible."[16]

In addition, it is important to the Soviet Union (as to any great power) that it have a reputation for supporting its allies. If it allows communist or pro-Soviet regimes to fall or be attacked without coming to their aid, other

"WE HAD TO GO INTO AFGHANISTAN TO PROTECT OUR SOUTHERN BORDER. NOW, TO PROTECT AFGHANISTAN'S BORDERS—"

©1980 HERBLOCK

FIGURE 3. Herblock's View of the Soviet Invasion. "We had to go into Afghanistan to protect our southern border. Now to protect Afghanistan's borders—." From *Herblock on all Fronts* (New American Library, 1980). Reprinted with permission.

regimes will be reluctant to cast their lot with the USSR. The Soviet record on this score prior to the 1979 invasion was far from perfect: It had not sent its army to defend North Korea when it was invaded by UN forces. It had not given North Vietnam as much support as it wanted during its long war with South Vietnam and the United States. It had not protected Egypt and Syria from defeat by Israel. And, more recently, it had not attacked China in retaliation for China's invasion of Vietnam. The Soviet leaders may have decided that they could not risk another such loss of face.[17]

Tsarist and Soviet Expansion

The invasion of Afghanistan was not merely a defense of communism but also a continuation of the centuries-old tradition of Russian imperialism. Tsarist armies conquered Central Asia and the Caucasus in the eighteenth and nineteenth centuries, and the Red Army conquered them again after the revolution. The tsarist regime imposed protectorates over Outer Mongolia and Tannu Tuva, and the Soviets imitated it in 1921.[18] Russian tsars invaded and annexed Estonia, Latvia, and Lithuania, and Russian communists repeated the move in 1940. In addition, during and after World War II the Soviets continued the imperialist tradition by annexing territories from Finland, Poland, Czechoslovakia, Romania, Germany, and Japan, as well as by establishing puppet regimes in East Germany, Poland, Czechoslovakia, Hungary, Romania, Bulgaria, and North Korea.[19]

Russian history is a history of invasions—invasions *of Russia* by powerful neighbors and invasions *by Russia* of countries along its borders. Tsarist Russia at one time or another attacked all of its neighbors, both European and Asian, and Soviet Russia has continued the tradition. Since 1917 the Soviets have attacked all of their neighbors except Norway and Turkey, and they carried out three minor invasions of Afghanistan in the 1920s and 1930s. The surprising thing about the 1979 invasion, therefore, is not that the Soviets did it, but that they had not staged a major invasion of Afghanistan earlier.

The Russian tsars tried to bring Afghanistan into their sphere of influence, but Great Britain prevented it. When the British abandoned South Asia after World War II, however, the Soviet regime was finally able to fulfill the old imperialist goal of extending Russian dominance over Afghanistan. Thus the Soviet invasion of Afghanistan can be viewed as just the latest step in the centuries-old process of Russian expansion.

There is also the frightening possibility that some of the members of the Politburo voted to invade Afghanistan because they looked upon it as a stepping-stone toward the Gulf. When Molotov was trying to negotiate a pact with the Germans in 1940, he declared that the Soviets would accept the treaty if (among other things) "the area south of Batum and Baku in the general direction of the Persian Gulf is recognized as the center of the aspirations of the Soviet Union."[20] Since the Gulf—and its oil—was one of the chief aims of Molotov and Stalin in 1940, it is logical to suppose that it was not entirely absent from Brezhnev's mind in 1979.

The "Tar Baby" Syndrome

Another factor in the Soviet decision to invade was the chaotic situation in Afghanistan: conditions became so bad that the Soviets decided they *had* to go in. Initially, when the communists first seized power, the Soviets were pleased. But disappointment soon crept in as Taraki and Amin goaded thousands into revolt, making it necessary for Moscow to increase its support—in arms, advisers, and money. A situation developed like that of Brer Rabbit and the Tar Baby—the more the Soviet Union intervened, the more it got stuck, and the more difficult it became to get loose. Soviet involvement in Afghanistan was somewhat similar to American involvement in Vietnam. In both cases intervention grew and grew, step by step. In both cases the big power hoped that sending arms and economic aid would suffice, but decided to send its own troops, since the native forces were doing so poorly. As with the United States, Soviet prestige became involved. (Of course the *differences* between Vietnam and Afghanistan are many.)

As the situation in Afghanistan deteriorated, the Soviets decided that they could not tolerate Amin any longer, especially since they had someone "better" to take his place—Babrak Karmal, who would be more obedient and more competent and who was not personally identified with the unpopular policies that Amin and Taraki had imposed. Thus intervention would have three objectives: to eliminate Amin, replace him with Babrak, and suppress the armed resistance.

As Ambassador Neumann said, "the Russians had a difficult choice to make—either to get in or to get out."[21] A Soviet official described the decision as follows:

> When it became clear that the revolution could be defeated as a result of external aggression, . . . the Afghan Government called on the USSR to send limited units of Soviet forces. . . . The USSR responded to this request. This was in fact a very difficult decision. . . . When all the positive and negative aspects were weighed from the point of view of the revolutionary operation in Afghanistan and the general situation of forces in the world, it became clear that it was necessary.[22]

How the Soviets Expected the World To React

The Soviet leaders knew that the invasion of Afghanistan would alarm many governments around the world. As two Soviet officials admitted, "In Moscow it was realized that the Soviet troops' entry into the neighboring country would be regarded with hostility by many."[23] The most dangerous reaction would be, of course, some kind of military move by the United

States. But the Politburo probably concluded that the chances of a direct military clash with the United States were slight. They judged, correctly, that Washington would not go to war over Afghanistan. There was no way in which the United States could stop a Soviet army in a country so far from American shores and so close to the Soviet Union. Nor would President Carter want to order American troops to fight Soviet troops and thereby run the risk of escalation or defeat. In addition, the Soviets were not as afraid of U.S. military power as they had been ten or fifteen years before. On a global scale Russia had achieved military parity, and in the vicinity of Afghanistan Soviet power was overwhelming.

The Soviets could see that the Carter administration, especially the president, was wrapped up in the Iranian hostage crisis, and perhaps they expected that the United States would soon be involved militarily in Iran. According to Marshall Shulman, there was serious discussion in the U.S. government at the time about possible military action against Iran, and news of this leaked to the newspapers. He thought that the Soviets were waiting for the United States to move against Iran so that they could invade Afghanistan at the same time and thereby lessen the unfavorable publicity they would receive.[24]

Another consideration encouraging the Soviets to go ahead with their plans to invade Afghanistan was the apparent attitude in Washington that Afghanistan was an insignificant country. Ambassador Watson said that from the Soviet "point of view, there wasn't much risk, that we thought it to be a relatively unimportant area" and their invasion "wouldn't disturb us greatly."[25] The United States had tacitly accepted Soviet predominant influence in Afghanistan ever since the 1950s and had made no real attempt to change this. When the communists seized power in 1978, Washington did nothing, and when U.S. Ambassador Dubs was killed in 1979, the United States merely sent a note of protest. Moscow may have reasoned that, because Afghanistan already had a communist government and there were thousands of Soviet military personnel in the country, the United States would not care if one communist regime was replaced by another and the number of Soviet troops was increased.

The Soviets, moreover, had learned from past experience that they could invade neighboring communist states with impunity. The invasions of Hungary in 1956 and Czechoslovakia in 1968 had brought howls of condemnation, but within a few months these acts were overlooked, and Soviet foreign relations continued as before. Similarly, Soviet support for communist takeovers in Asia and Africa in the 1970s had brought little response from the United States. Washington, whether under Ford or Carter, had stood by and done nothing while the Soviet Union helped to establish communist regimes in Angola, Ethiopia, and South Yemen, and while Vietnam, with Soviet support, invaded Cambodia. So there was little reason to expect that the United States would do much about Afghanistan.

Furthermore, the Carter administration seemed weak and indecisive. It had declared the presence of a Soviet combat brigade in Cuba "unacceptable" and then had accepted it. Carter acted as though the most important goal of American foreign policy was the release of the hostages from Iran, yet seemed incapable of accomplishing that goal. He seemed to be all talk and no action. In addition, he had insisted that he would not use military force in crises of this sort. The Politburo probably concluded that when they invaded Afghanistan, Carter would express moral condemnation, make a few vague threats, and then adjust to the new situation.

The men in the Kremlin undoubtedly also were aware of the profound effect that the Vietnam trauma had had on American public opinion, particularly on the question of U.S. intervention abroad to prevent the spread of communism. They knew that, to many Americans, Vietnam had "proved" that it was immoral and unwise to send U.S. troops to fight communism in distant countries, particularly insignificant Third World countries like Vietnam and Afghanistan. The Senate some years earlier had forbidden President Ford to take any further steps to oppose the Marxist regime in Angola, and sentiment against foreign military intervention was still very strong. For these reasons, as well as for geographic ones, it seemed unlikely that the United States would think of intervening militarily in Afghanistan.

The Deterioration of Détente

The Politburo's decision to invade Afghanistan may have been influenced also by the deterioration of détente. The Soviet leaders may have reasoned that, even if the invasion did worsen American-Soviet relations, it did not matter because those relations were strained already. Détente had failed to produce the benefits they had hoped for. Former Secretary of State Cyrus Vance and his adviser on Soviet affairs, Marshall Shulman, feel that this was an important factor in the Soviet decision. "Relations between Washington and Moscow," says Shulman, "were already so bad that the Soviets had no inhibitions about displeasing us."[26]

Soviet commentators have been happy, of course, to claim that the decline of détente was entirely the fault of the United States and that the invasion of Afghanistan itself was forced on Moscow by hostile American actions. One Soviet official later described what he called "the atmosphere under which the decision of rendering Soviet assistance to Afghanistan was taken" and listed the following complaints against the United States and its allies:

1. Presidential Directive No. 18 of August 1977, calling for the creation of a Rapid Deployment Force.
2. The promise by North Atlantic Treaty Organization (NATO) countries in May 1978 to increase their military budgets.

3. The NATO decision to employ new medium-range missiles in Western Europe, "directed against the Soviet Union and its allies."

4. "The United States had frozen in practice the signing of the SALT II agreement."

5. "The flirtation which the United States is carrying on with China."[27]

All these acts, he pointed out, had occurred before the Soviets invaded Afghanistan.

Another Soviet official listed additional complaints against the United States and its allies:

6. "The theoretical ranking of relationships with the USSR as almost the last among the American foreign policy priorities."

7. "The effort to remove the Soviet Union from the peaceful settlement of conflict situations even in regions that lie in the immediate vicinity of its borders (recall the fate of the Joint Soviet-American Statement on the Middle East issued on October 2, 1977)."

8. "The intensified buildup of the U.S. naval presence near the USSR's southern borders."

9. "An active drive to modernize American strategic weapons."

10. "The refusal of the Carter Administration to carry on a constructive American-Soviet dialogue."[28]

Soviet officials might have added still more complaints about things the United States had done, or failed to do, prior to the invasion of Afghanistan:

11. The refusal of Congress to authorize large loans or to grant most-favored-nation status to the USSR in order to promote Soviet-American trade.

12. The linking of Soviet-American trade to the emigration of Soviet Jews (the Jackson-Vanik Amendment).

13. The refusal of the United States to permit the sale to Russia of some high technology items, including advanced computers.

14. President Carter's public intervention on behalf of Soviet dissidents such as Andrei Sakharov, Vladimir Bukovskii, and Anatolii Shcharanskii.

Brezhnev may have been personally affronted when Carter signed the SALT II treaty, embraced him in public, and then failed to push the treaty through Congress. Brezhnev said that he had formed an impression of the United States as being "an absolutely unreliable partner in interstate ties, . . . a state whose leadership, prompted by some whim, caprice, or emotional outburst,

. . . is capable at any moment of violating international obligations and canceling signed treaties and agreements."[29]

The above list of Soviet complaints against the United States is, of course, completely one-sided. Needless to say, the USSR has done many things in recent years that the United States did not like—intervening militarily in Angola, South Yemen, and Ethiopia; carrying out a massive buildup of its military power; supporting Vietnam's invasion of Cambodia; sending arms to Libya and other troublemakers around the world; and encouraging Castro in his anti-American activities, to name just a few. Surely Moscow has done at least as much as Washington to undermine détente; in my view it has done much more.

But the point to be made here is that in the fall of 1979, when the Kremlin was making preparations to invade Afghanistan, Soviet-American relations were bad already, so the Politburo may have felt that sending troops into Afghanistan would not make them much worse. It should be added, however, that the Soviets probably would have invaded Afghanistan even if Soviet-American relations had been excellent.

The Influence of the Generals

How much influence military leaders have on Politburo decisions is unknown, but it may be that some of the top officers helped persuade the Politburo to favor invasion. Afghanistan was primarily a military problem—the problem of the armed rebellion of hundreds of thousands of Afghans, the chance of some form of intervention by hostile powers, and the possibility that 1,500 additional miles of Soviet frontier would have to be defended against an anti-Soviet regime. It is striking that two of the Soviet military leaders who were conspicuous in the decision to invade Czechoslovakia in 1968 seem to have played similar roles in Afghanistan. General Alexei A. Epishev, chief of the Main Political Administration of the Soviet armed forces, visited Czechoslovakia prior to the invasion of that country and made a repeat performance in Afghanistan in April 1979. It is believed that he favored intervention in Czechoslovakia, and it is logical to suppose that he felt the same way about Afghanistan.[30] In November Epishev warned Soviet servicemen that they must be "on the alert" and must support the USSR's "new foreign policy initiative," which was required, he said, because "aggressive imperialist circles and the Beijing leaders who form an alliance with them" were opposing the Soviet Union and were trying to ensure their "military superiority."[31] After the Soviet invasion of Afghanistan, he declared that it was a defensive move and a just one.[32]

In August 1979, as noted in Chapter 11, General Ivan G. Pavlovskii arrived in Afghanistan with a large staff for a lengthy inspection tour.[33] Since the rebels were fighting with increasing ferocity and the Afghan army was gradually disintegrating, it is likely that Pavlovskii and others recommended a military solution—invasion. What could have been more natural than that they should have looked upon the inept Afghan armed forces with disgust and preferred instead the efficient, dependable Soviet forces? The generals probably convinced themselves, and the Politburo, that they could clean up the whole mess in three or four months.

Soviet military leaders also may have viewed Afghanistan as an opportunity to test new weapons, try new tactics, and get combat experience for their troops, as well as a chance to win medals, promotions, and glory for themselves.[34] Soviet soldiers had not had a chance to engage in real fighting since the invasion of Hungary in 1956, and Soviet military writers expressed envy of the experience the Americans had gained in Vietnam. In addition, both military and political leaders in the Soviet Union may have felt that a dramatic display of military prowess, while making some countries more anti-Soviet, might make others so fearful of Soviet power that they would seek an accommodation with Moscow.

Another military factor favoring invasion was the momentum of events. Week by week the Soviet military made plans and preparations for a possible invasion, until by December the troops, arms, tanks, airplanes, and other supplies were in place. Once all the steps had been taken, it probably became psychologically difficult for anyone to argue against invasion. The preparations were complete. Why not go ahead?

Fear of China

Numerous Westerners who have talked with Soviet leaders have commented on the profound, visceral fear that the Soviets have for China, and this might have been another factor involved in the decision to invade Afghanistan. Afghanistan has a short frontier with China, and Peking would be happy to give aid and encouragement to any anti-Soviet regime in Kabul. The Soviets suspected that Peking was sending arms to the Afghan rebels and would continue to do so.[35] Soviet uneasiness about China had of course grown in proportion to the improvement in the climate between Peking and Washington. The establishment of normal relations with China and Vice Premier Deng Xiaoping's visit to the United States in January 1979 was followed by the proposal that most-favored-nation trade status be granted to Peking. Then came the announcement in October that Defense Secretary Harold Brown would go to China. All these were seen by Moscow as moves toward "quasi-allied relations" between the United States and China.[36]

Natural Resources

Another motive for the invasion may have been a desire to ensure Soviet access to Afghanistan's mineral resources, especially natural gas, which the Soviets have been importing for many years at low prices. Little is known about other minerals in Afghanistan, but *Business Week* reported that Soviet experts had made a survey several years earlier and found significant quantities of oil, copper, barite, bauxite, beryl, iron ore, fluorspar, coal, and chrome.[37]

Thus it appears that the Soviet decision to invade Afghanistan was influenced by many complex factors. As Brezhnev put it, "the Party's Central Committee and the Soviet Government . . . took into account the entire sum total of circumstances."[38]

NOTES

1. A. Petrov, "K sobytiem v Afganistane," *Pravda,* December 31, 1979, p. 4.

2. On the invasions of Iran, Outer Mongolia, and Tannu Tuva see the following chapters in Thomas T. Hammond (ed.), *The Anatomy of Communist Takeovers* (New Haven, Conn.: Yale University Press, 1975): R.K. Ramazani, "The Autonomous Republic of Azerbaijan and the Kurdish People's Republic," pp. 448–474; Hammond, "The History of Communist Takeovers," pp. 8–10, and 32–33; Hammond, "The Communist Takeover of Outer Mongolia," pp. 107–144; and Robert A. Rupen, "The Absorption of Tuva," pp. 145–162. On the invasion of China in 1929 see Peter S.H. Tang, *Russian and Soviet Policy in Manchuria and Outer Mongolia, 1911–1931* (Durham, N.C.: Duke University Press, 1959), pp. 218–234.

Some might question the appropriateness of the term "invasion" to describe Soviet intervention in Iran in 1946, arguing that Stalin merely left in place the troops that had occupied the northern part of the country during World War II in agreement with the British and Americans. But as Ramazani points out, at the end of the war Stalin not only refused to withdraw Soviet occupation forces as he had promised, but also "moved fresh troops and heavy equipment into northern Iran, accompanied by unusual troop movements towards Teheran." Stalin did this in support of the two puppet governments that had been set up with the backing of the Soviet army. As Ramazani says, "The USSR was adding military invasion to political subversion in Iran." Ramazani, "The Autonomous Republic of Azerbaijan," p. 464.

3. Interview with the *Washington Post,* January 15, 1981, p. A7.

4. *Pravda,* January 13, 1980, p. 1.

5. One of the best statements of the Brezhnev Doctrine is by S. Kovalev, "Sovereignty and the International Duties of Socialist Countries," *Pravda,* September 26, 1968.

6. The contrast between Soviet and U.S. frontiers has often been pointed out. The United States has had the good fortune to be bordered by two oceans and two relatively weak states, thereby making enemy invasions unlikely. The United States has not experienced a real invasion since 1812, while Russia has suffered six during the same period. In the age of atomic missiles, borders have, of course, become less important, but they are still a matter of great anxiety for Moscow.

It is by no means certain, however, that the Soviet concern for the security of its frontiers is mainly a result of the many invasions Russia has undergone. Other nations—France and Poland, to name just two—have also been invaded many times, but, as Anthony Austin says, "no other country needs the extraordinary trappings of security the Russian government seems to require." He adds, "A good argument could be made for the proposition that all Russian governments have been prey to insecurity because of their inner doubts about their legitimacy, never having received the consent of the governed." Anthony Austin, "Russia: Shadow and Substance," *New York Times Magazine,* August 30, 1981, p. 34.

7. Soviet troops were withdrawn from Czechoslovakia in 1945, in return for the withdrawal of American troops. Soviet armed forces invaded again in 1968, and they have remained ever since.

8. *Pravda,* January 13, 1980, p. 1. Former Secretary of State Vance feels that the Soviets feared a U.S. invasion of Iran and that this made them more concerned about the possible overthrow of the Amin government. He writes: "There were background news stories coming out of Washington to the effect that there was a possibility of some form of U.S. military action against Iran. . . . U.S. military presence in the area would make a collapse of the Kabul regime more dangerous for the Soviets and thus enhance the possibility of Soviet intervention. In addition, a U.S. military move in Iran might diminish international reaction to a Soviet invasion, as the Anglo-French attack on Egypt had done in the Suez crisis in 1956." Cyrus Vance, *Hard Choices: Critical Years in America's Foreign Policy* (New York: Simon and Schuster, 1983), p. 387.

9. Drew Middleton in the *New York Times,* July 10, 1981, p. A9.

10. Henry (Genrikh Alexandrovich) Trofimenko, "The Third World and the U.S.-Soviet Competition: A Soviet View," *Foreign Affairs,* vol. 59, no. 5 (Summer 1981), p. 1032.

11. Nikita Khrushchev, *Khrushchev Remembers: The Last Testament* (Boston: Little, Brown, 1974), pp. 298–300.

12. Marshall Shulman thinks that this was the most important factor leading to the Soviet invasion. Interview with Shulman. "Top State Soviet Expert Sees Limited Reason for Invasion," *Defense/Space Daily,* February 12, 1980, p. 223, reported an interview with Shulman as follows:

> The man who advises Secretary of State Cyrus Vance on Soviet affairs believes that the Soviets invaded Afghanistan because of a "broad fear" of the creation of a crescent of militant Islamic, anti-Soviet nations on its southern border, with the added possibility of Chinese or U.S. influence, and not because it seeks to gain access to the Indian Ocean and control over Middle East oil.
>
> Marshall D. Shulman . . . says the new situation created by the takeover of Afghanistan "opens up the possibility" for the Soviets to consider attacks on Pakistan and Iran, but that he does not believe that was the intent of the invasion.

13. On the impact of Iran and Afghanistan on Soviet Muslims see the article by Alexandre Bennigsen, "Soviet Muslims and the World of Islam," *Problems of Communism,* vol. 29, no. 2 (March-April 1980), pp. 38–51. He says that the native elites in Soviet Central Asia probably would like to see all or part of Afghanistan annexed to the USSR, thereby strengthening their position in Soviet society.

14. On this point see Richard Pipes and George Kennan, "How Real Is the Soviet Threat?" *U.S. News and World Report,* March 10, 1980, p. 33.

15. Harriman to Secretary of State, September 20, 1944, U.S. Department of State, *Foreign Relations of the United States,* 1944, vol. 4 (Washington, D.C.:

Government Printing Office, 1966), p. 993; as cited in Vojtech Mastny, *Russia's Road to the Cold War* (New York: Columbia University Press, 1979), pp. 212–213.

16. *Washington Post,* October 17, 1980, p. A24.

17. On Soviet military involvement in other countries since World War II see Stephen S. Kaplan, *Diplomacy of Power: Soviet Armed Forces as a Political Instrument* (Washington, D.C.: Brookings Institution, 1981). This detailed book has extensive sections on Soviet involvement in the Korean War, the war in Vietnam, the Arab-Israeli conflicts, and many other such events.

18. For details see two chapters in Hammond (ed.), *The Anatomy of Communist Takeovers:* Hammond, "The Communist Takeover of Outer Mongolia," and Rupen, "The Absorption of Tuva."

19. For details see the various chapters in Hammond, ibid.

20. Raymond J. Sontag and James S. Beddie (eds.), *Nazi-Soviet Relations, 1939–41; Documents from the Archives of the German Foreign Office* (Washington, D.C.: Department of State, 1948), p. 259. Molotov made the statement to the German ambassador on November 26, 1940, in response to a German draft of a proposed four-power pact to include Germany, Russia, Japan, and Italy.

21. *San Diego Union,* March 9, 1980. This is a report of a speech made by Ambassador Neumann in San Diego.

22. Academician Evgenii Primakov, director of the Institute of Oriental Studies in Moscow, *Federal Broadcast Information Service* (hereafter cited as *FBIS*), Soviet series, January 23, 1981, p. D2.

23. Academician Evgenii Primakov and *Izvestiia* writer Aleksandr Bovin in *L'Unita,* April 25, 1980, as translated in *FBIS,* Soviet series, May 2, 1980, p. D6. The two Soviet officials held a press conference in Rome in March, at which they defended the invasion of Afghanistan, and their views were later criticized by *L'Unita.* They in turn responded with a letter to *L'Unita,* from which this quotation was taken.

24. Interview with Marshall Shulman. Former Secretary of State Vance makes a similar comment in his memoirs: Cyrus Vance, *Hard Choices,* p. 387. Vance gives his views on why the Soviets invaded on pp. 387–389.

25. *Washington Post,* January 15, 1981, p. A7.

26. Interviews with Cyrus Vance and Marshall Shulman.

27. Evgenii Primakov in *FBIS,* Soviet series, January 22, 1981, p. A5.

28. Trofimenko, "The Third World," p. 1031; *Washington Post,* January 16, 1980, p. A17.

29. *Pravda,* January 13, 1980, p. 1.

30. Jiri Valenta, "From Prague to Kabul; The Soviet Style of Invasion," *International Security,* vol. 5, no. 2 (Fall 1980), p. 124. Valenta is also the author of *Soviet Intervention in Czechoslovakia, 1968: Anatomy of a Decison* (Baltimore, Md.: Johns Hopkins University Press, 1979).

31. *Komsomol'skaia pravda* (Moscow), November 23, 1979, as cited in Valenta, "From Prague to Kabul," p. 124.

32. "Loyalty to Lenin's Banner," *Krasnaia zvezda* (Moscow), February 22, 1980.

33. Testimony by Prof. John Erickson, Great Britain, House of Commons, Foreign Affairs Committee, *Afghanistan: The Soviet Invasion and Its Consequences for British Policy* (London: Her Majesty's Stationery Office, 1980), p. 38.

34. Ibid., p. 250. According to Erickson, the Soviets have used Afghanistan as an opportunity to try out a new assault rifle, antipersonnel artillery rounds, modified infantry combat vehicles, multiple rocket launchers, and a battle management computer system.

35. See the article by Vladimir Solovyov and Elena Klepikova in *Los Angeles Times*, December 29, 1980, part 2, p. 5.

36. V.B. Likin, "Washington-Beijing: 'Quasi-Allies'?" *SShA: Ekonomika, politika, ideologiia*, November 12, 1979, pp. 50–55, as cited in Jiri Valenta, "From Prague to Kabul," p. 128.

37. *Business Week*, September 29, 1980, p. 62. Theodore Shabad of the *New York Times* and *Soviet Geography* reports that the Soviets, starting in 1970, greatly increased the amount of geological exploration equipment sent to Afghanistan and that this probably "marked the beginning of an intensified Soviet geological exploration effort in Afghanistan." From Theodore Shabad, "The Soviet Union and Afghanistan: Some Economic Aspects," a paper read at the annual meeting of the American Association for the Advancement of Slavic Studies, Monterey, Calif., September 20, 1981, p. 1.

38. *Pravda*, January 13, 1980, p. 1.

CHAPTER 14

Babrak Attempts to Sovietize Afghanistan

In the name of God, the compassionate, the merciful. Dear long-suffering Muslim brothers of Afghanistan, peace be upon you. Heroic men and women of the homeland . . . allow me to express the deepest sympathy . . . for the inordinate sufferings and the blood you have shed because of the imprisonment, enforced migrations, barbaric and inhuman tortures, the martyrdom and killing of tens of thousands . . . which have taken place under Hafizollah Amin and on the direct instructions of this bloodthirsty butcher. . . . Hafizollah Amin, this agent of the CIA and . . . spy of American imperialism, this traitor . . . received his punishment at the just revolutionary tribunal of the oppressed people of Afghanistan . . . for his satanic and devilish deeds.

—Babrak Karmal, December 27, 1979[1]

BABRAK'S NEW PROGRAM

With the killing of Amin, Babrak Karmal assumed all of the top positions in Afghanistan—general secretary of the People's Democratic party, president of the Revolutionary Council, prime minister, and commander-in-chief. The new cabinet included members of both factions of the party—Babrak's Parchamis, of course, but also Khalq leaders who were not identified with Amin. In an effort to broaden the base of support for the government, Babrak even named several noncommunists to the cabinet.[2]

It became clear from the start that Amin was to be the scapegoat for all the sins of the previous communist administrations. The first postinvasion issue of the *New Kabul Times* bore a streamer headline: "Sanguinary Amin band ousted," with the subhead, "United PDPA ends reign of terror; murderer meets his fate." Babrak denounced Amin as "Hangman Hafizullah . . . the

CIA agent and the scheming spy of American imperialism, . . . that historic murderer and rogue who even did not have pity on the late Noor Mohammad Taraki, our dear leader and noble founder of our party."[3] The media harped on these themes repeatedly, as if all of the unpopular measures adopted since April 1978 could be attributed solely to Amin. It is ironic that Taraki now was glorified as a hero and a martyr, as he had long been an enemy of Babrak's and had been president when Babrak and the other Parcham leaders were ousted from the government.

When Babrak took over, he had ready a program intended to avoid the mistakes of Taraki and Amin and win popular support. He announced this program under the slogan, "Forward toward peace, freedom, national independence, democracy, progress and social justice." The program included six points:

1. . . . the release of all political prisoners who have survived the hatchet of Hangman Hafizullah Amin and abolish execution. . . .
2. Abolish all anti-democratic and anti-human regulations and ban all arrests, incarcerations, arbitrary persecutions, house searches and inquisitions.
3. Respect the sacred principles of Islam, freedom of conscience, belief, and religious practice, protect family unity, observe the principle of legal, lawful, just and private ownership. . . .
4. Revive individual and collective security and immunity, revolutionary tranquility, peace and order in the country.
5. Ensure healthy conditions conducive to democratic freedoms such as the freedom to form progressive and patriotic parties and mass or social organizations, freedom of the press, of demonstrations, . . . immunity of correspondence and communications, travel, and immunity of domicile.
6. Pay serious attention to and help the younger generations, school pupils, university students and the intelligentsia.[4]

Babrak also made special efforts to convince the people that he was a good Muslim. His speeches opened with the traditional incantation, "In the name of God, the compassionate and merciful." Mullahs were brought to Kabul for conferences and were sent on free tours of Soviet Central Asia to convince them that Islam was thriving in the USSR.[5] A new flag containing the old colors of black, red, and Islamic green replaced the former flag of communist red.

Babrak declared that he would not make his predecessors' mistake of attempting to transform Afghan society overnight. He promised that all "progressive" parties except those supporting Amin would be allowed freedom of political activity.[6] Some of the unpopular measures introduced by Taraki and Amin were canceled, while others were slowed down. Amid much publicity, hundreds of political prisoners were released from the infamous Pul-i-Charkhi prison.[7] Amnesty was offered to all refugees, including deserters from the

Afghan army.[8] Elections were promised, although no date was mentioned.[9] And, in an appeal to the ethnic minorities, Babrak promised to "cultivate and develop various dialects and cultures of all fraternal nationalities and tribes."[10]

BABRAK FAILS TO WIN POPULAR SUPPORT

Despite his efforts and despite the fact that his program made more sense than those of Taraki and Amin, Babrak had no success in winning over the Afghan people, for many reasons. First of all, he was known to be a communist and an atheist, and that alone was enough to make him an infidel to 90 percent of his fellow Afghans. Also, he was looked upon as a puppet of the Russians. Whereas Taraki and Amin had gained power on their own, Babrak had been placed in power by the Soviet army and was identified with the Soviet occupation of the country. He was a traitor, a quisling who had sold out to the enemy. While Taraki and Amin had praised the Soviet Union, Babrak far surpassed them in fawning before Moscow, even going so far as to tell a meeting of party members: "The pursuance of eternal friendship and solidarity with the Leninist Communist Party of the USSR and friendship between our countries and our peoples are the basic measures and yardsticks for the appraisal of the work of every member of the party from top to bottom, and of party and government officials from top to bottom."[11] Babrak was rumored to be surrounded by Soviet citizens—his chauffeur, his doctor, his guards, his cook, his advisers—which strengthened the impression that he was a mere tool of the Russians.

Babrak has not even been able to gain the support of both factions of the People's Democratic party or to stop party feuds. He and most of the othe Parchamis had been ousted from the party under Taraki; some had been exiled, but others had been thrown into prison and tortured under Taraki's police chief, Asadullah Sarwari, who became deputy prime minister under Babrak. Not surprisingly, Sarwari was hated by those who had suffered at his hands. Babrak had brought Khalqis into his government because of Soviet pressure and because he needed them as administrators. The Khalqis greatly outnumbered the Parchamis, especially in the army, and Babrak could ill afford to antagonize them. But there were many personal scores to settle, and shootouts occurred more than once. One Afghan refugee described the situation as follows: "These are just two gangs who have killed each other. Khalqis know that if given a chance the Parchamites will kill them, and the Parchamites know that the Khalqis will kill them. There is no trust and no possibility of trust."[12]

After a violent confrontation in June 1980, Sarwari was "exiled" by being made ambassador to Outer Mongolia, but the conflicts continued.[13] When the pro-Khalq commander of the 14th Armored Division was replaced by a

Parchami, the soldiers mutinied.[14] Plots against the government by Khalqi officers were discovered in June, July, and October of 1980 and again in February 1981. Some Khalqis have even gone over to the rebels.[15]

According to one estimate, by February 1980 there were probably fewer than 3,000 Parchamis and Khalqis left to staff the government and the party.[16] As a result, offices in some ministries were empty or partly empty. One diplomat who was called back to be in charge of a department of the foreign ministry reported that his five-person office was completely empty. In an attempt to remedy the situation, Babrak has tried to recruit retirees from prerevolutionary days. Some of those approached have fled across the frontier, while others too old for this escape route have gone to foreign missions to see if they could emigrate.[17] A few noncommunists have agreed to join the government, however, including some fairly prominent former officials.[18]

Babrak's attempts to undo the unpopular reforms of Taraki and Amin have not been successful. Major revisions in the land reform were announced in August 1981, involving concessions to tribal leaders and religious leaders, but this means nothing to Afghans who have fled across the frontier or to others who mistrust Babrak. Amnesty has been offered to refugees, but few have accepted. And efforts to convince the people that the regime is not atheistic have fallen on deaf ears.[19]

Meanwhile, economic conditions have worsened, which is not surprising since the country has been racked by civil war since 1978, and the Soviets have deliberately destroyed crops and food stocks in some areas. There are shortages of such basic foods as wheat, rice, and meat, and the Soviets have to import food not only to feed their own army but also to supplement the diets of Afghan city dwellers. The cotton crop has dropped in size, and in Kabul firewood and charcoal are rationed. Farm output in 1981 was even lower than in 1980. Industry, meanwhile, suffers from shortages of labor, raw materials, and fuel.[20]

Babrak has tried to rally the population in support of his regime by creating a National Fatherland Front, similar to the mass organizations formed by the communists in Eastern Europe at the end of World War II. At a meeting in December 1980, Babrak announced that the purpose of the front was "to mobilize in pursuance of [PDPA] policy . . . all noble people of Afghanistan to take active and conscious part" in achieving the goals of the regime.[21] Not surprisingly, the front has elicited little enthusiasm among the people. Participation in the front has also been discouraged by the rebels' practice of assassinating some of its prominent members.

SOVIETIZATION

Under Babrak the sovietization of the country has two main characteristics: (1) Soviet citizens run many of the government offices and make the important decisions; and (2) the government, the party, the mass organizations, the educational system, and the economy are all being remodeled to imitate the Soviet pattern.

It is reported that every Afghan minister has Soviet advisers who attend all important meetings and give him orders as to how he should run his ministry.[22] Babrak himself has testified that some Afghan bureaucrats sit around and do nothing: "At our request the USSR has sent experts and advisers for nearly all areas of government and for the ministries and administration of Afghanistan. . . . We will learn from the technical expertise of our Soviet comrades. . . . Unfortunately, some of our staff close their eyes to these possibilities . . . and some of them even lay all the burden and responsibility for practical work on the shoulders of the advisers."[23]

The People's Democratic party is organized like the Communist Party of the Soviet Union, with a Central Committee and Politburo at the top, and the Afghan government apes the Soviet structure with the equivalent of a Supreme Soviet and Council of Ministers.[24] Sovietization extends also to youth organizations. The Democratic Organization of Afghan Youth is modeled after the Komsomol in the USSR, while younger boys and girls have been recruited into the Pioneers, a group similar to the Soviet organization of the same name. Pioneer camps, like those in Russia, are used to train and indoctrinate Afghan children. Young people are also required to join teams for the preservation of public order, like the Druzhba in the USSR, and hundreds of children are sent to the Soviet Union each month for education and indoctrination.[25]

Adults too are organized in Soviet style. There are government-controlled unions not only for ordinary workers but also for writers, artists, teachers, and jounalists. It has been made clear by the regime that these trade unions, like the Soviet ones, are designed primarily to get the workers to support government policies; the unions are not independent, but are under control of the party. Women have their own Democratic Women's Organization, and peasants supposedly are represented by the Central Council of Agricultural Cooperatives.[26]

The educational system also is being Sovietized. Afghan elementary teachers have had to adopt a Soviet-style curriculum, new textbooks preaching communism have been introduced, and Russian has replaced English as the compulsory foreign language. Soviet professors have been added to the faculty of Kabul University, and Afghan students are sent by the thousands to study in the Soviet Union, especially in the Central Asian republics. The government reportedly has told school teachers that they must join the party or lose their jobs.[27]

The Afghan economy, in addition, is bound ever tighter to the USSR. Hardly a week passes without the signing of some new Soviet-Afghan agreement on trade or economic aid. According to Babrak, by November

1980 the Soviet Union provided 80 percent of Afghanistan's foreign aid. The Soviets will even supply electricity for Kabul by erecting power lines from the USSR.[28] The chief Afghan export to the Soviet Union is natural gas, and plans are under way to greatly expand the volume of gas delivered.[29] The famous Khyber Pass leading to Pakistan and India, which for centuries was the main route for foreign trade, has been replaced by the Salang Pass, which leads north to the USSR. Technical assistance by Western experts, even when sponsored by the UN, is being phased out, and almost all foreign technicians today come from Soviet-bloc countries.[30]

News also has been sovietized. Most of the foreign news stories in Afghan newspapers come from Tass, the Soviet news agency, and the *Kabul New Times* contains articles by people with names like Borisov, Boikov, and Semenov. Even news about Afghanistan is sometimes derived from Soviet sources, and about 60 percent of the broadcasts of Radio Kabul actually originate from transmitters in the USSR.[31]

What the Soviets seem to have in mind for Afghanistan is that it become another Outer Mongolia, that Afghanistan be, in effect, but not in name, one of the constituent republics of the USSR—nominally independent, but controlled by Moscow. Apparently Soviet scholars think along these lines. An American professor studying at the Institute of Oriental Studies in Moscow in 1980 discovered that experts on Afghanistan and experts on Mongolia were working closely together on ways to apply the Mongol experience in Afghanistan.[32] The Buddhist Mongols, however, are passive people, quite unlike the tough, independent, and warlike Afghans. So the course of developments in Afghanistan may be less like what happened in Outer Mongolia than the Kremlin expects or desires.

NOTES

1. Recording of speech by Babrak that was broadcast on the Kabul domestic service in Dari on December 27, 1979, as translated in *Federal Broadcast Information Service* (hereafter cited as *FBIS*), Middle East and North Africa Series, December 31, 1979, p. S1. Some people believe that this broadcast did not originate in Kabul but came rather from a radio station on Soviet territory, since Babrak apparently was not in Afghanistan at the time.

2. The first issue of the postinvasion *Kabul New Times,* January 1, 1980, contains photos of the new cabinet on the front page. See also Richard Newell, "Soviet Intervention in Afghanistan," *The World Today,* vol. 36, no. 7 (July 1980), p. 257.

3. *Kabul New Times,* January 1, 1980, p. 1.

4. Ibid., p. 2.

5. Interview with State Department official, November 25, 1980.

6. Agence France Press report, quoting Radio Kabul, cited in *FBIS,* December 31, 1979, p. S7.

7. See the photos in *Kabul New Times*, January 1, 1980, pp. 3–4.

8. Newell, "Soviet Intervention in Afghanistan," p. 258.

9. Agence France Press report, quoting Radio Kabul, *FBIS*, December 31, 1979, p. S7.

10. *Kabul New Times*, January 1, 1980, p. 2.

11. Speech by Babrak, November 13, 1980, broadcast on Radio Kabul and translated in *FBIS*, November 17, 1980, p. C3.

12. *New York Times*, August 5, 1980, p. A3.

13. Eliza Van Hollen, *Afghanistan: A Year of Occupation* (Washington, D.C.: Department of State, February 1981, Special Report No. 79), p. 3. Sarwari reportedly returned to Kabul in the summer of 1981.

14. *New York Times*, August 5, 1980, p. A3.

15. Van Hollen, *Afghanistan: A Year of Occupation*, pp. 3, 5.

16. Mohan Ram, *Far Eastern Economic Review*, February 8, 1980, p. 28. Francis Fukuyama in his excellent study, *The Future of the Soviet Role in Afghanistan: A Trip Report* (Santa Monica, Calif.: Rand Corporation, September 1980), pp. 20–21, makes this comment: "To the extent that the Soviets have found loyal Afghans, they have been drawn from the cities; the bulk of the PDPA membership consists of such urban types as schoolteachers, bureaucrats, army officers, and factory workers."

17. Interview with State Department official, November 25, 1980.

18. Newell, "Soviet Intervention in Afghanistan," p. 257.

19. Van Hollen, *Afghanistan: A Year of Occupation*, p. 3; *New York Times*, August 20, 1981, p. A3.

20. Fukuyama, *The Future of the Soviet Role*, p. 27; interview with State Department official.

21. Henry Bradsher, *Washington Star*, April 26, 1981, p. 15. See also Eliza Van Hollen, *Afghanistan: 2 Years of Occupation* (Washington, D.C.: Department of State, December 1981, Special Report No. 91), pp. 2–3.

22. *Washington Post*, January 25, 1980, p. A20.

23. Speech by Babrak, broadcast on Radio Kabul and translated in *FBIS*, November 17, 1980, p. C3. See also "With the Russians Downstairs, Afghan Aides Have Little To Do," *New York Times*, January 27, 1980, p. 12.

24. Tyler Marshall in the *Los Angeles Times*, May 17, 1981, p. 1. The PDPA presumably is still operating under the constitution contained in the Appendix.

25. *New York Times*, August 14, 1980, p. A9; *Washington Post*, February 27, 1981, p. A20; *Los Angeles Times*, May 17, 1981, pp. 1, 11.

26. These organizations were formed already under Amin; *Neues Deutschland*, October 30, 1979, translated in *FBIS*, November 2, 1979, p. S2.

27. *New York Times*, August 14, 1980, p. A9; *Washington Post*, February 27, 1981, p. A20; *Los Angeles Times*, May 17, 1981, pp. 1, 11.

28. Speech by Babrak, broadcast on Radio Kabul, November 14, 1980, translated in *FBIS*, November 17, 1980, p. C5.

29. Zalmay Kalilzad, "Soviet-Occupied Afghanistan," *Problems of Communism*, vol. 29, no. 6 (November-December 1980), pp. 29–30.

30. *Los Angeles Times*, May 17, 1981, p. 11.

31. Ibid.

32. Professor Karen Eide Rawlings of the University of Maryland, speech at the Kennan Institute, Washington, D.C., September 24, 1980.

CHAPTER 15

The National Liberation Struggle

[The Afghan people], whether trained soldiers or simple peasants, would all sacrifice every drop of blood till the last man was killed, in fighting for their God, their Prophet, their religion, their homes, their families, their nation . . . their liberty and independence.

—Abdur Rahman Khan,
Amir of Afghanistan (1880–1901)[1]

O Gods from the venom of the cobra, the teeth of the tiger, and the vengeance of the Afghan deliver us.

—Old Hindu saying

THE RESISTANCE MOVEMENT INTENSIFIES

The Soviets probably expected that their invasion would lead to the suppression of the resistance movement, but the initial effect was just the opposite. What had been a civil war between competing Afghan factions was transformed into a national liberation struggle pitting Afghans of all classes against the Soviet invaders. The aggression by the hated Russians united the people around a goal that all but a few could agree on—freedom from foreign domination.[2]

During the first years following the invasion the rebels operated openly in about 80 percent of the country, while the Soviet and Afghan armies were restricted mainly to the bigger towns and principal highways. But the rebels frequently ambushed traffic even on the main roads, and at night they operated almost everywhere. Government officials were forced to abandon some of the district capitals, and even such major cities as Qandahar, Herat, and Jalalabad were largely in rebel hands for months at a time.[3]

Kabul itself was the scene of much opposition activity, including strikes, protests, sabotage, assassinations, gun battles, and bombings. In February 1980, soon after the invasion, a general strike of shopkeepers and civil servants broke out, accompanied by demonstrations and riots. Soviet troops and Afghan police fired on the crowds, killing or wounding hundreds.[4] On Soviet Armed Forces Day, also in February, Babrak and other Afghan dignitaries gathered at the Soviet embassy to toast the Soviet army, but hundreds of ordinary citizens stood on their rooftops and expressed their defiance by shouting "*Allah-u-Akbar!*" ("God is great!") until they were hoarse. Crowds also threw stones at Afghans leaving the embassy that night.[5]

Particularly dramatic was the "children's revolt" in April and May 1980 when high school and university students in Kabul showed their hatred for the Soviets and Babrak by boycotting classes and by demonstrating. Girls pulled off their scarves and veils and threw them at Afghan men, yelling, "You wear these, and we will take the guns and go after the Russians."[6] Dozens of students were killed, and hundreds more were wounded. One schoolgirl used the blood of a comrade to write "Freedom!" on her scarf, while others shouted "Death to Brezhnev!" and "Death to traitors!" as they marched through the streets.[7] Students also demonstrated in front of the home of Education Minister Anahita Ratebzad, whom they believed to be Babrak's mistress, complaining that Afghanistan's schools should not be run by a prostitute.[8]

Opposition activity in Kabul reached such a high level that in October 1980 the government extended the nightly curfew by two hours. Armed patrols circulated throughout the city day and night.[9] Western diplomatic sources reported in January 1981 that in one week rebels in Kabul killed twenty-eight government supporters, thirty-five Afghan officers and soldiers, and three Soviet soldiers.[10]

THE IMPORTANCE OF PAKISTAN AND IRAN

The resistance movement has been helped greatly by the open borders with Pakistan and Iran, where the terrain is so rugged that the Soviets cannot prevent the *mujaheddin* from moving back and forth—to flee from Soviet attacks, rest, obtain arms, resettle their families, and plan further incursions. Pakistan has been particularly important in this respect. Pakistani officials could not stop the movement of Afghans across the frontier even if they tried, not only because of the mountains but also because no outside government, British or Pakistani, has ever been able to control the fierce Pushtun tribes who live along the border. The Pakistani regime has continued the British practice of letting the tribal chiefs rule this area, under their own laws, and the Pakistani army cannot even enter it without permission.[11]

The passage of Afghan rebels across the Pakistani frontier is easy because the population on both sides consists of Pushtuns, often of the same tribe. Thus rebels and their families fleeing from Afghanistan can sometimes find refuge with friends or relatives. For centuries nomads with their flocks have migrated each year across this border, keeping their herds in Pakistan in the winter and grazing them in Afghanistan in the summer. These people neither obtained, nor needed, passports or visas. This frontier may be delineated in treaties and on maps, but as far as the local tribes are concerned, it does not exist.[12]

Most of the rebel political organizations have their headquarters in Pakistan, where they are accessible to reporters; thus these groups get a great deal of publicity in the Western media. But they control only a minority of the freedom fighters in Afghanistan. Deep in the interior, far from Pakistan, are rebels fighting under their clan and tribal chiefs, with no aid from abroad and no place of refuge but their remote valleys and rough-hewn mountains.[13] For example, the Hazaras in central Afghanistan, the Uzbeks in the north, and the Tadzhiks in the northeast near the Soviet frontier have continued to resist even though they have no nearby sanctuary to flee to.[14]

The rebel groups are divided along linguistic, cultural, tribal, ideological, and political lines, and efforts to coordinate their activities have had limited success. Different groups have cooperated at times, however, including tribes that had long been enemies.[15] Disunity among the resistance movements has made it impossible for them to mount any large-scale operations,[16] but even with complete unity they could not conceivably defeat the Soviet armies in a frontal assault. The existence of hundreds of local guerrilla bands, each under its own leader, is in one sense a strength, however; if the Soviets should succeed in destroying a few groups, many would still be left. Like a bear attacked by a swarm of bees, the Soviet army is being hit from all directions.

THE PROBLEM OF OBTAINING ARMS

Unfortunately for the freedom fighters, the Soviet troops are much better equipped, but the rebels have armed themselves in various ways. Many Afghan men already owned an old rifle, usually a British Enfield of the type used in World War I. However, the rebels have captured or stolen most of their weapons from the Soviet and Afghan armies. If they have enough money, the rebels also can buy arms from Pakistani gunsmiths, who reproduce by hand a great variety of weapons, but the prices are very high.[17]

Either arms or money or both have been sent to the rebels by the United States, China, Egypt, Saudi Arabia, Israel, Iran, and perhaps other Gulf states. Saudi Arabia announced early in 1980 that it would give $25 million to the rebels.[18] The Egyptian defense minister boasted in February 1980 that his country not only was sending arms but also training Afghans in guerrilla warfare.[19] The U.S. government, by contrast, has never officially admitted giving aid, although former President Carter in his memoirs finally acknowledged that he had arranged to have Soviet-made weapons delivered to the rebels.[20] Meanwhile, President Reagan, in March 1981, said that if the Afghan freedom fighters asked for assistance, he would give the request serious consideration.[21]

Carl Bernstein reported in the *New Republic* that a covert operation to supply the *mujaheddin* with arms was instituted under President Carter, with National Security Adviser Brzezinski and CIA Director Stansfield Turner in charge. According to Bernstein, only Soviet-made weapons or reproductions of Soviet weapons were sent so that Pakistan would not be blamed and could claim that the arms had been captured by the rebels in Afghanistan. Such a scheme is workable because the Soviets over the years have given or sold many weapons to foreign countries, including China and Egypt, while Israel has captured many more in its wars with the Arabs. Bernstein said that most of the money was supplied by the United States and Saudi Arabia; the bulk of the arms, including Kalashnikov assault rifles, came from Egypt, while the Chinese furnished most of the hand-held SAM missiles and antitank weapons. Pakistan reportedly was reluctant to let the arms pass through its territory, for fear of Soviet reprisals, but agreed on condition that the amount of arms be severely limited and that they be carried across the border into Afghanistan promptly. Nevertheless, said Bernstein, the quantity of arms was later increased under Carter and again under Reagan.[22]

Confirmation of Egypt's role in supplying arms for the rebels was provided by Anwar Sadat himself during a television interview in September 1981. Sadat told NBC News that shortly after the Soviet invasion, "the United States sent me airplanes and told me, 'Please open your stores for us so that we can give the Afghanis the armaments they need to fight,' and I gave the armaments."[23] As Brzezinski was the chairman of the president's special coordinating committee on covert operations, he exercised overall supervision of the arms program; he made a trip to see Zia and Sadat in January 1980, so it seems likely that he was the one who made the arrangements with them. According to Bernstein, Defense Secretary Harold Brown, who was going to Peking about that time anyway, closed the deal with the Chinese.

U.S. officials and rebel leaders have insisted that most of the rebels' arms have come from Soviet and Afghan troops, particularly soldiers deserting from the Afghan army. Desertion became so common that in 1980 the Soviets took all warplanes, as well as antiaircraft and antitank weapons, from the Afghan army, for fear they would fall into rebel hands.[24] The rebels need antitank and antiaircraft guns and rockets, but have not been able to obtain enough of them. That weapons and ammunition have been in short supply is indicated by the very high prices they have been selling for along the Afghan border—$1,500 for a Soviet AK47 rifle, for example.[25]

REBEL FANATICISM

Those who have talked with Afghan rebels testify to their fanatical determination to fight the Soviets to the death. There are many reasons why the rebels are willing to do so. First, their mullahs have declared the struggle a *jihad,* a holy war of true believers against infidels. As one rebel leader explained it, "To us killing a Russian or dying in battle represents an equal victory. If a Moslem kills an enemy in battle, he is a *ghazi,* an Islamic warrior, and if he is killed, he is a *shaheed,* a martyr for Islam, and the rewards are great in paradise."[26]

Second, Afghans fight because of *badal* ("blood for blood"), the tradition that if a member of one's family is killed, that death must be avenged. "Every time a Russian helicopter gunship strafes a village," said one rebel, "every man in it will not rest until he has drawn Russian blood."[27] Third, they fight to protect their right of self-rule, to run their own affairs as they please—a tradition so strong that no government in Kabul has ever overcome it. Fourth, they fight because they despise the Shourawi (the Russians). And, finally, they fight because Afghans have always fought against anyone who trampled on their country. A wounded guerrilla in a hospital in Pakistan told an American correspondent: "We have chosen the way of martyrdom. How can we be defeated?" An insurgent leader declared: "We will go on fighting. Time does not concern us. We have been fighting for centuries."[28] Facing this kind of multifaceted fanaticism, the Soviets are in for a long and bloody struggle.

Another factor that has made things difficult for the Soviets is the primitiveness of the country and the people. In a modern industrialized state any political group that controls the central governmental apparatus, economic offices, and means of communication can usually impose its will on the rest of the country. But in an underdeveloped country like Afghanistan the opposite is the case. Control of the government in Kabul means little in the provinces because Afghanistan has never been a united, centralized state, but has always operated according to the principle of local autonomy, under local tribal chieftains. It is also difficult to exercise *economic* control from Kabul because most of the people are independent agriculturalists, working in a village economy that is largely self-sufficient. Nor can the people be controlled through the press because most of them cannot read.

This means that the Soviets must subdue every village, must win over or eliminate every local leader. The Afghans, having been denied the benefits of a modern education, haven't sense enough to give up and surrender their freedom. And they love to fight. Pushtun attitudes toward fighting are summed up in folk sayings like the following:

The sweetest fellowship is that of the sword.

A dog surrounded turns tail, a man fights.

Fear and shame are father and son.

Die for the honor of family or friend.[29]

THE DISINTEGRATION OF THE AFGHAN ARMY

The Soviets probably assumed that the Afghan army would be of great assistance in suppressing the rebels, but they have been disappointed. In fact, one might say that the Afghan army has been a liability. Many Afghan soldiers, either individually or in groups, have deserted to the enemy, taking their arms with them. For example, in Kunar province Colonel Abdul Rauf defected to the rebels with 2,000 of his men.[30] In addition, there have been several mutinies. The continued infighting between the Khalq and Parcham factions of the People's Democratic party has been particularly ruinous in the army because Khalq traditionally has had more followers in the armed forces, and many of them resent the dominant position that Parcham now has in the government. As a result of desertions, casualties, and the difficulty of obtaining new recruits, the Afghan army, which numbered 90,000 to 100,000 at the time of the Soviet invasion, had dropped to about 30,000 by early 1981 and was still about that size at the beginning of 1983.[31]

The Babrak regime has had to resort to extreme measures to draft recruits for the army, sending out impressment gangs to make house-to-house searches and conscripting youths fourteen years of age or even younger.[32] In an attempt to prevent the army from getting still smaller, the government in January 1981 issued a new draft law that lengthened the term of service by six months, but this brought about riots in Kabul and mutinies by some army units.[33] Low in numbers and morale, the Afghan army has been doing little of the fighting, and some of the officers have even cooperated with the rebels.[34]

SOVIET TACTICS IN AFGHANISTAN

Anyone reading the Soviet press would get a rather strange view of the war in Afghanistan. Usually only rebel casualties are mentioned, not Soviet ones. Indeed, Soviet publications seldom admit that Soviet soldiers engage in actual combat; they merely help train the Afghan army and carry out "exercises," while Afghans do the fighting. The conflict continues, the Soviets say, solely because "thousands upon thousands of bandits, armed and trained abroad, pour across the border day after day" into Afghanistan. The Soviet soldiers in Afghanistan are good communists fulfilling their "internationalist" duty to help suppress the "counterrevolutionary bandits," who are supported by the United States, China, and other countries who are intervening in the internal affairs of Afghanistan. The Soviet Union, however, is *not* intervening. *Red Star,* the organ of the Soviet army, put it as follows: "Our coming to our neighbor's aid—at his urgent request—is not aggression or intervention, as ill-intentioned slanderers try to prove. The only duty of the Soviet military contingent is to help Afghanistan repel the threat from outside."[35]

The Politburo presumably intends to subdue all of Afghanistan eventually, but so far has not sent enough troops to accomplish this goal. Within a few weeks after the invasion in December 1979 the Soviets had about 85,000 soldiers in Afghanistan, and that number remained fairly constant until the latter part of 1981, when it was increased by about 5 percent.[36] By March 1982 the figure had grown to around 100,000, and later in the year it grew to 105,000.[37] Whether this means that the Soviets intend to make further increases is impossible to say, but it seems unlikely that they will double or triple their contingent in Afghanistan. It may be that with all its other military requirements, the Politburo feels it cannot afford to keep more than 100,000 to 110,000 troops in Afghanistan. Still another consideration may be a desire to minimize casualties.

The Soviets have used tactics designed to keep their losses low, substituting firepower for manpower and making fullest use of their superior weapons—helicopters, bombers, tanks, armored personnel carriers, rockets, and artillery. Soviet soldiers expose themselves as little as possible to Afghan sharpshooters, but hide safely in their tanks, which leads some Afghans to refer to them contemptuously as "beardless cowards living in iron tents."[38]

At times the Soviets have tried to pacify certain rebel areas by moving in with massive firepower. But although they could easily take over a village, a town, or a valley because the outgunned freedom fighters would flee, the rebels would return and reoccupy the area as soon as the Soviet forces left. As a consequence, the Soviets have often used brutal scorched-earth tactics—bombing and strafing hostile villages and towns into piles of mud and brick rubble. The Soviet forces have also deliberately wrecked irrigation systems, burned crops, killed livestock, and contaminated water sources in an effort to starve out those peasants who support the rebels. By destroying housing, food, and water supplies the Soviets have made it impossible for the Afghans to return to their homes, the idea being that an empty village offers no resistance.[39]

This has led Louis Dupree to refer to Soviet policy in Afghanistan as a combination of "rubblization" and "migratory genocide." According to him, "the Russians are not trying to control Afghanistan, but to destroy it; their aim is not to kill the Afghans, but to drive them out of the country."[40] Although this is an exaggeration, there is no denying that the Soviets have leveled many villages, destroyed sections of cities, and caused many Afghans to flee. It is impossible to get accurate statistics, but it is believed that by 1983 over 3 million Afghans had fled their homeland, going mostly to

Pakistan, but also to Iran, Europe, and the United States. This means that *more than one-fifth of the Afghan people have left the country!* A comparable figure for the United States would be about 50 million Americans abandoning their homes and escaping into exile![41]

Soviet Use of Chemical Weapons

In addition to strafing and bombing villages and cities, the Soviets have used chemical warfare extensively. Former Deputy Secretary of State Walter J. Stoessel, Jr., accused the Soviets of attacking Afghans with "irritants, incapacitants, nerve agents, phosgene oxime, and perhaps mycotoxins, mustard, lewisite, and toxic smoke."[42] Stoessel told Congress that the United States had collected reports from Western journalists and Afghan refugees who had witnessed chemical attacks, doctors who had treated victims, and Afghan army deserters who had been trained by the Soviets in chemical warfare. After collating these reports and checking them against one another, the State Department declared that it had convincing evidence that the Soviet and Afghan armies had killed over 3,000 Afghans in forty-seven chemical attacks between the summer of 1979 and the summer of 1981. The number of Afghans actually killed by chemical attacks, said the State Department, might be much higher—more than 6,000.[43] There also have been several eyewitness accounts by Western observers of the use of an incendiary weapon—white powder dropped by an airplane and ignited—that destroyed whole villages.[44] Such brutal measures naturally intensify the hatred felt toward the Soviet troops, and the rebels reciprocate by killing most of their Russian prisoners, sometimes mutilating their bodies.

Misbehavior by Soviet Troops

There have been reports of misbehavior and poor morale among Soviet soldiers in Afghanistan. A few have deserted. It is said that many engage in black marketeering, which is easy to believe because so many Soviet citizens deal in the illegal economy back home. In addition, there have been stories of looting, robberies, rapes, and murder by Soviet troops, as well as the use of drugs, especially hashish. It is even claimed that the rebels buy arms from Soviet soldiers on the black market or steal their guns after getting them high on hashish.[45]

RESISTANCE ACTIVITIES IN 1981

By the beginning of 1981, a year after the invasion, the Soviets had little to show for their efforts. The resistance movement was larger, better organized, and better equipped than it had been when it was fighting against the Amin regime.[46] As the months passed, conditions for the Soviets did not improve. In April 1981 the four Afghan army divisions that had been helping guard

Kabul were moved to the countryside, and Soviet troops took their places. Apparently these divisions—long considered the most reliable ones in the Afghan army—were no longer trusted. This is not surprising since there have been plots by Khalqi army officers ever since the Parcham regime was placed in power. It was reported in April 1981 that there had been "a rash of lawlessness and killings" in Kabul. Three of the four main highways leading out of the capital had been closed, there had been renewed disorders in Herat, and fighting had broken out again in twenty of Afghanistan's twenty-nine provinces, including all those that border on the Soviet Union.[47]

Throughout the spring and summer of 1981 the rebels continued to operate freely in many parts of the country, scoring minor victories over the Soviets. In April two American journalists said that the rebels they saw in two provinces were better armed and more self-confident than they had been the year before. Steven McCurry, a free-lance photographer on his eighth visit to various rebel groups, reported that in the southwest province of Helmand he saw no evidence of central government authorities. Baluch freedom fighters moved about openly during daylight hours, busily planted mines where they thought Soviet tanks might venture, and possessed enough Soviet AK47 rifles, ammunition, food, and other supplies. Tyler Marshall, a Los Angeles journalist, found similar conditions in Ningrahar province, whose capital, Jalalabad, sits astride the main road from Kabul to the Khyber Pass. He said that the rebels there were well supplied with arms and ammunition and were conspicuous on main roads and in market towns, as if they had no fear of the Soviet or Afghan armies.[48] A traveler reported that it took him seven hours to go from Kabul to Jalalabad because his convoy was stopped by rebels who collected a one-dollar fee from every passenger. This occurred only five kilometers from a Soviet garrison.[49]

The rebels continued to be active even in areas close to Kabul. In June 1981 a journalist hiked with rebels from Pakistan to within twenty miles of Kabul, where he saw them use rocket-propelled grenades to destroy Soviet armored patrol cars and trucks. The insurgents told him that their morale was better, partly because they had more arms than before. He said that he passed through one area after another that appeared to be under rebel control and never saw any sign of government officials.[50]

One rebel group even managed to set fire to the important military air base at Bagram, thirty-six miles north of Kabul, causing large explosions in ammunitions dumps.[51] In July 1981 a three-day battle broke out in Paghman, only twelve miles northwest of Kabul. The *New York Times* reported that more than 300 tanks, trucks, and armored cars were used by the Soviet side, and it was estimated that several hundred Soviet and Afghan soldiers were killed.[52] The rebels remained dominant in the Paghman area, however, and used it as a base for raids against Kabul. They even smuggled Western newsmen from Paghman into Kabul. As a result, the communists had to launch more attacks on Paghman in the spring, summer, and fall of 1982.[53]

Some areas of Afghanistan have never been conquered by the Soviets, even temporarily. This is true, for example, of the Hazarajat, the central area of massive mountain peaks that makes up about one-fourth of the country. One pro-rebel source reported:

> Since mid-1979, the Hazarajat . . . has been free of government control. A complete independent administration, . . . includes a functioning judiciary and a rotating draft for resistance fighters as well as district commissioners and local mayors. It even maintains the only functioning telephone network remaining outside the major cities. The 200 Soviet troops and 150 government militia at the sole government garrison in Shahr-i-golgola (at Bamiyan) do not venture out of their fortress. The Hazarajat is a natural fortress of high peaks and semi-arid plateaus (4,000 to 12,000 feet or more), but the topography that helped the Hazara ethnic group to fight off the Kabul regimes and the Soviets also makes it impossible for the population of 2-3 million to be entirely self-sufficient in food. All efforts to retake the region by force having failed, the Soviets are now trying to starve it into submission by cutting off the access routes into the area.[54]

The Soviet press rarely reports any Soviet casualties at all, and it probably never will reveal total casualty figures. Since claims by rebel groups are assumed to be exaggerated, it is impossible to get accurate statistics. The State Department announced in December 1982 that its estimate up to that time was a total of 10,000 to 15,000 Soviet casualties. Of these about 5,000 were believed to have died, while 5,000 to 10,000 had been wounded or were suffering from diseases such as hepatitis.[55] For a superpower like the USSR this is a tolerable number, particularly since public opinion has so little influence on Kremlin policy making.[56]

REPORTS BY WESTERN JOURNALISTS

One is inclined to be skeptical of accounts in the U.S. press about the victories of the rebels and defeats of the Soviets since Americans (including myself) naturally are sympathetic toward the insurgents. The same might be said about statements issued by the State Department, which one would expect to have an anti-Soviet and pro-rebel bias. Such skepticism is warranted when the reports are based on claims by exile leaders in Pakistan, who probably exaggerate the triumphs of their forces. But several Western reporters have slipped into Afghanistan, traveled extensively around the country, and published accounts that tend to confirm one another.

For example, Edward Girardet of the *Christian Science Monitor* spent a month in Afghanistan in August and September 1981 and trekked 700 miles through several provinces, spending most of his time in the Panjshir Valley, only about 60 miles north of Kabul. He reached the following conclusions, which generally agree with those of other Western journalists, as well as American academic and government experts: (1) The insurgents "are certainly better equipped than in the early days of the occupation. Most military supplies in the Panjshir Valley consist of captured Communist material. . . . Despite reports of substantial assistance from the United States, China, and the Gulf nations, resistance groups inside the country bitterly complain that even if outside aid *is* filtering through, they see very little of it." "The main problem . . . is still lack of weapons." (2) The rebels are "better trained and better organized." "A year before . . . the guerrillas were, on the whole, extremely disorganized." Now they plan their attacks carefully and use better strategy and tactics. There has been "a marked improvement in the overall ability of the Afghan resistance to strike back at the Soviets." (3) "Morale among the *mujaheddin* is high." (4) "Among the country's seven major resistance organizations, there is greater readiness to coordinate guerrilla activities." (5) "The Afghan resistance commands almost the entire countryside." "In most parts visited by this correspondent . . . there is little sign of Soviet presence." The area under Soviet control has shrunken. "The Soviets really only control—and I wouldn't say control, but they occupy the towns, and of course the highways—but at a risk." (6) In Kabul life "has become one of constant insecurity. While the city functions as a capital during the daytime, the resistance takes over at night." (7) "The Afghan Army . . . is largely ineffective and unreliable. Defections continue at an enormous rate."[57]

Western journalists who traveled inside Afghanistan in 1982 saw little change and agreed generally with Girardet's conclusions. For example, Aernout Van Lynden, a Dutch free-lance journalist who spent two months with the insurgents in 1982, wrote a series of articles for the *Washington Post* that painted a similar picture of the national liberation struggle.[58]

RUTHLESS SOVIET ATTACKS

In the first half of 1982 the Soviets showed signs that they had decided to use ruthless measures in order to eliminate some of the most troublesome rebel strongholds. Qandahar and Herat, Afghanistan's second- and third-most-populous cities, had become a serious embarrassment to Moscow because they continued to be largely under the domination of the rebels, who fixed curfew hours, controlled prices, and even collected taxes.[59] Concluding that they could not tolerate this any longer, the Soviets subjected both cities to savage aerial and artillery bombardments in which many civilians were killed. According to one account, in Qandahar "the Soviets staged a brutal, block-by-block, World War II-style assault."[60]

During 1982 the Soviets also made strenuous efforts to destroy rebel forces in areas near Kabul, and with some success. In January they launched an attack on the freedom fighters in Parwan province, north of the capital and reportedly killed 150 to 200 in the fighting, executed 400 "suspects," and sent 700 more to prison.[61] (Another account puts the rebel losses in the thousands.[62]) Similar assaults were successfully carried out against the insurgents in Wardak province, just west of Kabul, and in Farah province, on the Iranian border.[63] Insurgent leaders in Pakistan admitted that these were the worst losses the rebels had suffered since the Soviet invasion.[64] Whether these defeats were due to improved Soviet tactics or to rebel mistakes is not clear.

The biggest antiguerrilla operation of 1982 (and the biggest since the invasion), however, was in the Panjshir Valley, located about 60 miles northeast of Kabul. This seventy-five-mile-long valley is of great strategic importance because it is near the military air base at Bagram and lies astride the key highway leading from Kabul to the USSR. The Soviets tried repeatedly to get this valley under control, launching no fewer than six offensives there in 1981 and 1982.[65] The local Tadzhik people resisted successfully under the leadership of a twenty-eight-year-old former student named Ahmad Shah Massoud, known as the "Lion of the Panjshir." They created an autonomous state with its own schools, jails, security committees, food distribution system, training courses for guerrillas, and intelligence network. Their troops were well equipped, moreover, with boots, uniforms, and weapons, most of them captured from the Soviet and Afghan armies.[66]

On May 17, 1982, communist forces invaded the Panjshir Valley with one Soviet and three Afghan divisions, while jets and helicopter gunships bombed and strafed the villages, forcing many of the rebels to flee to the surrounding mountains. In early June the Kabul government proudly announced that "the centers of bandits and counterrevolutionaries have been liquidated forever."[67] Convinced they had triumphed, the Afghan government said it was sending 1,000 young party activists into the valley to consolidate communist control and "impart the ideals of the revolution" among the people.[68]

Kabul's "victory" proved to be limited, however. A convoy of trucks carrying the 1,000 communists was ambushed, with heavy losses.[69] The Soviet and Afghan troops ran into similar difficulties. Teams of guerrillas from nearby valleys joined the Panjshir rebels, bringing pack trains loaded with arms and ammunition. After the communist troops had been drawn far into the valley, the rebels attacked and inflicted many casualties. Meanwhile, hundreds of Afghan soldiers deserted, along with their tanks.[70] Later, in August and September 1982, the Soviet and Afghan armies tried again to subdue the Panjshir Valley, but the rebels inflicted heavy casualties, captured large quantities of arms, and forced the communist troops to retreat.[71] Once more the Soviets discovered that while it might be relatively easy to drive the rebels out of a valley temporarily, it was impossible to keep them from returning unless large-scale occupying forces remain. According to one estimate, an occupation army of 6,000 to 10,000 soldiers would be required to maintain control of the Panjshir.[72]

The rebels continued to resist actively during the last half of 1982. In a daring raid in September they set fire to a Soviet tank-and-truck depot in Kabul.[73] Later they attacked Bagram airport, Jalalabad airport, a hydroelectric plant, many factories and markets, the offices of the People's Democratic party, Soviet army headquarters, and even the Soviet embassy.[74] In December Babrak accused them of also destroying many schools, bridges, and roads.[75] At times the *mujaheddin* became so bold that they made raids across the Soviet border, where they received aid and recruits from kinsmen living in the USSR.[76] The insurgents were greatly aided in these various operations by the presence in the Afghan army and bureaucracy of many sympathizers, who regularly gave warnings about impending Soviet actions.[77] Afghans who collaborated with the Russians, however, were liable to be assassinated, as Babrak and the Soviet press admitted.[78]

In the first months of 1983 the rebels continued to harass the Soviets and their Afghan friends. In February guerrillas sabotaged four of the main transmission lines linking Kabul to power stations, and the lights went out in most of the capital for four days.[79] And in March the Soviet news agency Tass reported that "barbarous" bombing attacks had inflicted "heavy damage" to shops, a market, a bank building, and a bus depot in Kabul.[80]

Although one naturally admires the rebels and cheers their victories, it is difficult to see how they can win in the long run. The Soviet Union is so much stronger—in soldiers, arms, and economic resources—that it seems bound to win eventually, just as it finally defeated the anti-Soviet guerrillas (the Basmachi) in Central Asia in the 1920s and 1930s. The Muslims of Soviet Central Asia—Tadzhiks, Uzbeks, Turkmen, Kirghiz, and Kazaks—also resisted Russian domination and atheistic communism, but finally had to give up the struggle. The Bolsheviks over the years were able to persuade some natives that communism was a superior system, seduce others into becoming collaborators, and convince the rest that resistance was hopeless. Although the Afghans may be better fighters than their brothers to the north, it seems inevitable that, after some years, they too will be crushed by the Soviet military machine. Unless the Soviets decide to give up and withdraw, which seems unlikely, the communists will gradually extend their dominion over all but the most remote villages.[81]

NOTES

1. R. T. Klass, "The Great Game Revisited," *National Review*, vol. 31, no. 43 (October 26, 1979), p. 1368.

2. Eliza Van Hollen, *Afghanistan: A Year of Occupation* (Washington, D.C.: Department of State, February 1981, Special Report No. 79), p. 3; Zalmay Kalilzad, "Soviet-Occupied Afghanistan," *Problems of Communism,* vol. 29, no. 6 (November-December 1980), p. 35; Louis Dupree in *Los Angeles Times,* December 29, 1980, Part 2, p. 5.

3. Kalilzad, "Soviet-Occupied Afghanistan," pp. 35, 38; Eliza Van Hollen, *Afghanistan: 2 Years of Occupation* (Washington, D.C.: Department of State, December 1981, Special Report No. 91), p. 2; Eliza Van Hollen, *Afghanistan: Three Years of Occupation* (Washington, D.C.: Department of State, December 1982, Special Report No. 106), pp. 2–5, 9. An account of fighting in and near Jalalabad can be found in the *New York Times,* February 21, 1980, p. A8.

4. *Washington Post,* February 26, 1980, pp. A1, A16; February 27, 1980, pp. A1, A16; *New York Times,* February 24, 1980, pp. 1, 10.

5. Interview with Habibullah Karzai, an Afghan exile leader.

6. *Washington Post,* May 12, 1980, p. A1.

7. Interview with Habibullah Karzai.

8. *Washington Post,* May 12, 1980, p. A17; *New York Times,* May 11, 1980, p. 3.

9. *International Herald Tribune,* October 17, 1980, p. 1.

10. *Washington Post,* January 22, 1981, p. A30. For another report of rebel activity in Kabul see *Washington Post,* October 17, 1980, p. A25.

11. Francis Fukuyama, *The Security of Pakistan: A Trip Report* (Santa Monica, Calif.: Rand Corporation, September 1980), pp. 13–16.

12. Ibid., p. 16.

13. Nancy Peabody Newell and Richard S. Newell, *The Struggle for Afghanistan* (Ithaca, N.Y.: Cornell University Press, 1981), p. 130. One Afghan exile told Francis Fukuyama in mid-1980 that the exile groups in Pakistan did not control more than 3,000 of the rebels fighting in Afghanistan, while there were possibly as many as 90,000 rebels in the Hazarajat region alone. Fukuyama, *The Security of Pakistan,* p. 18.

14. *New York Times,* July 20, 1980, p. 12.

15. R. Lincoln Keiser, "The Rebellion in Darra-i-Nur," a paper presented at the meeting of the American Anthropological Association in Washington, D.C., on December 5, 1980. According to Edward Girardet in the *Christian Science Monitor,* September 23, 1981, pp. 1–6, the resistance organizations by that time were coordinating their military activities more than before.

16. According to a Tass report, in August 1981 a force of 700 rebels attacked a border post along the frontier with Pakistan. This report, however, may be propaganda, designed to demonstrate that Pakistan is allowing the rebels to form large groups on its territory. *New York Times,* August 13, 1981, p. A5.

17. *New York Times,* April 14, 1981, p. A3.

18. Kalilzad, "Soviet-Occupied Afghanistan," p. 33.

19. *Washington Post,* February 14, 1980, pp. A1, A26.

20. Jimmy Carter, *Keeping Faith* (New York: Bantam Books, 1982), p. 475.

21. Interview with Frank Reynolds on ABC-TV, March 9, 1981.

22. *The New Republic,* vol. 185, no. 3 (July 18, 1981), pp. 9–10. Also reported by Bernstein in the transcript of ABC, "20/20," "Afghanistan—The Secret War,"

June 18, 1981, pp. 5–7. See also the *Washington Post,* December 19, 1982, pp. A1, A38.

23. *San Francisco Chronicle,* September 24, 1981, p. 11.

24. Van Hollen, *Afghanistan: A Year of Occupation,* p. 4.

25. *New York Times,* August 7, 1981, p. A4; April 14, 1981, p. A3. The resistance also desperately needs doctors, nurses, and medical supplies. Few of the rebels who are injured can make it to the hospitals in Pakistan, so a seriously wounded mujahid usually means a dead one, while those who are hit in the arms or legs generally develop gangrene and must submit to amputation. In early 1983 there were 24 French doctors in Afghanistan serving approximately 200,000 insurgents, but apparently there were no American doctors, nurses, or, for that matter, volunteers of any kind. Peter Arnett, "Report from a War Zone," *Parade Magazine,* February 20, 1983, p. 19.

26. *New York Times,* July 20, 1980, p. 12.

27. Ibid.

28. Ibid.

29. Louis Dupree, *Militant Islam and Traditional Warfare in Islamic South Asia* (Hanover, N.H.: American Universities Field Staff Reports, 1980/no. 21, Asia), p. 4.

30. Kalilzad, "Soviet-Occupied Afghanistan," p. 31.

31. *Washington Post,* December 27, 1981; Van Hollen, *Afghanistan: A Year of Occupation,* p. 3; Van Hollen, *Afghanistan: Three Years of Occupation,* p. 5.

32. Van Hollen, *Afghanistan: A Year of Occupation,* p. 3.

33. Ibid., p. 5; *New York Times,* July 15, 1980, p. A6. In July 1982 the tour of duty was again lengthened by six months, to a total of three years. Van Hollen, *Afghanistan: Three Years of Occupation,* p. 6.

34. Van Hollen, *Afghanistan: Three Years of Occupation,* p. 5.

35. From an article in *Krasnaia Zvezda* (*Red Star*), the official newspaper of the Soviet army, as reported in the *Washington Post,* March 1, 1982, p. A15. In 1982 and 1983 the Soviet press began publishing more candid reports of the fighting in Afghanistan, particularly on the role of Soviet soldiers. *Washington Post,* November 9, 1982, p. A22; February 28, 1983, p. A14; March 5, 1983, p. A14. In February 1983 the Soviet newspaper *Komsomolskaia pravda* revealed that three Soviet soldiers had been killed in an ambush. *Washington Post,* February 6, 1983, p. A16.

36. Statement by William Casey, director of the Central Intelligence Agency, at a meeting of scholars specializing on Afghanistan, Washington, D.C., December 16, 1981.

37. *New York Times,* March 9, 1982, p. A8; Van Hollen, *Afghanistan: Three Years of Occupation,* p. 1.

38. Louis Dupree, speech at the Asia Society, Washington, D.C., December 4, 1980.

39. Drew Middleton in the *New York Times,* August 7, 1981, p. A4; Van Hollen, *Afghanistan: Three Years of Occupation,* p. 4; U.S. Department of Defense, *Soviet Military Power,* 2nd ed. (Washington, D.C.: Government Printing Office, March 1983), pp. 49–50.

40. Speech at the annual meeting of the American Anthropological Association, Washington, D.C., December 5, 1980.

41. Van Hollen, *Afghanistan: Three Years of Occupation,* p. 10, says that by the end of 1982 more than 2.7 million refugees had registered with the Pakistani government, and the number of refugees in Iran was estimated to be between 500,000 and 1 million. This gives a total of 3.2 to 3.7 million, plus a few thousand in Turkey, the United States, and elsewhere. The population of Afghanistan in 1979 was approximately 15,500,000, according to *Background Notes: Afghanistan* (Washington, D.C.: Government Printing Office, April 1980), p. 1. The comparison is based on a U.S. population at the beginning of 1982 of about 230 million. One-fifth of that would be 46 million.

Getting accurate figures on the exiles is difficult because many Pushtun refugees live with relatives in Pakistan and don't bother to register, while some refugees register in more than one place in order to obtain extra food. Pushtun exiles can integrate to a certain extent with fellow Pushtuns living in Pakistan, but the situation facing most other exiles is more difficult, as they have no second homeland they can escape to. A Tadzhik, for example, would hardly wish to flee to his kinsmen in the Tadzhik Soviet Republic.

The *Washington Post,* September 24, 1982, p. A12, reported that conflicts had broken out between the Afghan exiles and the Pakistanis living near the 282 refugee camps.

42. *New York Times,* March 9, 1982, p. A9.

43. Ibid. See also the detailed report, with maps and tables: U.S. Department of State, *Chemical Warfare in Southeast Asia and Afghanistan; Report to the Congress from Secretary of State Alexander M. Haig, Jr., March 22, 1982,* especially pp. 6–8, 14–17. The report is summarized in the *New York Times,* March 23, 1982, pp. 14–15. A letter by Richard Burt, director of the Bureau of Politico-Military Affairs, Department of State, in the *Washington Post,* March 19, 1982, p. A22, criticizes the *Post* for questioning the State Department's handling of the chemical warfare issue.

Also note the article by Tyler Marshall, "Is Our Chemical War Propaganda Backfiring?" *Washington Post,* May 13, 1982, p. A31, and the letter by Karen McKay, executive director of the Committee for a Free Afghanistan, in the *Washington Post,* May 30, 1982, p. C6. The *Washington Post,* September 9, 1982, p. A21, published an article about a captured Russian soldier who confirmed that the Soviets were using chemical warfare in Afghanistan.

The U.S. government's charge that the Soviet Union and its allies are using "yellow rain" in Afghanistan, Cambodia, and Laos sparked considerable controversy, with some scientists arguing that the evidence is not conclusive. One Harvard professor suggested that the State Department's samples of "yellow rain" were little more than bee droppings, while other scientists insisted that they were man-made poisons. See Robert L. Bartley and William Kucewicz, "'Yellow Rain' and the Future of Arms Agreements," *Foreign Affairs,* vol. 61, no. 4 (Spring 1983), pp. 805–826. See also *New York Times,* June 2, 1983, p. A16; June 3, 1983, p. A30; and June 21, 1983, pp. C1–C2. And *Washington Post,* April 11, 1983, p. A11; June 1, 1983, p. A14; June 2, 1983, p. A11; and June 13, 1983, p. A14.

44. Interview with Gary Crocker, June 15, 1981. A great deal of information on Soviet use of chemical warfare can be found in two collections of documents put together by Crocker and others for the State Department and distributed in duplicated form: "Reports of the Use of Chemical Weapons in Afghanistan, Laos and Kampuchea" (131 pp.), issued in the summer of 1980, and "Update to the Compendium on the Reports of the Use of Chemical Weapons" (33 pp.) issued in March 1981. See also Newell and Newell, *The Struggle for Afghanistan,* pp. 136, 138–139; *New York Times,* March 30, 1980, p. A6, and August 8, 1980, p. A3; Van Hollen, *Afghanistan: Three Years of Occupation,* p. 5.

45. *Washington Post,* February 6, 1981, p. A26; Van Hollen, *Afghanistan: A Year of Occupation,* p. 3. Several Soviet deserters were interviewed on the ABC program "20/20" on February 17, 1983.

46. Van Hollen, *Afghanistan: A Year of Occupation,* pp. 1–2.

47. *Washington Post,* April 2, 1981, p. A15.

48. *New York Times,* April 14, 1981, p. A3.

49. Interview with State Department official.

50. Aernout Van Lynden in the *Washington Post,* June 5, 1981, p. A1.

51. *Washington Post,* June 18, 1981, p. A24.

52. *New York Times* dispatch from New Delhi, July 23, 1981, p. A4.

53. *Washington Post,* May 26, 1982, p. A24; Van Hollen, *Afghanistan: Three Years of Occupation,* p. 4; *Washington Post,* December 27, 1982, p. A26.

54. *News Leads: Afghanistan* (New York: Afghanistan Information Center), Report No. 1, July 1, 1981, p. 4.

55. *New York Times,* December 23, 1982, p. A7. For other estimates of casualties see *Time,* January 10, 1983, p. 30; *New York Times,* December 17, 1982, p. A3; December 8, 1982, p. A5; and August 7, 1981, p. A4.

56. Unlike the American public during the Vietnamese war, Soviet citizens do not get a daily diet of mutilated bodies and burned villages on their TV sets.

57. Edward Girardet, "With the Resistance in Afghanistan," *Christian Science Monitor,* September 23, 1981, pp. 1, 6, and September 24, 1981, pp. 1, 6; transcript of Public Broadcasting System, "MacNeil-Lehrer Report," "Afghanistan: War Continues," October 16, 1981, pp. 2–4. For a general evaluation of the military situation at the end of 1981 see the article by Stuart Auerbach in the *Washington Post,* December 27, 1981, pp. A1, A24. See also the report of the travels in Afghanistan by Peter Grant in Jack Anderson's column, *Washington Post,* November 8, 1981, p. C7. Van Hollen, *Afghanistan: 2 Years of Occupation,* p. 5, says: "In many parts of the country, the *mujahidin* are still seriously underarmed in relation to the numbers of potential fighters."

58. The Van Lynden articles can be found in the following issues of the *Washington Post:* September 10, 1982, p. A21; November 2, 1982, pp. A1, A14; November 15, 1982, p. A14; December 10, 1982, pp. A1, A31; December 13, 1982, pp. A1, A18; December 19, 1982, pp. A1, A38; December 27, 1982, pp. A1, A26; December 28, 1982, p. A10; and January 1, 1983, pp. A1, A14.

59. Van Hollen, *Afghanistan: 2 Years of Occupation,* p. 2.

60. *Washington Post,* April 13, 1982, p. A9.

61. UPI dispatch in the *Charlottesville Daily Progress,* March 10, 1982, p. A12.

62. *Washington Post,* April 13, 1982, p. A9.

63. Ibid.

64. UPI dispatch in the *Charlottesville Daily Progress,* March 10, 1982, p. A12.

65. *Washington Post,* June 4, 1982, p. A15; *New York Times,* June 9, 1982, p. A3, and June 23, 1982, p. A5.

66. *Time,* July 5, 1982, p. 39; *Washington Post,* July 9, 1982, p. A27.

67. *Washington Post,* June 4, 1982, p. A15.

68. Ibid., June 17, 1982, p. A28.

69. *New York Times,* June 23, 1982, p. A5, and June 30, 1982, p. A3.

70. *Time,* July 5, 1982, p. 39; *Washington Post,* December 27, 1982, p. A26.

71. Van Hollen, *Afghanistan: Three Years of Occupation,* p. 4.

72. *New York Times,* June 9, 1982, p. A3.

73. *Washington Post,* November 2, 1982, pp. A1, A14.

74. *Izvestiia,* December 17, 1982, p. 5; Van Hollen, *Afghanistan: Three Years of Occupation,* p. 9; *The Guardian* (Manchester), December 30, 1982, p. 7; *New York Times,* December 8, 1982, p. A5; *Washington Post,* November 2, 1982, pp. A1, A14; November 15, 1982, p. A14; December 10, 1982, p. A31; January 1, 1983, p. A14.

75. *New York Times,* December 21, 1982, p. A3.

76. Van Hollen, *Afghanistan: Three Years of Occupation,* p. 9.

77. *Washington Post,* December 27, 1982, p. A26; *Le Monde,* November 10, 1982.

78. *Izvestiia,* December 17, 1982, p. 5; *New York Times,* December 21, 1982, p. A3.

79. *Washington Post,* February 9, 1983, p. A21.

80. *Washington Post,* March 5, 1983, p. A14.

81. The situation of the Afghan insurgents is not identical with that of the Basmachi in every respect. Professor Leon B. Poullada explained this in a letter to me as follows: "In the 1920s Central Asia was even more remote from the concerns of the outside world than Afghanistan is now. Media coverage of the Soviet repression of Central Asian Muslims was practically non-existent. There was no Third World group of countries, no nonaligned organization, no Islamic Conference. In other words, the situations are comparable, but not parallel. Afghanistan is going to be a much tougher nut than Central Asia not only because the Afghans are better fighters, but also because world conditions are very different."

CHAPTER 16

Soviet Losses and Gains from the Invasion

LOSSES

The End of Détente

The invasion of Afghanistan has been costly to the Soviets in a number of ways. Perhaps the most obvious loss has been the killing of détente with the United States. The tone of the dialogue between the two superpowers changed dramatically under Carter and became even more antagonistic under Reagan. The embargoes on grain and advanced technology hurt the Soviet economy some, if not seriously, and the SALT II treaty lost whatever chance it had of getting Senate approval.

The Politburo must have known that invading Afghanistan would have a devastating effect on détente, but went ahead anyway, thereby demonstrating again that improving relations with the West does not have top priority in Soviet foreign policy. The number-one goal of the Soviets is to hang on to what they have, to maintain and strengthen their control over the Soviet empire, even if this means sending troops into neighboring countries. Retaining and expanding Soviet power and influence is considered more important than the variable and uncertain rewards of trying to bring about a lasting rapprochement with the United States.

American Rearmament

Another Soviet loss from the invasion has been the speeding up of American rearmament. Indeed, the Soviet invasion of Afghanistan may have the same effect on the United States that the Cuban missile crisis reportedly had on the Soviet Union. It has been said that after President Kennedy faced down Khrushchev in 1962, a top Soviet official blamed Krushchev's defeat on U.S.

military superiority and declared: "Never will we be caught like this again."[1]
It is widely believed that the humiliation of 1962 gave the Soviet leaders
much of their motivation for the rapid military buildup that they have been
carrying on ever since. The invasion of Afghanistan is serving as a similar
catalyst for American defense spending. The result has been an intensification
of the arms race and a worsening of the prospects for arms control. The
eventual, long-term consequences of this for Russia and the world are incalculable.

A Blow to Soviet Prestige

The invasion of Afghanistan and the continued slaughter of Afghans by
the Soviet invaders has of course had a negative effect on the Soviet image
around the world, not only in the West but almost everywhere. At a special
session of the United Nations General Assembly in January 1980, 104 states
voted for a resolution calling for the immediate withdrawal of foreign troops
from Afghanistan, while only 18 voted against it. In November 1980 a
similar resolution was passed by a larger margin—111 to 22—including 40
Third World nations.[2] Equally one-sided votes were cast in 1981 and 1982.[3]
Conferences of Islamic nations have repeatedly denounced Soviet "military
aggression" against Afghanistan, and several of these states have sent aid to
the Afghan rebels.[4]

Soviet prestige in the Third World has suffered a severe blow; in the
future such states presumably will view Soviet attacks on imperialism with
greater skepticism than in the past. As one Asian ambassador put it, "We
have to rethink our basic concepts that imperialism is fundamentally synonymous
with the West."[5] Indeed, it will be difficult for Moscow to support its claim
that it is the staunchest foe of imperialism when it is engaged in a campaign
of blatant imperialism or its claim that it is the most faithful supporter of
the national liberation movement when it is using tanks, jets, helicopter
gunships, and chemical weapons against a genuine national liberation struggle.
Jimmy Carter agrees that the invasion was very damaging to Russia's reputation
in Asia, Africa, and Latin America. In his memoirs he refers to "the great
diplomatic losses suffered by the Soviets among the less developed countries
of the world. Decades of propaganda efforts to project themselves as the
peace-loving defender of small countries had gone down the drain."[6]

The Soviet invasion of Afghanistan has also worsened Soviet relations with
its neighbors in the Far East. Communist China has repeatedly stated that
Sino-Soviet relations cannot be significantly improved as long as Soviet armed
forces are occupying Afghanistan. Japan seems to have been affected even
more than China, as a Japanese scholar explained:

> The Soviet invasion of Afghanistan in December 1979 had a major impact
> on Japanese foreign policy—both in its general orientation and its attitude
> toward the USSR. By the very act of military intervention in Afghanistan,

the Soviet leaders destroyed their bargaining position in relations with Japan. The Japanese government of prime minister Masayoshi Ohira adopted a policy of even closer cooperation with the United States that was exemplified by the suspension of personal exchanges between high officials of the USSR and Japan and the freezing of joint economic projects with the Soviets, together with the boycotting of the Moscow Olympics. Furthermore, the "Pacific Basin Cooperation Design" which was promulgated by Ohira and his foreign minister, Saburo Okita, appeared to mark a departure from Japan's policy of balancing relations, since it excluded specific reference to the Soviet Union. Finally, the Soviet invasion of Afghanistan resulted in expanded concern in Japan for military security.[7]

Soviet use of chemical warfare in Afghanistan (and the use of Soviet-made chemical agents by client regimes in Laos and Cambodia) presumably also will serve to blacken the reputation of the Soviet Union in the eyes of the world. Apparently the Soviets hoped that they could get away with this cruel and illegal tactic if the chemicals were only in remote jungle and mountainous areas, where concrete evidence is hard to find. But the U.S. government has systematically collected eyewitness testimony from many different sources and has given the matter much publicity in the hope that this would force Moscow to stop. Since Afghanistan, Laos, and Cambodia are all Third World countries, perhaps this communist practice, when it becomes well known, will be particularly harmful to the Soviet Union's influence in less-developed parts of the world.[8]

It also seems likely that some countries close to the USSR are wondering if the day will come when the Soviets will invade them or encourage local communists to overthrow their governments. For example, it probably was not mere coincidence that President Saddam Hussein launched a crackdown on communists in Iraq in 1978, in the aftermath of the coup in Afghanistan. Twenty-one communists in the armed forces were executed, and several thousand communists or suspected communists were arrested that June, perhaps in a move designed to make sure that a similar coup would not occur in Iraq.[9] Other countries in that area also are apprehensive about Soviet intentions regarding them. For example, since the invasion, six of the Gulf states have formed the Gulf Cooperation Council, indicating not only increased fear of the USSR but also determination to resist any further Soviet advances.

Another result of the invasion was to put strains on Soviet relations with Cuba. Jimmy Carter in his memoirs describes how the invasion caused Castro to go so far as to request a secret meeting with U.S. officials:

> One surprising development was Cuba's adverse reaction to the Soviet invasion. Fidel Castro had been trying to get his country elected to a seat on the United Nations Security Council and seemed likely to prevail even against firm United States opposition. After he first refused to criticize the

Soviet action, he lost support and had to withdraw from contention. It happened that during this time, Cuba was scheduled to host a meeting of the NAM (Non-Aligned Movement) countries. . . . Most of the . . . [members] became irate because of Cuba's reluctance to condemn the Soviet invasion, and Castro was apparently feeling the heat. He sent me word that he wanted to discuss Iran and Afghanistan, and I asked Robert Pastor, Latin American specialist on the National Security Council staff, and Peter Tarnoff, Executive Secretary of the State Department, to go to Cuba for a secret meeting with him.[10]

Carter then quotes from his diary for January 18, 1980, on what happened during the meeting with Castro:

Our emissaries to Cuba reported a startling frankness in an 11-hour discussion with Castro. He described without any equivocation his problems with the Soviet Union; his loss of leadership position in NAM because of his subservience to the Soviet Union; his desire to pull out of Ethiopia now, and Angola later; his involvement in the revolutionary movements in Central America but his aversion to sending weapons or military capability to the Caribbean countries; and so forth. He is very deeply hurt by our embargo. Wants to move toward better relationships with us, but can't abandon his friends, the Soviets, who have supported his revolution unequivocally. . . .

The reasons for this long discourse were unclear to us, but it was at least obvious that Cuba was embarrassed to be aligned with the Soviet Union in the public debates.[11]

There is no doubt that the Soviet invasion weakened Cuba's influence in the Nonaligned Movement. At the 1979 meeting of the Nonaligned Movement in Havana (before the invasion), Castro was able to steer the movement in a pro-Soviet direction, but at the 1981 meeting in New Delhi a resolution was adopted calling for the withdrawal of "foreign troops" from Afghanistan. Arguments by the Cuban representative that the USSR was the true friend of nonaligned states were rejected.[12] Although some Third World states close to the USSR have refused to *criticize* the Soviet invasion, very few have been willing to *defend* it.

It seems likely that the longer the conflict between the Soviet forces and the rebels continues, the greater will be the damage to the reputation of the USSR around the world. Since the fighting has already dragged on for many months and promises to continue much longer, this invasion may hurt Soviet foreign relations much more than the invasions of Hungary and Czechoslovakia. This will not be the case, however, if Afghanistan disappears from the news media and people forget about it. Afghanistan is, after all, a distant land to Americans and West Europeans, and there is a tendency in many circles to resume business as usual.

Unpopularity at Home

Aside from damaging Russia's image, the involvement in Afghanistan is also costing a great deal in money and manpower—resources that could better be used to improve the Soviet economy. There is also the possibility that it is undermining morale among Soviet citizens, as more and more coffins are shipped home. We cannot take public opinion polls in the USSR, of course, but there are reports that some Soviet citizens refer to the Afghan conflict as "that dirty little war." An American professor who visited the USSR in the fall of 1981 reported that Soviet citizens told him the war was unpopular among important segments of the population:

> Because the regime doesn't share information about the actual level of casualties, rumors circulate wildly within the Soviet Union, and it may be that there is an exaggerated notion of what the losses are in Afghanistan. . . . The rumors that circulate are not only that there are Soviet soldiers dying in Afghanistan—which is an unpopular idea among their people—but there are also ugly rumors of the way in which the soldiers die, . . . the way the soldiers are mutilated.[13]

The Soviet leaders themselves may be looking upon it increasingly as a "dirty little war," a quagmire they somehow got stuck in and from which there is no easy escape. It would not be surprising if the Soviet leaders sometimes think how nice it would be to return to the good old days when President Daoud or King Zahir was in power.

GAINS

Despite the many negative consequences the Soviets have suffered from the invasion of Afghanistan, their gains have been substantial. For one thing, they achieved their immediate objective of removing an unreliable communist ruler and replacing him with an obedient puppet. They also prevented the overthrow of communism in Afghanistan, thereby maintaining the principle of the Brezhnev Doctrine. And they preserved the military security of their border by keeping Afghanistan from falling into the hands of anti-Soviet insurgents.

An Improved Geostrategic Position

Perhaps the most important gain for the Soviets, however, was the improvement of their geostrategic position, particularly in regard to the Gulf and its oil. Through the use of Afghan airfields, especially those at Shindand and Qandahar, Soviet fighter-bombers are now much closer to the Strait of Hormuz. And if Backfire bombers are stationed at these fields, they will constitute a serious threat to the American naval task force operating in the

Indian Ocean. (These airfields will not be of much use to the Soviets, however, as long as they are vulnerable to raids by Afghan rebels.)[14] By land the Soviets could drive from Afghanistan to the Strait of Hormuz in a short time, although the roads are very poor.

Russia's geostrategic position has improved not only in relation to the Gulf but also in relation to the whole Indian subcontinent, by ending Afghanistan's historic role as a neutral buffer between Russia and India. In the nineteenth century, Britain saw to it that Afghanistan remained independent so as to protect India from further Russian expansion, and the tsarist government had to accept this in order to avoid war with England. Under Brezhnev, however, Russia finally attained its long-time ambition of extending its power to the Khyber Pass, the gateway to Pakistan and India. This means that Moscow is in a better position to exert pressure on these two countries, especially Pakistan. Iran, which also has been an object of Russian ambitions for centuries, is likewise more vulnerable than before to Soviet influences or to a possible Soviet invasion. (These points are discussed in greater detail in Chapter 18.)

Another geostrategic gain from the invasion has been the de facto annexation of the strategic Wakhan Corridor, the long arm of land that sticks out from northeastern Afghanistan, separates the USSR from Pakistan, and gives China a small frontier with Afghanistan. Since Soviet troops have occupied this area and most of the local inhabitants have fled or been evacuated, the Chinese no longer have a direct land route for sending aid to the Afghan rebels.[15]

Combat Experience and Testing of Weapons

The invasion and the subsequent fighting against the insurgents also provided the Soviets with valuable military experience and opportunities to test many new weapons—an assault rifle (the AKS), automatic mortars, self-propelled artillery, shells with needlelike projectiles, new types of cluster bombs, mine-laying and mine-clearing equipment, modified infantry combat vehicles, multiple rocket launchers, helicopters, a new tactical fighter-bomber (the FU-25), and battle-management computers.[16] Afghanistan also gave many officers and troops their first opportunity for actual combat and their first chance to try out various military tactics. To get some idea of the value of Afghanistan as a training ground it should be pointed out that by early 1983 more than 400,000 Soviet soldiers had served in Afghanistan.[17] Just the task of planning the invasion, mobilizing the personnel, assembling the supplies, organizing the communications system, and carrying out the operation must have been a valuable educational experience for the Soviet military machine.

Access to Afghan Minerals

Invading Afghanistan also guaranteed Soviet access to valuable minerals, especially natural gas. While the amount of gas imported from Afghanistan is small in comparison with total Soviet consumption, the Soviets seem eager to get as much of it as possible—no doubt partly because they pay low prices for it. Soon after the invasion a second gas field began production, with the result that in 1980 the value of gas exported to the Soviet Union rose by 400 percent over the 1978 figure. In addition, the Soviets have found deposits of oil and other minerals in Afghanistan.[18] With large parts of the country in rebel hands, however, it is doubtful that the Soviets have been able to do much to develop these mineral resources.

Finally, the invasion also may have increased the respect and fear that many nations have for the Soviets. The invasion has demonstrated again that the USSR is tough and determined, while the United States, by contrast, often appears weak and indecisive.

NOTES

1. Soviet Deputy Foreign Minister Vasilii Kuznetsov to John J. McCloy, as quoted in *Newsweek,* June 12, 1978, p. 31.

2. *Washington Post,* November 21, 1980, p. A27.

3. Eliza Van Hollen, *Afghanistan: 2 Years of Occupation* (Washington, D.C.: Department of State, December 1981, Special Report No. 91), p. 2; Eliza Van Hollen, *Afghanistan: Three Years of Occupation* (Washington, D.C.: Department of State, December 1982, Special Report No. 106), p. 2.

4. *Washington Post,* January 2, 1980, p. A3, and January 29, 1980, pp. A1, A7; *New York Times,* May 23, 1980, p. A10; Eliza Van Hollen, *Afghanistan: A Year of Occupation* (Washington, D.C.: Department of State, February 1981, Special Report No. 79), p. 5.

5. *Washington Post,* January 11, 1980, p. A1.

6. Jimmy Carter, *Keeping Faith* (New York: Bantam Books, 1982), p. 480.

7. Hiroshi Kimura, "The Impact of the Afghanistan Invasion on Japanese-Soviet Relations," in *Soviet Foreign Policy and East-West Relations,* ed. by Roger E. Kanet (New York: Pergamon Press, 1982), pp. 144–145.

8. See the comments about Soviet chemical warfare in Chapter 15. See also *Chemical Warfare in Southeast Asia and Afghanistan: Report to the Congress from Secretary of State Alexander M. Haig, Jr., March 22, 1982* (Washington, D.C.: Department of State, March 1982, Special Report No. 98).

9. *New York Times,* June 29, 1981, p. A3.

10. Carter, *Keeping Faith,* p. 479.

11. Ibid., pp. 479–480.

12. *Washington Post,* February 14, 1981, pp. A1, A21.

13. Comment by Professor Robert Legvold, transcript of Public Broadcasting System, "MacNeil-Lehrer Report," "Afghanistan: War Continues," October 16, 1981, p. 6.

14. Drew Middleton in the *New York Times,* March 10, 1980, p. A12. The Qandahar airfield was built by the United States, in part with the idea that U.S. bombers returning from attacks on the Soviet Union could land there.

15. Yaacov Vertzberger, "Afghanistan in China's Policy," *Problems of Communism,* vol. 31, no. 3 (May-June 1982), pp. 10–11.

16. Professor John Erickson in Great Britain, House of Commons, Foreign Affairs Committee, *Afghanistan: The Soviet Invasion and Its Consequences for British Policy* (London: Her Majesty's Stationery Office, 1980), p. A8; interview with Rear Admiral Robert P. Hilton, vice-director, operations, U.S. Joint Chiefs of Staff; Eliza Van Hollen, *Soviet Dilemmas in Afghanistan* (Washington, D.C.: Department of State, June 1980, Special Report No. 72), p. 3.

17. Interview with Gary Crocker, expert on Soviet military matters in the State Department; Philip Jacobson, "The Red Army Learns from a Real War," *Washington Post,* February 13, 1983, p. C4. Lessons learned from operating helicopters in Afghanistan are described in an article by Lt. Colonel B. Budnikov in *Aviatsiia i kosmovnatika* (Moscow), no. 9, 1980, pp. 8–9.

18. Theodore Shabad, "The Soviet Union and Afghanistan: Some Economic Aspects," a paper read at the annual meeting of the American Association for the Advancement of Slavic Studies, Monterey, Calif., September 20, 1981, pp. 1, 4, 5. Shabad goes on to say that "the Soviet economic presence in Afghanistan, which has been pervasive since World War II, greatly intensified after the 1978 revolution and especially after the military intervention, which appears to have largely cut off Afghan trade with the non-Soviet partners." Ibid., p. 8.

CHAPTER 17

What Will the Soviets Do in the Future?

OPTIMISM ABOUT A SOVIET PULLOUT

Is there a chance that the Kremlin can be persuaded to withdraw its 100,000 troops from Afghanistan, abandon the communist regime of Babrak Karmal, and permit the formation of a neutral coalition government? Evidently some important officials in the United Nations and the State Department, as well as some specialists on South Asia, think so.

Diego Cordovez, under secretary general of the United Nations, announced in June 1982 that he had held successful talks with Afghan, Pakistani, and Soviet representatives in Geneva. Both sides, he said, showed great flexibility, and they worked out a "package of understandings" which he would refine later in trips to Kabul, Islamabad, and Teheran.[1]

Shortly thereafter the State Department revealed that the U.S. ambassador in Moscow had conducted a series of secret conversations with the Soviet Foreign Ministry. These were designed to get the USSR to withdraw from Afghanistan and thereby remove a major impediment to better Soviet-American relations.[2] In February 1983 the Afghan desk officer in the State Department declared: "The Reagan administration is convinced that a dialogue with the Soviet Union over Afghanistan is possible. Unlike Poland, where Soviet intentions are unbreakable, the United States does detect a Soviet willingness to eventually leave Afghanistan to its traditional neutrality."[3]

Some specialists on South Asia also are optimistic that diplomatic negotiations will lead to a Soviet withdrawal from Afghanistan. Selig Harrison in the *New York Times,* (July 12, 1982), claimed that "some Soviet leaders [unnamed] show interest in finding a graceful way out." He added, without citing his source, "Moscow says that it would seek to broaden the base of the Kabul regime, possibly replacing Mr. Karmal."[4]

Lewis M. Simons, who covered Afghanistan as a journalist from 1972 to 1978, takes a similar stand. Writing in the *New Republic,* he saw "an emerging Soviet inclination toward a face-saving resolution" of its Afghan occupation. He also quoted an anonymous "senior U.S. government official" as saying that many people in Washington felt the chances for a peaceful settlement were growing.[5]

It is easy to understand why the UN, the State Department, and friends of Afghanistan are eager to see a Russian withdrawal. It would end the suffering of the Afghan people, permit the more than 3 million refugees to return to their homes, and reduce the Soviet threat to Pakistan, India, Iran, and Gulf oil. Unfortunately, however, it is doubtful that the Soviets will get out of Afghanistan. They went into Afghanistan to establish their domination of that country, and they probably will not withdraw until that domination is ensured one way or another.

The difficulties standing in the way of an agreement between the USSR and the Babrak regime on the one hand and Pakistan and Iran on the other hand is illustrated by the conditions under which Cordovez conducted the UN negotiations. The foreign minister of Pakistan would not talk to the foreign minister of Afghanistan because Islamabad does not recognize the Kabul government. Consequently, Cordovez had to act as a courier between the two diplomats. Iran refused to participate in the talks even in this indirect fashion. Likewise absent were the foreign ministers of the two states that probably will have the deciding voice in any settlement—the Soviet Union and the United States.[6] The millions of Afghan rebels and refugees were not consulted at all.

The Kremlin probably has encouraged the diplomatic discussions for several reasons: (1) to lessen the condemnation of the Soviet Union by encouraging hopes that it will withdraw, (2) to gain international legitimacy for the Babrak regime, (3) to improve the USSR's world image by appearing to be reasonable and conciliatory, (4) to discourage the sending of further aid to the rebels, and (5) to undermine the morale of the *mujaheddin,* who fear that a deal will be made behind their backs. Perhaps the Kremlin also hopes that through persistent negotiations it eventually can get a settlement that leaves communists in control of Afghanistan.

This does not mean that the United States should oppose the UN initiative or abandon its own talks with Moscow. One always tries to achieve peaceful solutions, even if the prospects appear hopeless. But it does mean that we should not permit the negotiations to serve as a means of taking pressure off of the Soviets or as an excuse to reduce aid to the rebels in Afghanistan or the refugees in Pakistan and Iran.

While negotiations for a peaceful settlement should not be opposed or boycotted, they should be viewed realistically and skeptically, bearing in mind Afghan national character and traditions, as well as the record of Soviet foreign policy. Let us do that now by examining each of the main options faced by the USSR in Afghanistan and seeing which ones it is most likely to adopt.

SOVIET ALTERNATIVES IN AFGHANISTAN

These Soviet alternatives are to: (1) form a coalition government, (2) restore the king, (3) let Afghanistan become neutral and nonaligned, (4) follow a policy of "Finlandization," (5) withdraw Soviet troops, (6) send more troops, (7) annex all or part of Afghanistan, or (8) continue present policies.

Before discussing each of these alternatives it should be noted that the best way to anticipate Soviet behavior in the future is to examine Soviet behavior in the past. To understand what the USSR is likely to do in Afghanistan, one should recall what the Soviets did after they invaded other small states on their borders and installed communist regimes—in Outer Mongolia and Eastern Europe. In those countries the USSR followed a rather consistent pattern of policies, and it seems reasonable to suppose that their policies in Afghanistan will be similar.

1. Form a coalition government. Some commentators have suggested that the Soviets might tire of the struggle in Afghanistan and accept a coalition government. It is difficult, however, to imagine which political groups would join such a coalition. Judging from past Soviet actions in Eastern Europe, Moscow will not accept a coalition unless it is dominated by the communists, that is, unless it is a sham coalition. As for the rebel leaders, most of them hate the communists so passionately that they probably would not join a cabinet containing even a single communist, and they surely would not join one controlled by communists. Edward Girardet, a journalist who has spent a great deal of time in Afghanistan with the insurgents, says that the ones he talked with insisted they would never compromise with the Soviets or the Afghan communists: "They were adamant that the only way they would accept a solution would be for the Russians to leave. And they're also adamant that there would be no Communists left. . . . I asked them, 'What would you do with these people.' And they said, 'Well, obviously they cannot live here; otherwise, we'd kill them.'"[7]

Rebel opposition to the idea of a coalition government is matched by the equally vehement opposition of Babrak. When he was asked what he thought of the proposal for a coalition with the rebels, he rejected it emphatically. "Afghanistan has no tradition of compromising with gangsters," he said.[8]

Undoubtedly the Soviets could put together some kind of bogus coalition consisting of communists and noncommunists, but it is doubtful that it would attract much of a following. In the present atmosphere of mutual hatred, any Afghan who cooperated with the Soviets or Babrak would be looked upon with contempt by most of his fellow countrymen. The Soviets might remove Babrak and form a new cabinet under a new prime minister, but it is most unlikely that any leader installed under Soviet sponsorship would be accepted by the rebels.

In my view it will be difficult, if not impossible, to negotiate an agreement that will satisfy both communists and noncommunists. One Soviet citizen put his finger on the key point when he said, "In terms of a political settlement, there's nothing we can offer that the other side—that is, Pakistan, Iran, or the West—will accept. There's nothing that they're going to offer which will allow Babrak Karmal's regime to be established which we can accept. And therefore, here we sit."[9]

2. Restore the king. Various people have suggested that the best man to head a coalition regime would be the former king, Mohammad Zahir, who was overthrown in 1973 and has lived in exile ever since. Nicholas Gage in the *New York Times* reported from Pakistan as follows: "In diplomatic circles here discussion frequently turns to personalities who might be suitable to head such a [coalition] government and gain enough support to make it work. One of the names mentioned is former King Zahir, now living in Rome."[10]

Selig Harrison, a long-time specialist on Afghan affairs, asserted on the op-ed page of the *New York Times* that "King Mohammad Zahir may yet have a role to play" in a transition to a new regime.[11] Lewis Simons wrote in the *New Republic:*

> Zahir Shah . . . has emerged as a possible central player in unifying the disparate factions within the country. . . . He could provide a centrifugal [*sic*] force needed to pull into reasonable proximity the diverse essential elements in Afghanistan—the Communists and the Moslem fundamentalists. . . . Although there is hostility toward Zahir Shah from the ultrafundamentalist Ekhawani Musalmin (Moslem Brotherhood) faction among the mujahidin . . . a mounting number of resistance members consider him their best hope.[12]

At first glance there is much plausibility to these statements. Zahir is certainly the best-known Afghan exile, as he was the nominal king of Afghanistan for forty years, and no other former ruler is still alive. Zahir got along well with Soviets; it was during his reign that Moscow began giving Afghanistan large amounts of military and economic aid. The Soviets know that he is not an able leader, and they may look upon him as someone they could easily control.

Despite these considerations, however, it is unlikely that Zahir will be moving back to Kabul. Many Afghans oppose him precisely because he did have good relations with Moscow; they despise him as the man who opened the gates to Soviet influence.[13] He was never very popular; when he was ousted in 1973, almost no one came to his defense. And since he is not a strong person, he would have a difficult time—anybody would—uniting the many contentious émigré factions. Zahir, moreover, is weak and lazy. Throughout much of his reign he let various relatives run the country for him, and he has continued his indolent ways in exile, making no effort to regain power.

More important, however, the Soviets are unlikely to restore the monarchy for ideological reasons. Moscow has at times left monarchs on their thrones as a temporary measure to camouflage communist domination. They did this with the bogdo gegen of Outer Mongolia in the 1920s and with King Michael of Romania in the 1940s.[14] But there has never been a case where the Soviets allowed a communist regime to be replaced by a monarchical one. This would be too much of an ideological retreat, almost like restoring the tsar in Russia. It is conceivable that Zahir or some other member of the royal family might be used as a figurehead president or in some other position, but not as king.

3. Let Afghanistan become neutral and nonaligned. Some writers, such as Jagat S. Mehta, former foreign secretary to the government of India, suggest that Afghanistan be restored to the status it enjoyed from the nineteenth century down to the communist coup of 1978—neutral, nonaligned, and independent. As Mehta put it, "Since 1880 the rulers of Afghanistan have maintained a sagacious policy of not becoming involved in the European political game or serving as the strategic instrument of any power. In its strategic location, Afghanistan recognized that to preserve its independence the country must remain neutral in great power conflicts but with special care not to provoke the security sensitivities of its powerful neighbor to the north."[15]

According to Mehta, the Soviets regret their invasion of Afghanistan and, in all likelihood, want to restore the pre-1978 status quo. "In retrospect," he said, "the USSR probably recognizes that a genuinely non-aligned Afghanistan pursuing non-radical policies was a better guardian of Soviet interests."[16]

With the Soviets coming around to this point of view, said Mehta, a "broad concensus exists among contending and interested powers."

> A surprising measure of common ground on the broad ingredients of an ultimate solution has emerged among the various interested parties. Many have implicitly recognized that stability cannot be restored unless Afghanistan is neutralized against great-power competition. . . .
> All these proposals in effect call for the restoration of Afghanistan to its prerevolutionary status—non-aligned although sensitive to Soviet interests, free to develop economic relations with all countries, and able to develop according to its own religious and social ethos.[17]

Most Afghans undoubtedly would be delighted to see their country restored to its pre-1978 status, but it would be difficult if not impossible to turn the clock back in this fashion, and it is highly doubtful that the USSR would permit it. Moscow has spent millions of rubles and sacrificed thousands of casualties to make sure that the Afghan government remains firmly pro-Soviet, and it is unlikely to settle for less. Allowing the formation of a neutral, nonaligned government, like the restoration of the monarchy, would be an impossible ideological retreat for Moscow. The Brezhnev Doctrine, we must remember, proclaims the principle that once a country becomes communist it must remain communist, especially if it borders on the USSR.[18]

Moscow has not permitted the neutralization of any of its client states in Eastern Europe, so what reason is there to believe that it would allow this in Afghanistan? Hungary tried to become neutral in 1956, but was prevented from doing so by Soviet tanks. Austria, true enough, was allowed to adopt a policy of neutrality in 1955 when Soviet troops were withdrawn, but Austria was in quite a different situation from that of Afghanistan. In the first place, Austria was not communist. Second, in return for Soviet withdrawal, the United States, Britain, and France also pulled their occupation forces out of Austria. For Russia to agree to the neutralization of Afghanistan it would have to get an equivalent reward as compensation for the loss of an obedient satellite on its frontier.

Creating a neutral, nonaligned Afghanistan would be difficult also because of the hatred that has grown during the last few years—hatred between communist and noncommunist Afghans and hatred of Afghans for Russians. Judging from the resistance movement, the great majority of Afghans are anything but neutral in their feelings about communists and Russians, and their passions presumably are growing stronger as the fighting continues. Since hundreds of thousands of people have been killed since 1978, either by the Afghan communists or by the Soviets, there are probably no neutrals left.

4. Follow a policy of "Finlandization." Selig Harrison in an article in *Foreign Policy,* "Dateline Afghanistan: Exit Through Finland?"[19] put forward the suggestion that the Afghan problem be solved by making Afghanistan another Finland. He proposed a regional security agreement containing these elements: (1) "A precise timetable" for the withdrawal of Soviet forces from Afghanistan "over a period of several years"; (2) "Acceptance by Moscow that its residual forces in Afghanistan would keep out of Afghan internal affairs"; (3) "In return for agreeing not to give help or sanctuary to Afghan resistance groups, Islamabad and Teheran could seek reciprocal Soviet and Afghan pledges barring their help to Baluch and Pushtun separatist movements"; (4) "Pakistani and Iranian inspection of Soviet bases" and "Soviet inspection of Pakistani and Iranian border areas"; (5) "A companion accord stabilizing the disputed Afghan-Pakistan boundary"; and (6) "Parallel understandings between the United States, the Soviet Union, and China designed to neutralize Pakistan and Iran as arenas of great-power conflict."[20]

After proposing this rather comprehensive series of agreements, Harrison then said: "The real question is not whether Finlandization would be desirable but whether it is possible."[21] Precisely. In my opinion it clearly is *not* possible.

Even a whole team of Talleyrands could not carry off all these diplomatic miracles.

What incentive would the Soviet Union have for agreeing to these proposals? It would get nothing in return but promises by Pakistan and Iran to cease aiding the rebels—promises that would have little value to Moscow if it withdrew its forces form Afghanistan and abandoned the struggle against the rebels. At times Harrison himself seemed to realize the impracticality of his plan, admitting that "such a proposal is likely to be dismissed out of hand by Moscow." But then, in a moment of resurgent optimism, he added: "In time, however, some such formula might win Soviet acceptance."[22]

Even if all of Harrison's proposed agreements could be negotiated, it is doubtful that Finlandization could work in the case of Afghanistan because the Finns and Afghans are so different. The Finns are united, disciplined, and have a strong central government, whereas the Afghans are a heterogeneous collection of independent, unruly tribes who have never fully recognized the jurisdiction of any government in Kabul. The Finns, moreover, have had postwar leaders who were realistic, moderate, and determined to get along with Moscow—men like former President J. K. Paasikivi. What Afghan statesman can one name today who could imitate Paasikivi's delicate balancing act of mollifying Moscow and keeping his people in line?

The Finns, moreover, have considerable experience in adapting to the domination of a powerful neighbor. They were ruled by the Swedes until the Russians conquered them in 1812, and Finland remained a part of Russia until 1917. At the end of World War II, when Finlandization as we know it began, the Finns were in a helpless state. They had been beaten twice by the Russians, first in the Winter War of 1939–1940, and then again, with their Nazi allies, in the great battles of the German-Soviet war. Seeing the Red Army impose communist regimes on the Baltic States, Poland, and elsewhere, the Finns were only too happy to give Moscow a veto over Finnish foreign policy in exchange for independence in domestic affairs.

The Afghans, by contrast, have never been conquered by the Russians or anyone else. They are not accustomed to foreign domination. They are fiercely independent and love to fight. Since they have not been defeated by the Soviets, they are in no mood to compromise, and their traditional hatred of the Russians has doubtless been intensified by the bloody conflicts of the past few years. All in all, it seems doubtful that the Afghans have the self-restraint, discipline, and submissiveness needed to carry out the kind of relationship that Finland has with the USSR. Finns are Finns, and Afghans are Afghans.

It is also doubtful that Moscow would be willing to give Afghanistan the kind of freedom that Finland enjoys. The Finnish case is exceptional, quite unlike Russia's usual policies towards its small neighbors. Much more typical was what happened, for example, to Poland at the end of World War II.

None of the other states along Russia's European borders were allowed the independence granted to Finland. All of them were subjected to communist seizures of power, carried out with the aid of Soviet intervention in one form or another. It seems likely that Afghanistan will continue to follow this pattern, not the Finnish example.

Jagat Mehta also favors the Finlandization of Afghanistan, but with an added twist—"Swedenization" of the whole area, particularly Pakistan, India, and Iran. The Soviets allowed Finland to be independent, he says, because Sweden remained neutral and refused to join NATO. Afghanistan cannot become another Finland, therefore, unless its neighbors follow the path of Sweden and disassociate themselves from any of the power blocs. "The Kremlin's attitude toward withdrawal from Afghanistan," he adds, "will depend on whether Pakistan becomes a heavily armed, pro-Western ally or a neutral state between the superpowers."[23]

It is easy to understand why an Indian diplomat is attracted to the idea of Pakistan weakening its ties to the United States and canceling its military buildup. From the Pakistani point of view, however, this buildup is necessitated by the proximity of Soviet power in Afghanistan, as well as by India's large-scale acquisitions of arms from the USSR. Pakistan is unlikely to curtail its arms program unless India does the same and unless Russia withdraws its armies from Afghanistan. The Finlandization of Afghanistan will probably have to precede any Swedenization of its neighbors, but neither is very likely.

5. *Withdraw its troops.* There has been much talk about the Soviet Union withdrawing its forces from Afghanistan, under one condition or another. President Carter solemnly warned that unless the troops were withdrawn by a certain date, the United States would boycott the Olympics. The UN General Assembly, the Islamic Foreign Ministers Conference, the Nonaligned Foreign Ministers Conference, the European Community, and various other groups have called for Soviet withdrawal. Soviet leaders have encouraged talk of withdrawal by saying over and over again that their forces in Afghanistan are only "limited military contingents" who are there "temporarily" and that they will be pulled out as soon as "outside interference" comes to an end.

For example, Brezhnev stated soon after the invasion, on February 23, 1980, that the Soviet Union would withdraw its armed forces from Afghanistan—under these conditions:

> The USSR will withdraw its military contingents from Afghanistan as soon as the factors that caused their presence there no longer exist. . . . I want to state quite definitely that we will be ready to begin withdrawing our troops as soon as all forms of outside interference directed against the government and people of Afghanistan completely end. Let the U.S., together with Afghanistan's neighbors, guarantee this, and then the need for Soviet military assistance will no longer exist.[24]

But there is little likelihood that Soviet military forces will leave Afghanistan this year, next year, or in ten years. Soviet troops occupied Poland in 1945, and they are still there today, as they are in East Germany, Czechoslovakia, Hungary, and Outer Mongolia.[25] In those cases where the Soviets did pull their soldiers out of nearby communist countries (such as China, North Korea, Yugoslavia, and Romania), these countries later adopted anti-Soviet policies of one degree or another. If Moscow in the past has stationed troops in neighboring countries to ensure their loyalty, provide military security for the USSR, and prevent their communist regimes from being overthrown, what reason is there to suppose that Afghanistan would be an exception? Indeed, there is so little support for communism in Afghanistan that the presence of Soviet military force is essential for the survival of any communist government.

Withdrawal would also involve a loss in Soviet prestige. Through its invasions of Hungary, Czechoslovakia, and Afghanistan the Soviet Union has acquired a reputation for being tough, determined, and ruthless. Withdrawing from Afghanistan would create an image of weakness; it might even encourage other client states to rebel from Moscow's control. One Soviet citizen expressed Soviet determination to remain in Afghanistan as follows: "It's a mess." But he added, "We're not going back. It's a test for the Red Army."[26]

Pulling Soviet troops out of Afghanistan might also lead to trouble in Soviet Central Asia. Uzbeks and other Central Asians who are unhappy under Russian rule might be encouraged to think that if the Russians could be forced to leave Afghanistan, perhaps they could be made to leave Central Asia also.

Withdrawal from Afghanistan would likewise mean sacrificing the political and strategic advantages that Moscow has gained from its occupation—its closer proximity to the Gulf and the Indian Ocean and its increased ability to exert pressure on Pakistan and Iran.[27]

Despite vague promises to withdraw at some unspecified date in the future if certain conditions are met, the Soviets give every indication that they plan to stay a long time. For example, the barracks and other installations they have built for their armed forces are permanent installations. Similarly, the Soviet Union has constructed the first bridge ever across the Amu Darya, is building a railroad from the Soviet frontier to Kabul, and has greatly enlarged the air bases at Shindand and Qandahar. In addition, it must be remembered that, unlike the United States in the case of Vietnam, there is no chance that public opinion in the Soviet Union will force the government to pull out.

Of course there may be, some day, a *partial* withdrawal of Soviet military units. If the Soviets are able to increase the size and reliability of the Afghan army, there could be a commensurate reduction in Soviet forces. And if the day ever comes when the communists in Afghanistan gain firm control of the country, the Soviets may feel that they can withdraw their forces completely.

In the summer of 1981 the U.S. government, in an effort to defuse the Afghanistan issue, made several approaches to the Soviet Union, indicating that it understood Soviet interests in Afghanistan, was willing to compromise, and would accept a solution that provided the Soviets with a face-saving way of withdrawing from Afghanistan. These approaches were rebuffed by Moscow. The Soviets said that there was no point in holding discussions until the United States recognized the Babrak regime and guaranteed that the insurgents would not be able to pass back and forth across Afghanistan's frontiers. They also indicated that they must be certain that Babrak would not fall after the Soviet forces were withdrawn.[28] Along with these diplomatic efforts, the United States tried to convince the Soviets that they were in a no-win situation with the Afghan rebels and would do well to extricate themselves. But the Soviets were not interested.

Later Moscow did permit the Babrak regime to participate in the peace negotiations conducted by the UN, but it dictated terms that made an agreement impossible. While making vague promises to withdraw its troops, the USSR demanded that there be no fixed timetable, so that the pullout could be adjusted to the level of the resistance movement. The Soviets also insisted that Kabul must have a "friendly" regime, which they defined as a regime that would continue to use Soviet military advisers and would invite Soviet troops back in case of a military threat in Afghanistan or Iran![29] It was not surprising, therefore, that the UN talks in June 1983 ended "with no sign of major progress on any of the significant issues."[30]

6. Send more troops. There seems little doubt that the mighty Soviet Union could defeat the Afghan rebels and pacify most of the country if it decided to commit enough men to do the job. But it would take a lot more than the 100,000 or so troops that had been sent there by the spring of 1983. Some have estimated that as many as 400,000 men would be required to eliminate resistance completely, while others think 400,000 would not be enough.

If the Soviets sent three, four, or five times as many troops to Afghanistan, they could control more of the country than they do now. They could maintain garrisons in the district capitals as well as the provincial ones, make more sweeps through the countryside, prevent the rebels from blocking the highways, and perhaps seal the borders with Pakistan and Iran. If they were unable to suppress the resistance movement entirely, they could surely reduce it. They could bring to an end the embarrassing spectacle of simple Afghan peasants, with few arms and little help, defying one of the world's superpowers.

Why have the Soviets been unwilling to send more troops? There are probably several reasons. First, a dramatic increase in Soviet forces would get Afghanistan into the headlines again, while at present it gets little attention from the news media. The invasion did great damage to the Soviet image around the world, and the Politburo may feel that it has enough public relations problems elsewhere, as in Poland.

Second, the Soviet leaders perhaps think they cannot spare many more forces in Afghanistan. Those of us on the outside, looking at the huge Soviet army, are inclined to think that they could easily send a few hundred thousand more to Afghanistan, but the Soviet army has enormous tasks, such as guarding the vast stretches of frontier with Europe and China. Theater commanders in these areas would probably object to any suggestions that they send some of their troops to Afghanistan. This would be particularly true, one would think, along the Polish frontier, at least as long as the situation there remains volatile.[31] If all the troops on duty are needed at their present posts, this means that no more could be sent to Afghanistan without calling up reservists, and that would disrupt the Soviet economy, already plagued by labor shortages.

A third reason for not sending more Soviet troops to Afghanistan is that it would increase costs. The occupation has already cost a great deal, probably much more than the Soviets anticipated. They have to ship in supplies for their own soldiers and much of the food and fuel for Afghan cities.[32] The Politburo may well feel that it is already overextended economically. Aside from economic problems at home, there is the economic disruption throughout Eastern Europe caused by the Polish crisis, not to mention Soviet commitments to Cuba, Ethiopia, South Yemen, and other countries around the world. All in all, the Soviet leaders may have decided that they cannot afford to invest any more manpower and resources in Afghanistan.

Fourth, the Soviets may be trying to avoid duplicating the American experience in Vietnam, where half a million foreign soldiers were not enough to win a guerrilla war against determined natives. Perhaps the Soviets decided from the beginning that they were going to limit their investment in Afghanistan and be satisfied for the time being with controlling the principal towns and highways.

Finally, the Politburo knows that sending significantly more troops to Afghanistan would increase casualties. While they do not have to pay as much attention to public opinion as a democratic government does, they cannot ignore it entirely. Soviet tactics in Afghanistan so far have been designed to minimize the loss of Soviet lives, losses that obviously would rise if they sent in more troops and engaged in more active military operations.[33]

With all of these considerations in mind, the Soviets so far have not made any large increases in their occupation forces since the initial invasion. Of course they could do so at any time. They did send about 15,000 more at the end of 1981, and they may send additional troops in the future. They may decide that in order to take advantage of their strategic position vis-à-vis the Gulf, Pakistan, and Iran, they will have to bring Afghanistan under much firmer control. But so far there are no signs that they are planning to double or triple their forces in Afghanistan.

7. *Annex all or part of Afghanistan.* Some people have suggested that Moscow may annex all of Afghanistan, making it the sixteenth republic of the USSR.[34] Such suggestions are probably erroneous since they are contrary to past Soviet performance. So far the Soviet government has never annexed all of an independent country unless (like Estonia, Latvia, and Lithuania) that country had previously been a part of the tsarist empire. The Red Army invaded Outer Mongolia in 1921 and put it under firm Soviet control, so that Mongolia today has little more independence than, say, the Uzbek Soviet Republic. But Moscow has never formally annexed Mongolia because nothing would be gained and world opinion would be offended. It looks much better for Moscow to pretend that Outer Mongolia is a free and independent state—annexing it would be evidence of Soviet expansion. In addition, having an independent Mongolia gives the Soviet Union one more vote in the United Nations and other international organizations. These considerations also explain in part why Stalin did not annex Eastern Europe or North Korea at the end of World War II.

Thus is is unlikely that Moscow will annex all of Afghanistan. It isn't necessary. Afghanistan is a relatively small, backward country with no powerful neighbor other than the USSR, so there is no danger of it breaking away from the Russian bear's grasp. Annexation would not strengthen Moscow's control, but would simply tarnish its image.

It has also been suggested that the USSR might annex *part* of Afghanistan. From an ethnic point of view this makes some sense because in northern Afghanistan there are large numbers of Tadzhiks (about 3.5 million), Uzbeks (about 1 million), and Turkmen (about 125,000) who could logically be annexed to the Tadzhik, Uzbek, and Turkmen Soviet republics.[35] For this type of annexation—based on an ethnic claim—there are several precedents in Soviet history. To name just three cases, the eastern half of Poland was annexed with the justification that it was populated mainly by Belorussians and Ukrainians, while northern Bukovina was taken from Romania and Carpatho-Ukraine from Czechoslovakia on the grounds that they were predominantly Ukrainian.

Soviet annexation of the northern part of Afghanistan would be somewhat logical also from the point of view of geography. The towering ranges of the Hindu Kush divide Afghanistan roughly into two halves—north and south. These mountains, some of which are over 18,000 feet high, offer much more of a natural barrier to travel than the Amu Darya, the river that marks a large part of the present boundary between Afghanistan and the Soviet Union.

Soviet Muslims would probably be delighted to see all or part of Afghanistan added to their Central Asian republics. According to Alexandre Bennigsen, a leading authority on Islam in the USSR, "It is likely that the present-day elites [in Soviet Central Asia] favor Soviet annexation of, if not the whole of Afghanistan, then at least Afghan Turkestan north of the Hindu Kush. Such an annexation would considerably strengthen the Soviet Muslims' demographic and political position vis-à-vis the Russians."[36]

It is precisely because it would strengthen the Soviet Muslims' "demographic and political position vis-à-vis the Russians" that the Kremlin probably will *not* annex northern Afghanistan. The Politburo, which is dominated by Russians, is already faced with serious problems caused by the high birthrate among the 43 million Muslims of the USSR, as compared with the low birthrate among Russians.[37] This threat of growing Islamic population and power would be aggravated by the addition of more Muslims, especially those who are fanatical in their religion and in their hatred of Russians. Many of the Muslims in northern Afghanistan are former Basmachi or children of Basmachi—the anticommunists who fought against the Soviet regime in the 1920s and 1930s before fleeing to Afghanistan. Since Soviet leaders presumably are already worried that the virus of Islamic nationalism will spread from Iran and Afghanistan to Soviet Central Asia, it is unlikely that they will increase the danger of infection by annexing northern Afghanistan. A minor exception should be noted, however. As mentioned in Chapter 16, the Soviets have already de facto annexed the small, remote, but strategically important Wakhan Corridor.[38]

8. Continue present policies. The Soviets have occupied Afghanistan ever since December 1979. Thus the Politburo has had plenty of time to consider changing its policies, but has not done so. This must mean that they think the present course of action is basically correct or at least preferable to any alternative. Apparently they assume that over a period of time they can strengthen their position and gradually wear down the opposition—as they did in Outer Mongolia, Eastern Europe, Central Asia, and, indeed, in the whole Russian Empire after the Bolshevik seizure of power in Petrograd.

The Soviets seem to be willing, at least for the time being, to accept the present stalemate. They can't suppress the rebels, but the rebels can't drive the Soviets out of Afghanistan. The war is costing the USSR men and resources, but the costs are bearable. As far as world opinion is concerned, they probably think that the worst is over, that if many countries don't like what Moscow is doing in Afghanistan, they have resigned themselves to it and are not going to do much about it. Other matters have drawn the world's attention away from Afghanistan. Thus the Politburo sees its intervention in Afghanistan continuing at a relatively low level, and foreign opposition continuing at the same level.[39]

This is not the first time the Soviets have been faced with the task of establishing communist rule in a country where the majority of the people are anticommunist; in fact, nowhere has it been otherwise. Nor is it the first time the Russians have fought against Muslims; they have been fighting Muslims for centuries. Under the tsars they subdued the Muslims of Kazan, Astrakhan, and the Crimea, drove the Turks out of the Ukraine, and conquered the Muslims of the Caucasus and Central Asia. After 1917 the Bolsheviks conquered the Muslims of the Caucasus and Central Asia again, not finishing the fight against the Basmachi until the 1930s. The Soviets can be expected to show their usual patience and persistence in Afghanistan, anticipating a slow, gradual triumph.

While the Soviets apparently intend to pursue more or less the same policies as they have so far in Afghanistan, they undoubtedly want to suppress the rebels more effectively. They might do this in part by greater use of chemical warfare and other ruthless measures such as destroying villages and cities, burning crops, and driving Afghans out of the country. That is, they could adopt a systematic policy of what has been called rubblization and migratory genocide, especially in areas near the Pakistan border. Two Soviet actions in early 1982 seemed to indicate that they had indeed decided on such a policy. At that time the Soviets subjected Qandahar, Afghanistan's second-largest city, to an artillery and aerial bombardment in which hundreds of civilians were killed. According to Walter Stoessel, former deputy secretary of state, "after the bombardment, Soviet forces entered the city and engaged in wanton looting and killing among the civilian population. Many of the city's buildings were severely damaged; two-thirds of its population fled."[40] A similar attack was launched against Herat, another major city.[41] As a result of harsh measures like these, the number of Afghan refugees increased dramatically in late 1981 and early 1982, rising from 2 million to about 3 million.[42]

In addition to bombarding cities, the Soviets also have tried to suppress the resistance by using chemical warfare. It is possible that the Soviets will decide that the best way to win the war quickly and cheaply is through greater use of various chemicals. It is to be hoped, however, that the publicity given to these violations of the Geneva Convention will restrain Moscow, lest world public opinion be aroused by such inhuman tactics.

Another military measure the Soviets might attempt would be to close the frontier with Pakistan and Iran. The Soviets have already tried to do this by scattering small antipersonnel mines along the frontier trails.[43] So far these mines have not proved to be a major hindrance to the rebels, but might if used on a larger scale.[44] It is also conceivable that Moscow will decide to do in Afghanistan what it has done along its European borders—build barbed-wire fences with watch towers and mine fields. This would be difficult and expensive in Afghanistan's rocky, mountainous terrain, but the Soviets have seldom counted the cost where matters of security are concerned.

In the long run the most effective means for establishing Soviet control in Afghanistan is education and indoctrination. The crippling weakness of the

USSR in Afghanistan is that so few Afghans favor communism. Most Afghan adults probably cannot be converted to communism, but it may be possible to win over a significant portion of the youth. To accomplish this goal, several thousand Afghan young people are presently being educated in the USSR, and there are plans to send many more.[45] Some observers maintain that this will not work, that the Afghan students will come home hating the Russians more than ever.[46] Against this one can argue that the communist coup of 1978 was carried out largely by officers who had been trained in the USSR and were eager to make Afghanistan communist. If they learned to hate the Russians, they were nonetheless impressed by the factories, hospitals, and other manifestations of modernization in Soviet Central Asia and were convinced that communism was the solution for Afghanistan.[47]

The Soviets are trying to obtain reliable cadres for communizing Afghanistan not only by training youth in the USSR but also by transforming the Afghan educational system, hoping thereby to create a "New Afghan Man." One factor that aids the Soviets is the low life expectancy in Afghanistan—only forty years.[48] This means that young people constitute an unusually large percentage of the population, and the older generation will be dying off rather rapidly.

Although it is more difficult to make communists out of Afghan adults, the Kabul regime is making an effort here also. The population is subjected to a barrage of communist propaganda on the radio, television, and in the newspapers. Unfortunately for the government, about 90 percent of the people cannot read, which makes them safe from the poisonous influences of the printed word, so it would not be surprising if the regime institutes a crash program to eliminate illiteracy. It probably also will expand the national television network so as to make thought control easier. Television programs from the Soviet Union are being received in Kabul on a regular basis.[49]

The training of new cadres is the key to the future of communism in Afghanistan; if this succeeds, everything else has a chance to succeed. Young people trained and indoctrinated in the USSR or at home can provide officers and soldiers for the army, bureaucrats for the ministries, administrators for the provinces, spies for infiltration of the rebels, and so on. This is not to say that it will be easy for the Soviets to subdue the people of Afghanistan. They are tough, independent, stubborn, loyal to their kin, and accustomed to fighting. But it is hard to see how they can long continue to withstand the overwhelming military, economic, and political power of their mighty neighbor. The people of Eastern Europe, like the people of Afghanistan, are anticommunist and anti-Soviet, but this has not prevented the communist regimes of those countries, with Soviet support, from maintaining themselves in power ever since World War II. The Afghans will probably suffer the same fate.

PROSPECTS UNDER ANDROPOV

Casting an aura of uncertainty over all of these comments is the death of Leonid Brezhnev. No one can predict what Yurii Andropov's policies toward Afghanistan will be or how long he will retain his present position. There has always been a great deal of continuity in Soviet foreign objectives and strategies, but past changes in leadership have also brought significant changes in foreign policies. Although it seems unlikely that Brezhnev's demise will produce any radical alteration in Afghanistan's situation, this possibility cannot be ruled out.

There have been reports (perhaps spread by Soviet disinformation agents) that Andropov opposed the invasion and is eager to reach a settlement that would lead to a Soviet withdrawal. Vladimir Kuzichkin, a former KGB major who defected, claims that the KGB, then headed by Andropov, warned Brezhnev not to invade Afghanistan.[50] President Zia of Pakistan had a talk with Andropov after Brezhnev's funeral and said later that he believes Andropov is sincere in pursuing negotiations about Afghanistan.[51] Zia also reported that he detected a "hint of flexibility" in Andropov's attitude toward a peaceful settlement.[52] Zia went on to say, however, that the Soviets made it clear that "they are not going to pull out in the near future."[53] He added, "We have no proof, no indications, no promises. I do not see a quick or a very early solution to the problem."[54] The Soviets would never permit an anti-Soviet government in Kabul, he said, while Pakistan would never recognize or negotiate with the Babrak regime.[55]

Some observers had expected Andropov to come forward with a new and promising proposal, but their hopes were diminished by an editorial in *Pravda* on December 16, 1982, that reaffirmed the Brezhnev line and showed no signs of Andropov's hoped-for "flexibility." The revolution in Afghanistan, said *Pravda* (quoting Brezhnev) "is irreversible." "The path to a political settlement," it said (again imitating Brezhnev), lies through direct negotiations between the Babrak government "and the governments of its neighbors"— a procedure that Pakistan and Iran have rejected. The editorial also noted that the Afghan regime so far had not availed itself of its "legitimate right" to pursue the rebels "when they are returning to their foreign operational bases"—a threat that the Soviets might increase their armed attacks across Pakistan's border. Finally, *Pravda* repeated the line that Brezhnev had stated many times: "The Soviet Union . . . has expressed its readiness to withdraw its troops, under an accord with the DRA government, just as soon as foreign interference in Afghan affairs ends and guarantees have been given that such interference will not be resumed. . . . Nothing in the principled Soviet position has changed."[56]

There has been speculation that Andropov might pull out of Afghanistan in order to bring about a reconciliation with China. In 1979, as a protest over the Soviet invasion of Afghanistan, the Chinese broke off discussions with Moscow designed to improve Sino-Soviet relations. In the fall of 1982, however, the talks were resumed as a result of a deterioration of Chinese relations with the United States. The Chinese apparently decided to put their relations with Moscow on a footing more equal with Sino-American relations. The Chinese continued to insist, however, that any significant improvement in the atmosphere between Moscow and Peking could come only after the Soviets had made certain concessions, including the removal of their troops from Afghanistan.[57] If getting out of Afghanistan would bring a restoration of truly friendly Sino-Soviet relations, Andropov might be willing to pay the price; a friendly China is obviously more important to the USSR than a friendly Afghanistan. There are many sources of conflict between China and the Soviet Union, however, and it seems unlikely that all of these problems can be resolved. China, moreover, has indicated that it wants only "normal" relations with Moscow, not a return to its former status as a junior partner in a communist bloc dominated by Russia.[58]

Russia's leadership may have changed, but Russia's reasons for going into Afghanistan have not changed. That being the case, it seems likely that Andropov's policies in Afghanistan will be basically similar to Brezhnev's policies.

NOTES

1. *New York Times,* June 26, 1982, p. A3, and July 12, 1982, p. A15. According to the *New York Times,* December 7, 1982, p. A7, Pakistan and Afghanistan agreed in Geneva that a settlement must include these four elements: "A timetable for the departure of the Soviet troops; guarantees by each side that neither would promote armed intervention against the other; the United States, Soviet Union and China should insure the guarantee; Afghanistan would take back the 2.8 million refugees in Pakistan and about one million in Iran, offering amnesty to all, complete civil rights, their inclusion in the nation's land redistribution, access to jobs, and the right to move about freely."
2. *New York Times,* July 24, 1982, p. 3.
3. Peter Arnet, "Report from a War Zone," *Parade Magazine,* February 20, 1983, p. 19. The State Department officer quoted was Ernestine Heck.
4. "Rough Plan Emerging for Afghan Peace," *New York Times,* July 12, 1982, p. A15.
5. Lewis M. Simons, "Standoff in Afghanistan," *The New Republic,* vol. 187, no. 7 (August 16 and 23, 1982), pp. 23–24. Simons covered South Asia for the *Washington Post.*
6. *New York Times,* June 17, 1982, p. A5.
7. Transcript of Public Broadcasting System, "MacNeil-Lehrer Report," "Afghanistan: War Continues," October 16, 1981, p. 7.
8. *New York Times,* December 21, 1982, p. 3.

9. Public Broadcasting System, "MacNeil-Lehrer Report," pp. 7–8. The quote was reported by Professor Robert Legvold of Columbia University.

10. *New York Times,* July 20, 1980, p. 12.

11. *New York Times,* July 12, 1982, p. A15.

12. Simons, "Standoff in Afghanistan," pp. 23–25.

13. Professor Louis Dupree says that neither Zahir nor his son-in-law, Abdul Wali, is popular with the Afghan people. Conversation with Dupree, December 16, 1980.

14. Thomas T. Hammond, "The Communist Takeover of Outer Mongolia: Model for Eastern Europe?" in *The Anatomy of Communist Takeovers,* ed. by Thomas T. Hammond (New Haven, Conn.: Yale University Press, 1975), pp. 122–124 and 133.

15. Jagat S. Mehta, "A Neutral Solution," *Foreign Policy,* no. 47 (Summer 1982), p. 141.

16. Ibid., p. 144.

17. Ibid., p. 145.

18. *Literaturnaia gazeta* (Literary Gazette), an important Soviet newspaper, published an article on March 12, 1980 (p. 9), that described neutralization as an American plot to overthrow the communist regime:

> The "neutralization" label conceals a course aimed at the elimination not only of the government now in power in Afghanistan but also of the very system set up by the April revolution. . . . The authors of the "neutralization" idea . . . are trying to decide the fate of the Afghan people for them. But have the Afghan people accomplished a revolution in order to exchange independence for the status of a trust territory, in the guise of "neutrality"?

Pravda, however, on December 16, 1982 (p. 4), declared that "the Soviet Union is interested in having Afghanistan remain a neutral and nonaligned state." *Pravda* is, of course, the most authoritative publication in the USSR.

19. *Foreign Policy,* no. 41 (Winter 1980–1981), pp. 163–187. See also Harrison's article in the *New York Times,* December 22, 1980, p. A23. For a critique of Harrison's proposal see Leon B. Poullada's letter in the *New York Times,* January 12, 1981, p. A18.

20. Harrison, "Dateline Afghanistan: Exit Through Finland?," pp. 183–185.

21. Ibid., p. 186.

22. Ibid., p. 183.

23. Mehta, "A Neutral Solution," pp. 146–147. See also the critical letter by Joseph J. Collins and Mehta's reply in *Foreign Policy,* no. 49 (Winter 1982–1983), pp. 186–190.

24. *Pravda,* February 23, 1980, p. 1.

25. Soviet troops entered Poland, East Germany, and Hungary during World War II and never left. They withdrew from Czechoslovakia in 1945 in return for the evacuation of American troops from the western part of the country. Soviet forces left Outer Mongolia in 1957 but returned in 1967.

26. Public Broadcasting System, "MacNeil-Lehrer Report," p. 7.

27. On this point see Francis Fukuyama, *The Security of Pakistan: A Trip Report* (Santa Monica, Calif.: Rand Corporation, September 1980), passim.

28. Leslie H. Gelb, citing unnamed State Department officials, in the *New York Times,* August 7, 1981, pp. 1A, 4A. Gelb formerly held a high position in the State Department and presumably has good connections there.

29. *New York Times,* June 25, 1983, p. 3; Selig S. Harrison, "Nearing a Pullout from Afghanistan," *New York Times,* June 7, 1983, p. A23. See also the letter by Paul H. Kreisberg criticizing Harrison's article, *New York Times,* June 12, 1983, p. 18E.

30. *New York Times,* June 25, 1983, p. 3. A good summary of the obstacles to an agreement is given by William Claiborne in the *Washington Post,* May 21, 1983, pp. A17–A18.

31. Professor Robert Legvold, after talking with Soviet policymakers and foreign-policy analysts in Moscow in October 1981, reported: "They [the Soviets] feel there is an interconnection between Afghanistan and Poland. People . . . said to me that one of the constraints on their action in Poland is Afghanistan, and one of the constraints on the degree to which they escalate in Afghanistan is Poland." Public Broadcasting System, "MacNeil-Lehrer Report," p. 8.

32. Interview with State Department official.

33. This discussion of why the Soviets have not significantly increased the number of troops in Afghanistan is based in large part on a conversation with Gary Crocker of the State Department.

34. Alexandre Bennigsen, "Soviet Muslims and the World of Islam," *Problems of Communism,* vol. 29, no. 2 (March-April 1980), p. 49; Zalmay Kalilzad, "Soviet-Occupied Afghanistan," *Problems of Communism,* vol. 29, no. 6 (November-December 1980), p. 40.

35. The population figures are taken from Louis Dupree, *Afghanistan* (Princeton, N.J.: Princeton University Press, 1980), pp. 59–61. See also Dupree's ethnic map on p. 58.

36. Bennigsen, "Soviet Muslims," p. 42.

37. On the problems the Politburo faces as a result of the high birthrate of Soviet Muslims, see: Michael Rywkin, "Central Asia and Soviet Manpower," *Problems of Communism,* vol. 28, no. 1 (January-February 1979); Murray Feshbach and Stephen Rapawy, "Soviet Population and Manpower Trends and Policies," in U.S. Congress, Joint Economic Committee, *The Soviet Economy in a New Perspective* (Washington, D.C.: Government Printing Office, 1976); S. Enders Wimbush and Alex Alexiev, *Soviet Central Asian Soldiers in Afghanistan* (Santa Monica, Calif.: Rand Corporation, January 1981).

38. Yaacov Vertzberger, "Afghanistan in China's Policy," *Problems of Communism,* vol. 31, no. 3 (May-June 1982), pp. 10–11.

39. See the comments by Robert Legvold and Robert Neumann in Public Broadcasting System, "MacNeil-Lehrer Report," pp. 5–7.

40. *New York Times,* March 9, 1982, p. A9.

41. *Washington Post,* March 9, 1982, p. A8.

42. *New York Times,* March 9, 1982, p. A9.

43. Gérard Chaliand, "Bargain War," *New York Review of Books,* vol. 28, no. 5 (April 2, 1981), p. 31.

44. According to Gary Crocker of the State Department, the mines caused many injuries at first, but then the rebels learned how to handle them.

45. Eliza Van Hollen, *Afghanistan: A Year of Occupation* (Washington, D.C.: Department of State, February 1981), Special Report No. 79, p. 4.

46. Alexandre Bennigsen in a speech at the Kennan Institute, Washington, D.C., March 16, 1981.

47. Unfortunately, no one seems to have published a study of the composition of the People's Democratic party, with statistics on how many of its members were trained in the USSR. Anthony Arnold reportedly is working on a book about the PDPA.

48. U.S. Department of State, *Background Notes: Afghanistan* (Washington, D.C.: Government Printing Office, April 1980), p. 1.

49. *Pravda,* August 3, 1982, p. 6.

50. *Time,* November 22, 1982, p. 33.

51. *Washington Post,* December 9, 1982, p. A16.

52. *New York Times,* December 10, 1982, pp. 1, 8.

53. *New York Times,* December 9, 1982, p. A12.

54. *Washington Post,* December 9, 1982, p. A16.

55. Ibid.

56. *Pravda,* December 16, 1982, p. 4.

57. *Washington Post,* October 19, 1982, p. A15.

58. Flora Lewis in the *New York Times,* October 15, 1982, p. A27. See also the *Washington Post,* March 2, 1983, p. A18.

CHAPTER 18

Possible Soviet Moves in the Gulf Area

 The road to Paris and London lies through the towns of Afghanistan, the Punjab, and Bengal.

—Leon Trotsky, 1919[1]

The area south of Batum and Baku in the general direction of the Persian Gulf is . . . the center of the aspirations of the Soviet Union.

—V. M. Molotov, 1940[2]

THE THREAT OF SOVIET OIL BLACKMAIL

Former Secretary of State Edmund Muskie once described a conversation he had with Soviet Foreign Minister Andrei Gromyko: "Gromyko asked me, 'Why are you so upset about Afghanistan?' I said, 'It's the geography of Afghanistan that disturbs us. Whatever your present intentions are, if you move into Afghanistan and stay there you will become a more serious potential threat to our vital interests in the area than you were before you moved in.'" And Muskie added later: "The consequences of a cutoff of the Persian Gulf oil, for us in the West, are too catastrophic to ignore."[3]

Muskie made a crucial point: It is not Afghanistan itself that worries the United States, because Afghanistan is one of the poorest countries in the world and borders on no vital waterways. What is worrisome is what lies this side of Afghanistan, especially the oil of the Gulf (see Figure 4). Afghanistan is important because it is next to Iran, where anti-American fanatics hold sway, and because it is close to the Gulf, where highly vulnerable regimes are in power. As another former secretary of state, Henry Kissinger, put it: "We are on a roller coaster to disaster. Our future is now at the mercy of a precarious political status quo in what is probably the most

201

FIGURE 4. Afghanistan's Strategic Position. This map originally appeared in Yaacov Vertzberger, "Afghanistan in China's Policy," *Problems of Communism,* vol. 31 (May–June 1982), p. 7. Adapted for *Problems of Communism* by the Cartographic Services Laboratory of the University of Maryland from the U.S. Department of State map "Azimuthal equidistant projection centered on Kabul, Afghanistan." Reprinted by permission of *Problems of Communism.*

volatile, unstable and crisis-prone region in the world."[4] The situation in the Gulf today is frightening for the United States and its allies because more than half of the oil involved in international trade comes from the Gulf, including a significant portion of U.S. imports and much higher percentages for several of our key allies, including West Germany, France, Italy, and Japan.[5] This vital area is far from the United States but only a few hundred miles from the Soviet Union; so defending our interests there poses formidable logistical problems. Figuring out how to get significant quantities of troops, weapons, and supplies to the Gulf before the Soviets do is a nightmare for American military planners.

The crucial question about the Soviet invasion of Afghanistan, therefore, is the one Muskie referred to: Will the Soviets use Afghanistan as a stepping-stone to the Gulf? As indicated above, I do not think this objective was the main motivation for the Soviet invasion; there were other reasons having to do with Afghanistan itself that were more compelling. But the Soviet leaders can look at a map as easily as we can, and they are hardly ignorant of the fact that the occupation of Afghanistan put them much closer to the Strait of Hormuz. Whether they went into Afghanistan for defensive or offensive reasons, the fact remains that they are there, and the temptation to take advantage of this is great.

The big temptation for the Soviets is to get into a position whereby they could interdict the shipment of oil out of the Gulf—by securing a base along the Strait of Hormuz, gaining a commanding position along the sea lanes leading out of the strait, or establishing their domination over one of the major Gulf states. If the Soviets were to acquire the ability to control the oil flow, they could blackmail Western Europe, Japan, and many other states. Then the whole postwar struggle between the United States and the Soviet Union might well be over, and Moscow would be a big step along the road to world domination.

How would this blackmail work? The Soviets probably would *not* attempt to cut off the flow of oil, for this would mean war. They wouldn't have to cut it off, however, as long as other states knew that they *could* cut it off. Instead the Soviets would go to the West European states and Japan and say something like this:

> We know that Gulf oil is very important to you, and we are happy to be able to tell you that you never need to worry about it again because we have established stability in that area. Through our strengthened position in the Gulf, we can guarantee that from now on you will get all the oil you need. We are your friends, and we will protect your interests. That being the case, there is no need for you to ally with the imperialistic Americans or to spend so much money on arms, and there is obviously no longer any need for NATO.

Thus a dominating Soviet position in the Gulf could lead to the Finlandization of Western Europe, Japan, and the many other states who are dependent on this oil and who therefore would be afraid to antagonize Moscow.

Even if the USSR does not actually obtain bases near the Strait of Hormuz or place a pro-Soviet regime in power in one of the Gulf states, an uncontested increase of Soviet military and political power in the area could bring about the gradual Finlandization of our allies and of the Gulf states themselves. If Soviet power and influence in the area increases more than that of the United States in the next few years, all these states may decide that they cannot depend upon the United States to defend their interests and may choose to make their peace with Moscow.

Of course it is not a foregone conclusion that Western Europe and Japan would succumb to such Soviet oil blackmail, or that the United States would be powerless to respond. A Soviet move of this kind might have the opposite effect of strengthening NATO and binding the industrial powers even closer to the United States. It might be that an American threat to use nuclear weapons (tactical or strategic) would be sufficient to deter the Soviets. It is also possible that sending additional American and allied warships to the Gulf would protect the flow of oil and prevent the Soviets from making their blackmail effective. But in view of the fainthearted reaction by most West European states to the invasion of Afghanistan and the imposition of martial law in Poland, we have little reason for confidence that our allies will stand firm against Soviet intimidation.

It seems likely that the Soviets will move cautiously in the Gulf area, lest they trigger a war with the United States. But one should not rule out the possibility that they will make a major, overt move, such as an invasion of Iran. Although the Soviet leaders in recent years generally have followed low-risk foreign policies, it is conceivable that they will decide that the time has come to strike in the Gulf area, that the prize is too great to be missed, and that the chances of success are better now than later. The Politburo might conclude that, given the present status of the Soviet-American military balance, the United States would not be able to make an effective response and that it makes no sense to wait until Washington has strengthened American strategic weaponry, built up the Rapid Deployment Force, and established bases in proximity to the Gulf. And if the Soviets should decide to stage a massive invasion of Iran in the near future, i.e., within the next five or six years, it is hard to see how the United States could stop them, except through the use of tactical nuclear weapons, with all the dangers of escalation that this would involve.[6] Still, the Soviets probably would not want to take this risk, and it seems more likely that they will move slowly, cautiously, and covertly, camouflaging their actions, and using natives or proxies rather than Soviet citizens.

POSSIBLE SOVIET SCENARIOS

It might be useful to outline a number of possible scenarios whereby the USSR could acquire the ability to threaten the flow of oil out of the Gulf. Some of these scenarios may be quite unlikely, but none of them, I think, is inconceivable, and they are worth thinking about and trying to guard against. The Soviets probably could not carry them out this year or next year, and they may never be able to do so, but the Western powers need to plan for the worst possible contingencies, including these.

Iranian Scenario No. 1. Iran offers the greatest possibilities for the expansion of Soviet influence in the Gulf, for several reasons: (1) It is the only Gulf state that borders on the USSR. Since 1979 that border has, in effect, been greatly lengthened: Soviet troops today are stationed along the Iranian frontier not only in the north but also in the east, in Afghanistan. (2) Iran occupies the whole northern shore of the Strait of Hormuz, the most strategic point in the Gulf. (3) Iran is one of the few states in the Middle East that has a sizable communist party, the Tudeh party. (4) Since the fall of the shah, the country has been in chaos and may become even more chaotic when Khomeini dies. (5) Azerbaizhan and Kurdistan, two large and populous areas in northern Iran, have long been the object of Soviet intrigues.

Meddling in Iran is an old Russian custom; tsarist Russia invaded Iran on occasion, and Soviet Russia has continued the tradition. In 1920 Bolshevik soldiers invaded the Caspian province of Gilan, and they refused to leave until Iran signed a treaty (February 27, 1921) that Russia claims gives it the right to intervene militarily if it ever feels threatened.[7] (Iran has repudiated articles 5 and 6 of this treaty, but the Soviets have not; perhaps they may want to use them in the future.) During World War II the Soviet Union occupied all of northern Iran, in agreement with the United States and Britain. But in 1945–1946 Soviet troops refused to evacuate Azerbaizhan and Kurdistan and proceeded to set up two puppet states with the help of communist Azeris and Kurds from the USSR. Only strong pressure from the United States and the UN forced the Soviets to withdraw.[8]

That Stalin's successors continued to cast covetous eyes on Iran is indicated by a revealing passage in Khrushchev's memoirs:

> The Afghans asked us to help them build several hundred kilometers of road near the Iranian border. It cost us a hefty sum since we had to tunnel through the mountains. However, because Afghanistan didn't have railroads, such a highway would be a main artery, carrying the economic lifeblood of the country. The road also had great strategic significance because *it would have allowed us to transport troops and supplies in the event of war with either Pakistan or Iran* [emphasis added].[9]

Today the Soviets probably would be reluctant to invade Iran, lest this lead to war with the West. But they will certainly do all they can to help the Tudeh party seize power. Although Tudeh is at present rather small, it is the only well-organized, tightly disciplined party in the country—an advantage that is especially valuable during a period of political and economic turmoil.[10]

During the first few years after the Khomeini revolution the influence of the USSR and the Tudeh party in Iran grew significantly. When the U.S. Navy blockaded Iranian ports on the Gulf, Moscow gave Iran permission to transport goods across Soviet territory, and this transit trade grew from 1 million tons in 1978 to 3.4 million tons in 1981. Direct trade between the two countries also rose—from 671 million rubles in 1978 to 800 million rubles in 1981.[11] As a result of its isolation from the West, Teheran was forced to turn increasingly to Moscow for goods, arms, advisers, and technology. In February 1982 Iran concluded an agreement with the Soviet Union for increased economic and technical cooperation, and the Iranian minister who signed the agreement even referred to the USSR as a "friendly country."[12] The Soviets also helped with numerous Iranian construction projects, including electrical power stations and a metallurgical combine.[13]

Meanwhile members of the Tudeh party increased its influence by showing respect for Islam and pretending to be loyal followers of Khomeini. As a result of this tactic, the party grew in numbers, and communists managed to obtain a number of positions in the government, especially in the ministry of foreign trade.[14]

Although Soviet-Iranian economic relations prospered, the Islamic regime took many steps that angered Moscow. *Pravda* on March 9, 1982, presented a long list of complaints:

> The Iranian authorities have reduced the size of the diplomatic staff of the Soviet embassy in Teheran and closed down the consulate in Resht completely. . . . The Iranian Society for Cultural Relations with the USSR and the Russian-language courses that it conducted have also been shut down. The Russian-Iranian Bank and the branches of the Soviet Insurance Society and the Transport Agency have been closed.
>   . . . The Iranian authorities have taken these actions in an atmosphere of greatly intensified anti-Soviet propaganda. For example, the slogan of "two threats"—one from the south (that is, from the U.S.) and the other from the north (that is, from the Soviet Union)—has been advanced.[15]

The Soviets no doubt became even more angry at the Iranian government when in July 1982 it arrested a number of Tudeh officials. Then, in February 1983, it arrested many more Tudeh leaders, including the top two, Nurredin Kianuri, the general secretary, and Ehsan Tabari, the chief theoretician. All of them were charged with spying for the USSR. In April Kianuri made a dramatic confession on Iranian television that Tudeh, ever since its founding, had been "an instrument of espionage and treason." Shortly thereafter the party was dissolved, and in June Kianuri was executed.[16]

Tudeh has often been suppressed before, but has always managed to recover. If it recoups its losses this time, it might still be able to stage a coup at the death of Khomeini or at some other time of crisis.[17] Although Tudeh is small, we should remember that communist parties just as small have carried out revolutions in numerous countries around the world, Afghanistan being the most recent example. If Tudeh did succeed in seizing power, the door would then be open for a massive increase in Soviet influence, especially if the new regime requested Soviet intervention. A natural consequence would be Soviet bases near the Strait of Hormuz, putting the USSR in a position to engage in oil blackmail. A Tudeh coup without overt Soviet participation is probably Moscow's favorite scenario for Iran. Certainly it would involve much less danger of world war than a blatant invasion by the Soviet army.[18]

Iranian Scenario No. 2. A Tudeh coup is not the only way in which the Soviets might gain influence in Iran; dismemberment of Iran is another possibility. Only about half of the population of Iran are Persians; the rest are Azeris, Kurds, Arabs, Baluch, Turkmen, and so on. The biggest threat of dismemberment comes from the Azeris and the Kurds, who have repeatedly risen up in rebellion since Khomeini came to power. They have "brother" Azeris and Kurds living across the frontier in the USSR and they had their own Soviet-sponsored communist republics in 1945–1946. (These are not small minorities; the Azeris in Iran number about 8 million, while there are about 2.5 million Kurds.)[19] Culture, language, and religion serve as barriers between these two nationalities and the Persians. While most Persians are Shia Muslims, the great majority of the Kurds are Sunnis. The Azeris are Shia, but they have their own ayatollah, Shariat-Madari, and do not recognize Khomeini. Islam, therefore, is not as strong a bond among the three groups as it might be otherwise.

As the government in Teheran does not have firm control over what goes on in Azerbaizhan and Kurdistan today, it has become easy for the Soviet Union to increase its influence in the area, both openly and covertly. Cultural relations with fellow ethnics in the USSR have increased, and Soviet propaganda and infiltration have become more extensive. Some of the Azeri and Kurdish communists who earlier fled to the USSR have returned, and the political parties that ruled the left-wing republics in 1945–1946 have been revived. Since Azeris and Kurds from the USSR look and talk just like their brothers and sisters in Iran, Soviet agents have little difficulty operating in Azerbaizhan and Kurdistan.[20]

Under these circumstances, it would be feasible for Moscow to arrange a repetition of the events of 1945—the proclamation of independent Azerbaizhan and Kurdistan republics, led by pro-Soviet communists. The new governments could then call upon the USSR for economic and military aid, including military advisers. Over a period of time the number of such advisers could be increased to the point where Azerbaizhan and Kurdistan would be, in effect, under Soviet occupation. Moscow would then have control of provinces that contain a large part of the population of Iran, produce most of Iran's food, border on the crucial Shatt-al-Arab waterway, and are close to the oil fields of both Iran and Iraq.[21]

Again it should be emphasized that the Soviet Union probably will *not* march its army into Azerbaizhan and Kurdistan, since this might prompt a military response by the West. However, gradual infiltration by Soviet military and political advisers, buttressed by economic and military aid, could lead to Soviet domination without giving the Western powers any specific act to protest about—just as the West failed to do anything about the growth of Soviet influence in Afghanistan in 1978–1979. The Azeris and the Kurds, for their part, would have no choice but to seek close ties with the Soviets, since nobody else would protect them from Iran and Iraq.

The establishment of strong Soviet influence in independent Azerbaizhan and Kurdistan states would give Moscow several strategic advantages: (1) Soviet intervention in the rest of Iran, either covertly or openly, would be easier. (2) The Soviets would be closer to the oil fields of Iran and Iraq, putting them in a better position to exert pressure on those two countries or, if feasible, to occupy the oil fields. (3) Since there are large and troublesome Kurdish minorities in Iraq and Turkey, the Soviets could gain considerable leverage on those two countries by threatening to support Kurdish territorial claims or by supplying arms to Kurdish rebels. (4) The Soviet position in the Gulf area would be strengthened so those states getting most of their oil from the Gulf would be more fearful about doing anything to antagonize Moscow.[22]

Arguing against a Soviet move into Azerbaizhan and Kurdistan, however, is the fact that these are not the most important parts of Iran—they do not contain oil. If the Soviets did succeed in establishing their dominance over the two northern provinces, this might produce retaliatory action on the part of the United States and its allies, moves that would deny Russia control over the oil fields.

The Baluchistan Scenario. The Soviet occupation of Afghanistan provides opportunities for Soviet expansion also in Baluchistan. The Baluch are a separate ethnic group who have no state of their own, but live in an area of 207,000 square miles that stretches across three countries—southwest Pakistan, southeast Iran, and southern Afghanistan. Like many other peoples in the world today, the Baluch are infected by the spirit of nationalism, resent being ruled by foreigners, and wish to have their own independent national state, uniting all Baluch peoples into a greater Baluchistan. This is particularly true of the Baluch in Pakistan, who fought a bitter and bloody insurrection against the Pakistani government from 1973 to 1977. The Baluch in Iran are also dissatisfied, in part because they are Sunni Muslims in a country dominated by Khomeini's Shiites.[23]

Some of the Baluch in Pakistan are pro-Soviet in varying degrees, and others would be willing to accept support from any country, including the USSR. After the insurrection, many of the Baluch rebels fled from Pakistan to Afghanistan. Among them were members of the Marxist Baluchistan People's Liberation Front, who have been training and preparing for the day when they can return to Pakistan and start a new uprising.[24] This situation presents Moscow with an opportunity to carry out the Baluchistan scenario— i.e., promoting a Baluch rebellion against Pakistan and Iran that would lead to the formation of a pro-Soviet independent Baluchistan, which might then grant military bases to the USSR on the Arabian Sea.

Aside from the Baluch rebels who fled from Pakistan, there are about 100,000 or more Baluch who are natives of Afghanistan and about 15,000 who live in the USSR.[25] This means that the Soviets could organize, arm, and train a Baluch "liberation army" in Afghanistan or the USSR and smuggle weapons and agents into Pakistan and Iran to prepare for the day when the "national liberation struggle" would begin.[26] A Baluch revolutionary government could proclaim the independence of Baluchistan and, if it proved unable to defend itself, could appeal for aid from Soviet troops stationed along the frontier.

An independent Baluchistan indebted to the Soviet Union and dependent upon Soviet support against Pakistan and Iran might then be willing to let Moscow build naval and air bases at the ports of Gwadar, Pasní, and Ormara.[27] If the Baluch-populated areas of Iran also became parts of an independent Baluchistan, the Soviets might get even better bases at the Iranian port of Chah Bahar, which is only about 250 miles from Hormuz. Moscow would then be in an excellent position to threaten the sea lanes leading out of the Gulf.

What is not clear about the Baluch is how much the Soviet invasion of Afghanistan has antagonized them. According to Francis Fukuyama, "the primary concern of most politically active Baluchis now is the freedom of their kinsmen living under Soviet occupation in Afghanistan."[28] Louis Dupree also reported that in the latter part of 1981 the Soviets sent a group of about thirty Baluch from Afghanistan into Pakistan to stir up trouble, but they betrayed the Soviets and reported to the Pakistan authorities.[29] If this is typical and most Baluch now hate the Russians more than the Pakistanis, the Baluchistan scenario obviously is much less feasible than it seemed to be earlier. Of course the Soviets will not be able to intervene actively in Baluchistan until they have improved their military position in Afghanistan. No sizable Soviet force could be supported in Baluchistan without overland logistical lines that are secure from Afghan rebel attacks.

The Pakistan Scenario. A variation of the Baluchistan scenario would be the complete partitioning of Pakistan. The Baluch would create their own independent state, while Afghanistan and India would seize the rest, thereby wiping Pakistan off the map. Afghanistan has long coveted the Northwest Frontier Province of Pakistan because it is populated predominantly by Pushtuns and formerly belonged to Afghanistan. India, for its part, would be happy to get the Punjab, the Sind, and the Pakistani part of Kashmir. The remainder could become the People's Democratic Republic of Baluchistan, under the protective wing of the USSR. One advantage of this scenario for the Soviets is that they would not have to use their own troops, but could stay on the sidelines as "innocent" bystanders.

Through such a partition the Soviet Union could simultaneously achieve several objectives: (1) create an independent Baluchistan, beholden to Moscow; (2) acquire military bases on the coast of Baluchistan, near the entrance to the Gulf; (3) enlarge its satellite state, Afghanistan; and (4) destroy Pakistan, which is the chief refuge for Afghan rebels, the main route through which arms are sent to the rebels, and a friend of the United States.

How India would react is another story. It might be happy to get some of Pakistan's territory and see its most hated enemy destroyed, but it would probably be uneasy about becoming an immediate neighbor of Soviet-occupied Afghanistan. India also would have to consider possible moves by the United States and China, which would be unlikely to stand idly by and watch the dismemberment of Pakistan. Combined Chinese and American pressure probably would be sufficient to deter India from such blatant aggression. Only U.S. involvement in Vietnam allowed India the freedom to invade Bangladesh in 1971. A similar invasion of Pakistan in the future would probably be impossible unless the United States were deeply engaged elsewhere at the time.

Other Possible Scenarios for the Persian Gulf Region. Moscow also might use its client state, South Yemen, as a tool for expanding Soviet influence in the Gulf. If South Yemen should ever succeed in uniting with North Yemen, it then might be powerful enough to promote a revolution in Saudi Arabia by a direct attack and also by arming and organizing the million-plus Yemenis and Palestinians who work in Saudi Arabia.[30]

North Yemen and South Yemen together have a population of about 9 million, almost twice that of Saudi Arabia, so a unified Yemen could pose a real threat to the Saudis. This is especially true because the Soviets have sent large quantities of arms to the Yemenis: beginning in 1979 Moscow sent North Yemen somewhere between $1 billion and $2 billion in military equipment, including MIG-17s, Sukhoi fighter-bombers, helicopters, tanks, armored personnel carriers, and various types of artillery. In addition, Moscow increased the number of military advisers in North Yemen to about 600, while about 1,500 Yemenis, mostly military personnel, were brought to the USSR for training. During the same period the Soviet Union sent arms to the National Democratic Front, a guerrilla movement led by dedicated Marxists.[31]

Noting the similarities with Afghanistan, which also obtained most of its arms from Moscow and sent most of its military officers to Russia for training, some observers predict that within a few years North Yemen may repeat the Afghan pattern—a communist coup carried out by officers indoctrinated while studying in the USSR. A Marxist North Yemen united with a Marxist South Yemen would then pose a serious threat to Saudi Arabia—and to the West.

Another possible danger spot is Oman. It might be subjected to an invasion by the Marxist regime of South Yemen, combined with a revival of the Dhofar rebellion that plagued southern Oman for many years. Although Oman is a small, poor country, it is of great strategic importance: it occupies the southern side of the Strait of Hormuz and has agreed to let the United States use some of its facilities for military purposes. The threat to Oman was highlighted in March 1981 when South Yemen massed troops along the frontier and provoked several border clashes.[32]

Whether the Soviet Union will try to promote any of these scenarios, or some combination of them, is anybody's guess. But the occupation of Afghanistan surely improved Moscow's ability to move in the direction of the Gulf, to exacerbate the problems of states in that area, and to threaten the interests of the United States and its allies. It should be borne in mind, however, that carrying out some of these scenarios is dependent upon Moscow getting Afghanistan under much firmer control than it has achieved so far.

Finally, we should remember that the situation in the Gulf could worsen for the West and improve for the USSR even if the Soviets do nothing. The biggest change in the region in recent years was the fall of the shah, and the Soviet Union was not responsible for that. This area is plagued by great political instability, due largely to the strains that arise when conservative Islamic societies undergo modernization. Saudi Arabia and other Gulf states are grappling with the problem of how to introduce Western education and technology without disrupting Muslim traditions, how to build modern industries and cities without creating social ferment, how to absorb sudden and enormous wealth without stirring up class antagonisms, and how to preserve monarchical governments against the threat of revolution by radicals on the Left or Right. If other regimes in the Gulf succumb to revolution in a manner reminiscent of Iran, the West will probably be hurt, while the USSR will probably gain.

NOTES

1. Cited by Professor Albert L. Weeks in the *New York Times Book Review,* June 21, 1981, p. 13. Trotsky made the statement on August 5, 1919, in a secret message to the Central Committee of the Russian Communist party, in which he argued that "we have up to now devoted too little attention to agitation in Asia."

An English translation may be found in Jan M. Meijer (ed.), *The Trotsky Papers, 1917–1922*, vol. 1 (London-The Hague-Paris: Mouton, 1964), p. 625.

2. Raymond J. Sontag and James S. Beddie (eds.), *Nazi-Soviet Relations, 1939–41: Documents from the Archives of the German Foreign Office* (Washington, D.C.: Department of State, 1948), p. 259. Molotov, who was commissar of foreign affairs at the time, made the statement on November 26, 1940. He indicated that the USSR would sign a pact with the Axis powers if they made certain concessions regarding Finland, the Turkish Straits, the area south of Batum and Baku, and other matters considered vital to Russia.

3. *Washington Post,* February 1, 1981, p. C5.

4. *Time,* September 22, 1980, p. 29.

5. *Washington Post,* January 28, 1980, p. A16; *New York Times,* January 27, 1980, sec. 3, p. 1. For further details see Alvin J. Cottrell (ed.), *The Persian Gulf States* (Baltimore, Md.: Johns Hopkins University Press, 1980), especially Chapter 9, "Oil in the Persian Gulf Area," by Keith McLachlan, pp. 195–224; and Rouhollah K. Ramazani, *The Persian Gulf and the Strait of Hormuz* (Alphen Aan den Rijn, Holland: Sijthoff & Nordhoff, 1979).

6. I wish to thank Francis Fukuyama for suggesting this paragraph. The U.S. Joint Chiefs of Staff in February 1982 declared that a Soviet invasion of Iran was the "least likely" threat to U.S. interests in Southwest Asia, but that, if it occurred, it could be very dangerous. They pointed out that an invasion through the mountains of northern Iran would be difficult. *Washington Post,* February 10, 1982, p. A12.

7. Cottrell, *The Persian Gulf States,* p. 173; Rouhollah K. Ramazani, *The Foreign Policy of Iran, A Developing Nation in World Affairs, 1500–1941* (Charlottesville: University Press of Virginia, 1966), chap. 7.

8. Rouhollah K. Ramazani, "The Autonomous Republic of Azerbaijan and the Kurdish People's Republic," in *The Anatomy of Communist Takeovers,* ed. by Thomas T. Hammond (New Haven, Conn.: Yale University Press, 1975), pp. 448–474.

9. Nikita Khrushchev, *Khrushchev Remembers: The Last Testament* (Boston: Little, Brown, 1974), p. 299. He added, quite innocently, "It took some time for the . . . Afghan leaders to understand that we weren't pursuing mercenary or military goals in their country."

10. Interview with Alvin J. Cottrell. For a good discussion of Tudeh, see Shahram Chubin, "Leftist Forces in Iran," *Problems of Communism,* vol. 29, no. 4 (July-August 1980), pp. 1–25.

11. *Izvestiia,* February 11, 1982, p. 4.

12. *Washington Post,* February 16, 1982, p. A16.

13. *Izvestiia,* February 11, 1982, p. 4; *Washington Post,* February 16, 1982, p. A16.

14. *Washington Post,* April 10, 1982, p. A11, and April 16, 1982, p. A20.

15. *Pravda,* March 9, 1982, p. 4.

16. Karen Dawisha, "The U.S.S.R. in the Middle East: Superpower in Eclipse?" *Foreign Affairs,* vol. 61, no. 2 (Winter 1982/1983), p. 447; interview with Rouhollah K. Ramazani; *Time,* May 16, 1983, p. 27; *Washington Post,* May 2, 1983, p. A14; *New York Times,* June 22, 1983, p. A2. The regime previously had cracked down on the left-wing Mujaheddin-i-Khalq party.

17. Comment by Professor Bernard Lewis of Princeton University at the Woodrow Wilson International Center for Scholars, December 9, 1980. There may be some possibility that the Soviet Union and Tudeh will cooperate with the leftist Mujaheddin-i-Khalq party, which is much larger at present than Tudeh.

18. Tudeh made a bid for power as far back as 1953 when the shah was first forced to flee from Iran. For details see Rouhollah K. Ramazani, *Iran's Foreign Policy, 1941–1973: A Study of Foreign Policy in Modernizing Nations* (Charlottesville: University Press of Virginia, 1975).

19. Interview with Rouhollah K. Ramazani. Estimates of the population of the various ethnic groups in Iran vary widely.

20. Interviews with Alvin J. Cottrell and Rouhollah K. Ramazani; Chubin, "Leftist Forces in Iran," pp. 1–2.

21. For more information on the Azeris and Kurds, as well as other minorities in Iran, see Rouhollah K. Ramazani, *The Northern Tier: Afghanistan, Iran, and Turkey* (New York: Van Nostrand, 1966), pp. 29–38. An account of Kurdish rebelliousness is in the *Washington Post,* February 10, 1981, p. A12. In April 1981, the Iranian government offered to grant legal recognition to the Kurdish Democratic party and other rebellious ethnic groups if they would renounce their opposition to the regime and turn in their arms. Teheran has made many such amnesty offers to the Kurdish guerrillas, but without result. *Washington Post,* April 9, 1981, p. A24. See also *Washington Post,* February 10, 1981, p. A12, and *New York Times,* May 31, 1980, p. A5.

22. It is interesting to note that the shah told George Bush in April 1978 that he looked upon the communist seizure of power in Afghanistan as one more example of a Soviet grand design, as part of a communist drive to encircle Iran. In the same conversation with Bush, the shah spoke of his concern about the other Gulf states, which he said were "run by a bunch of bedouins" who had no plans and were no match for the forces determined to overthrow them. Secret cable from Ambassador William Sullivan in Teheran to State Department, cable no. 04062, April 30, 1978, p. 1.

23. *New York Times,* January 13, 1980, p. 2E; Selig S. Harrison, "Nightmare in Baluchistan," *Foreign Policy,* no. 32 (Fall 1978), pp. 139, 148–150; *Washington Post,* February 8, 1980, p. A20.

24. *Time,* January 15, 1979, pp. 32–33.

25. Population statistics in these countries are unreliable. The 100,000 figure comes from Louis Dupree, *Afghanistan* (Princeton, N.J.: Princeton University Press, 1980), p. 62. The figure of 15,000 Baluch in the USSR is an estimate based on a population of 13,000 in 1970, as reported in Alexandre Bennigsen, "Soviet Muslims and the World of Islam," *Problems of Communism,* vol. 29, no. 2 (March-April 1980), p. 40. The Baluch were not counted in the 1979 census.

26. Bruce Stannard of *The Observer* (London) was admitted to Afghanistan in the summer of 1981. He wrote: "Afghan government ministers we spoke to would neither confirm nor deny reports that up to 12,000 Baluchi rebels were now being trained in Afghanistan with Soviet assistance. The Baluchi tribesmen, who are demanding independence could . . . easily destabilize Pakistan if the Americans continue to step up their aid to the Afghan rebels through that country." *Boston Globe,* August 30, 1981, p. 13.

27. Amaury de Riencourt, "India and Pakistan in the Shadow of Afghanistan," *Foreign Affairs,* vol. 61, no. 2 (Winter 1982/1983), p. 433.

28. Francis Fukuyama, *The Security of Pakistan: A Trip Report* (Santa Monica, Calif.: Rand Corporation, September 1980), p. 12.

29. Statement by Professor Louis Dupree at a meeting of specialists on Afghanistan, Washington, D.C., December 16, 1981.

30. David Ottoway, "Saudis Cast Wary Eye on Foreign Workers," *Washington Post,* March 4, 1981, p. A16.

31. David Ottoway in the *Washington Post,* April 21, 1982, p. A19.

32. The *Washington Post* on March 27, 1981, p. A4, published the following story: "Oman has accused South Yemeni forces of firing on an Omani aircraft and at an Army patrol during a number of border incursions last month. . . . The firing incidents were followed by the massing of Yemeni troops on the border with Oman. The statement accused the Soviet Union, East Germany and Cuba of supporting the moves."

CHAPTER 19

What Should the United States Do About Afghanistan?

In view of Soviet Actions in Afghanistan and possible future Soviet moves in the area of the Gulf, what should the United States do?

SEND AID TO THE REBELS AND THE REFUGEES

The most obvious and most urgent need is to send arms, food, medicine, and money to the Afghan rebels. We should do this not only because we admire these brave people but also because it serves our own interests. The longer the Soviets have to fight in Afghanistan, the harder it will be for them to cause trouble elsewhere—in Pakistan, Iran, the Gulf, or other areas. Afghanistan cannot be used as a staging area for Soviet moves toward the Gulf as long as more than half of the country is in the hands of guerrillas. The military airfields at Shindand and Qandahar cannot serve as bases for flights to the Strait of Hormuz or the Indian Ocean if the runways and fuel dumps are vulnerable to rebel raids.[1] Thus it is to the advantage of the United States to support the Afghan resistance movement.

It is also worth remembering that throughout the Vietnam war the Soviets supplied the arms that were killing American soldiers and made no attempt to hide that fact; indeed, they boasted to the world that Soviet support for the "national liberation struggle" in Vietnam was a sacred duty. The U.S. government, by contrast, has never admitted that it is sending aid to the "national liberation struggle" in Afghanistan. Now that the Soviets are involved in "their Vietnam," we should make it as expensive as possible for them. If they have to pay a heavy price for their invasion of Afghanistan, this may discourage them from undertaking similar adventures in the future. Our main goal should not be to get them to withdraw; rather our chief goal should be to discourage them from invading other countries in the future.

215

Robert G. Neumann, former U.S. ambassador to Afghanistan, made another important point: "If we refuse to help the Afghans, we . . . would demonstrate that we are all talk and no action. . . . Our failure to act would give a signal to Saudi Arabia and the other Gulf states that we are simply not to be counted upon. . . . If we do nothing for Afghanistan, they will draw their own conclusion. They will then have to consider how to respond to Russian pressure to cut a deal with Moscow."[2]

Some have argued that the United States should not send arms to the rebels, on the grounds that their cause is hopeless: the more weapons the Afghans get, the more of them will be killed. The argument is made that we would increase the slaughter by encouraging the freedom fighters to wage a war they cannot win. To this one can reply that the rebels have shown that they are going to fight whether we help them or not; indeed, many of them have already been fighting for years without outside assistance or encouragement. As one Afghan put it, "It is not up to Washington whether we fight or not; it is up to Washington whether we will fight with reasonably good weapons or with stones."[3]

We should also send more aid to the Afghan refugees. As mentioned above, by the beginning of 1983 there were approximately 3.5 million Afghan refugees in Pakistan and Iran—the largest refugee population in the world. Most of the exiles have been driven out of their homes by Soviet attacks in which whole villages were demolished by bombing, strafing, and the use of incendiary chemicals. Despite aid from Pakistan, the UN, the United States, and others, the refugees live in miserable conditions, with inadequate housing, food, clothing, and medical care. The people of the United States are traditionally generous to those in need, but so far the plight of the Afghan refugees has attracted little attention in this country.

The Soviet Threat to Pakistan

Unfortunately, transporting sophisticated arms or large quantities of arms across Pakistan to the rebels poses problems. If the supplies reaching the rebels via Pakistan were to increase a great deal, the USSR might take military action against Pakistan. In fact, the Soviets have already given Pakistan a taste of what they could do; refugee camps and border posts in Pakistan have been bombed and strafed, and Pakistani soldiers have been killed in small-scale border incidents.[4] It would be easy for the Soviets to increase these attacks, make larger incursions across the frontier, occupy small salients of Pakistani territory, or seize key mountain passes.[5]

Pakistan is also vulnerable to Soviet political pressures. For example, the Soviets could back Afghan claims to Pushtunistan, i.e., the Northwest Frontier region of Pakistan. Nationalistic Pushtuns in Afghanistan have long demanded that these territories be returned, and the Babrak regime could perhaps gain some popular support by championing this cause. The Soviets also could threaten Pakistan by endorsing Baluch demands for independence, as explained in Chapter 18.

Another handy weapon Moscow could use against Pakistan would be to support President Zia's political opponents, particularly the followers of former President Bhutto. They are already doing this indirectly, through the Babrak regime. Bhutto's sons are living in a house in Kabul supplied to them by the Afghan government, and apparently it was from Kabul that they planned the hijacking of a Pakistani airliner in March 1981.[6] As Zia's rule is rather shaky, he is probably worried that the Soviets will give further aid to his enemies in the future.

Another way in which the Soviets could punish Pakistan for aiding the Afghan rebels would be to encourage India to attack Pakistan and seize some of its territory. Finally, as the ultimate form of punishment, the Soviets could launch a full-scale invasion of Pakistan and dismember it, with or without the aid of India.[7]

For all of these reasons it would be risky for Pakistan to allow arms to flow to the rebels openly or on a scale big enough to seriously damage Russia's position in Afghanistan. Once the Soviets feel they are suffering major setbacks because of Pakistan, they will be tempted to take retaliatory action. This means, in effect, that the rebels may never get enough sophisticated arms to improve their present position significantly. Even if the U.S. government should decide to send large quantities of antitank and antiaircraft weapons, Zia might feel he could not allow them to pass through Pakistani territory.

American policymakers have the delicate task of "trying to maintain a balance between having the insurgents armed well enough to make it too costly for the Russians to want to stay in Afghanistan, while not providing so many weapons that the Soviets will be provoked to attack Pakistan."[8] In public statements Pakistani officials reject the notion that the Soviet Union might launch a large-scale invasion of Pakistan, but some of them admit in private conversation that the prospect worries them. As one high official put it,

> Pakistan provides sanctuary for villagers who support the insurgents. If they had no place to go, the insurgents might knuckle under, the way the Russians see it. They are wrong because the Hazaras in central Afghanistan, the Uzbeks in the east, even the Tadjiks in the north near the Soviet border, are resisting successfully without such a sanctuary. But in their frustration Pakistan has to be a tempting target for the Soviets when they see all the Afghan activity on the North-West Frontier.[9]

Ways To Strengthen Pakistan

Pakistan today is in a very difficult position. To the east it is bordered by its big and bitter enemy, India, with a population of 650 million compared to Pakistan's 80 million—an enemy with which it repeatedly has been at war. India, moreover, signed a treaty of friendship with the USSR in 1971 and made a massive arms deal with the Soviets in 1980. On the west and north Pakistan is now bordered, in effect, by the Soviet Union. Pakistan feels threatened by these two powerful neighbors and naturally looks to the United States for support. But if Pakistan accepts large-scale American aid or moves closer to Washington, it will alarm its neighbors and possibly provoke them into retaliatory action.

It was not surprising, therefore, that in 1980 President Zia rejected as "peanuts" President Carter's offer of $400 million in aid. A senior Pakistani official described the situation very well:

> The $400 million we were being offered was over a two-year period, and half of it was military sales credits that we would have had to pay back, so what we would be getting this year [1980] to build up our forces to face the Soviets was $100 million in credit. And what does $100 million buy these days when it comes to arms?
>
> If we accepted the $400 million we would not be buying any real security and we would be provoking the hostility of both the Soviet Union and India. And we would be endangering our position in the nonaligned bloc and in the Islamic group of nations. We concluded, therefore, that we would be worse off accepting the American offer than rejecting it.[10]

The Carter administration's policy, said President Zia, lacked "credibility and durability." That is, the smallness of the offer indicated a feeling in Washington that it must be cautious about making a substantial, long-term commitment to Pakistan. It simply was not worth it to Zia to line up with the United States against the Soviet Union unless Washington gave evidence that it would be a generous and dependable ally. Speaking of Russia, Zia commented: "You cannot live in the sea and create enmity of the whales. You have to be friendly with them. The Soviet Union is on our doorstep. The United States is ten thousand miles away."[11] Zia knew, moreover, that Pakistan's defenses along the border with Afghanistan were weak, which meant that the Soviets could strike there "with impunity."[12]

Zia may have questioned American credibility also because he had seen the United States pull out of Vietnam, Cambodia, and Laos and do little or nothing to stop the spread of Soviet influence in Angola, Ethiopia, South Yemen, and Afghanistan.[13] American opposition to Soviet-supported Marxist takeovers in the Third World had appeared weak and unpredictable, whether under Nixon, Ford, or Carter. In the post-Vietnam era the American people seemed reluctant to do much to stop the spread of communism and Soviet power around the globe.

Carter's 1980 aid offer came only a few months after he had cut off all aid to Pakistan because he believed it was secretly trying to develop nuclear weapons. This hardly seems fair since in 1974 Pakistan's chief enemy, India, exploded a nuclear device manufactured with the use of heavy water supplied by the United States.[14] While the policy of trying to prevent the proliferation of nuclear weapons is admirable, the United States has not been able to prevent Pakistan from pushing its nuclear program in the past and is not likely to be able to do so in the future. During President Zia's trip to the United States in December 1982, he assured President Reagan that Pakistan was not interested in manufacturing or acquiring nuclear weapons, but administration officials told Congress at the same time that Pakistan's nuclear arms program was continuing without halt.[15]

The Carter administration hestitated to make a major commitment to Pakistan in part because the country is ruled by an unrepresentative, authoritarian military dictatorship, headed by an unpopular general. Opposition to Zia is so widespread that he may well be overthrown within the next few years. If the United States sends Zia massive economic and military aid, there may be a repetition of what happened in Iran under the shah, and Pakistan could end up as an adversary rather than a friend of the United States.[16]

While this is a real danger, it seems imperative that the United States make use of Pakistan for the defense of the Gulf, if for no other reason. To dramatize the importance of Pakistan to the West, one should picture what it would be like if the Soviet Union gained control of southern Pakistan. Then the Soviets could build air and naval bases at the ports of Karachi, Gwadar, and other ports astride the sea lanes leading from the Gulf. This would largely nullify American sea power in that area and place oil shipments to the United States and its friends in jeopardy.

Strengthening Pakistan would have several benefits. Pakistan could continue to serve as a refuge and source of arms and other supplies for the Afghan insurgents. It also would be encouraged to persist in its refusal to recognize the Babrak regime. In addition, if we give substantial support to Pakistan, perhaps it will permit the shipment of larger quantities of the munitions the rebels need, including antiaircraft and antitank rockets. American support for Pakistan might also cause it to facilitate the buildup of U.S. military power in the Gulf area. While the Pakistanis do not want to have American bases on their territory, they might permit the stationing of supply ships, loaded with tanks and other military equipment, in Karachi and other harbors, for use by our Rapid Deployment Force.[17]

For these and other reasons, the Reagan administration decided to make a more generous aid offer to Pakistan than had the Carter administration. In June 1981 it announced that the United States and Pakistan had agreed to a program of assistance over a five-year period amounting to more than $3 billion, about half of it economic and half military. The economic aid will make it easier for Pakistan to care for the 3 million or so Afghan refugees on its territory. (Pakistan is currently bearing about half of the cost of this refugee support.) The United States has promised to sell Pakistan a variety of weapons, including some F-16 fighter-bombers, the most advanced plane in the American arsenal. However, President Reagan will have to convince Congress to grant the money and exempt Pakistan from the Symington Amendment, which prohibits the sale of arms to any country trying to develop nuclear weapons.[18]

While India objects to Reagan's arms sales to Pakistan, there seems to be little justification for such objections. India is ten times the size of Pakistan, has eight times the population, has a much larger army, air force, and navy, and recently concluded an arms deal with the USSR worth more than $8 billion. It seems unlikely, therefore, that Pakistan will be so foolish as to attack India. As Drew Middleton pointed out in the *New York Times,* "the proposed American assistance falls short of what Pakistan needs to balance India's increasing military strength."[19]

The Reagan administration is understandably disgusted by the Indian government's unprincipled, immoral defense of the Soviet invasion of Afghanistan. Friends of India defend its stand by arguing that India's geographic position, next door to Russia, forces it to follow a pro-Soviet policy. But Pakistan is even closer geographically to the USSR and is even more vulnerable to Soviet pressure, yet Pakistan has vigorously opposed the Soviet occupation of Afghanistan.

Although India's behavior, especially its policy toward the USSR, is often annoying, the United States cannot afford to ignore Indian feelings. U.S. aid to Pakistan is essential, but it should be handled in such a way as to minimize anti-American and anti-Pakistani sentiment in India. Our policies must be designed to win friends not only in Pakistan but in the whole Indian subcontinent. So far, however, Washington has appeared insensitive to Indian fears. For example, the Reagan administration has "pointedly refused to give public or private assurances to New Delhi that Washington would not permit American weaponry to be used in an Indian-Pakistani conflict."[20] In addition, the United States has promised to give Pakistan not only defensive arms for resisting a possible Soviet attack but also offensive arms that could be used against India. Washington's decision to supply Pakistan with some F-16 fighter-bombers produced a storm of anti-American sentiment in India, much to the delight of the Soviet Union.[21] Indians also point out that most Pakistani troops are stationed along the border with India, rather than facing a possible threat from Soviet forces in Afghanistan.[22]

India, as the largest, most populous, and most powerful state in South Asia cannot be ignored in any plan to stop further Soviet expansion in that area. The only way to achieve lasting stability there is through reconciliation between India and Pakistan—a goal that has become even more urgent following the Soviet occupation of Afghanistan. At times Indian officials have given signs that they realize the two countries need each other. Prime Minister Gandhi, for example, commented in August 1982, "We want our neighbors to be stable and strong. Nothing is so dangerous as a weak neighbor."[23] Similarly, while making a visit to Pakistan the year before, Indian Foreign Minister Narasimha Rao declared that India has "an abiding interest, even a vested interest in the stability of Pakistan" because of "the geopolitical situation in which both of our countries find themselves."[24] In practice, however, neither India nor Pakistan has done much to reconcile their differences, and the Reagan administration, by the way it has handled the Pakistan aid program, has exacerbated the tensions between the two countries.

Although the arms aid promised to Pakistan by Reagan is much larger than that offered by Carter, it is, of course, far from enough to enable Pakistan to defend itself from a full-scale Soviet attack. No amount of aid could guarantee Pakistan security from Soviet aggression, but it could make a Soviet attack more costly, and thus might discourage Moscow from attempting it.[25] The aid package also makes the Pakistanis feel that the United States is more committed than before to the defense of their country.

Aid Through Iran

Another conduit for weapons to the rebels is Iran, although on a much smaller scale than Pakistan. Since relations between the United States and Iran are hostile, the Teheran government is not eager to cooperate with the United States. However, Khomeini has expressed sympathy for the rebels, and apparently he is permitting the shipment of arms across Iran to Afghanistan. As the southeastern part of Iran is populated predominantly by Baluch and that area today is largely autonomous, the sympathy of the Baluch for the rebels may be more important than Khomeini's attitude. In any case, American officials have confirmed that arms are reaching the insurgents via Iran. Some are sold to the rebels at high prices, while others are sent to them free of charge.[26]

DON'T FORGIVE AND FORGET

If the Soviet Union is to be discouraged from making future aggressive moves like the invasion of Afghanistan, it will have to pay some penalty for what it has done. Unfortunately, when the USSR invaded Hungary and Czechoslovakia, it got little more than a slap on the wrist. There was an uproar in the press for a while, but then the noise died down and the United States and Western Europe returned to business as usual. This has happened again. Afghanistan isn't news anymore; it is seldom mentioned in the press, and the U.S. government does relatively little to publicize the situation in

Afghanistan. Worst of all, President Reagan, despite his antipathy for the Soviet Union, canceled the grain embargo.

Professor Leon B. Poullada, who has spent many years in Afghanistan as a diplomat and a scholar, criticized the cancellation of the embargo in a letter to the *New York Times:*

> If I were sitting in the Kremlin, I would draw the following lessons from the lifting of the grain embargo:
>
> First, the USSR can invade and occupy a small neutral country like Afghanistan any time it sees fit. The United States may impose sanctions but they will be short-lived. In a matter of months the forces of capitalism, dollar greed and internal politics will force the U.S. to resume business as usual.
>
> Second, American policy toward the USSR is just as mushy and inconsistent under Reagan as it was under Carter. The rhetoric may be tougher but the actions are softer.
>
> Third, the way to extract favorable results from the United States is to threaten some country, preferably one with a large ethnic minority in America such as the Poles, and then withdraw the threat. The American Government will fall all over itself in gratitude for such restraint. Soviets can continue to kill Afghans in exchange for vague promises not to kill Poles. After all, there is no powerful Afghan-American community in America.
>
> The decision to impose a grain embargo to punish the USSR was perhaps unwise. Whether and how much it hurt the Soviets or if it hurt American farmers more are debatable questions.
>
> What is not debatable is the international psychological effect. The embargo was an American expression of shock and disgust at the barbarous Soviet move and a warning of more unpleasant results if Moscow tried to extend its aggression in the Middle East. Once imposed, consistency and deterrence required it be continued until Russia ended its odious aggression.
>
> Instead the message has gone out to the world and to the brave Afghan freedom fighters that the Soviets are forgiven. Considering that the Afghans are the only people anywhere in the world today actually fighting the Soviets and containing their uncivilized aggression, the American decision to undermine their morale seems shortsighted and unconscionable.
>
> American officials talk big about a Rapid Deployment Force for the Middle East but it has so far failed to materialize. The Afghans, however, have already provided us with such a force on the ground and in actual physical contact with the enemy. By sheer courage they are holding the invaders of the Middle East at bay. They have raised the spirits of free men everywhere by showing that a freedom-loving rag-tag guerrilla force can hold off the mighty Red Army.
>
> How does America reward this effort? Instead of supporting this Islamic indigenous fighting force with the weapons it needs, American officials keep talking about establishing American bases in the Middle East, which does

not want our presence. And now we have told the Afghan *mujahidin* that we are forgiving Soviet aggression in Afghanistan because the Russians were nice enough not to invade Poland.[27]

Unfortunately, few Americans have demonstrated such sympathy for the Afghan freedom fighters or such outrage at the U.S. government's halfhearted support for the Afghan cause. During the Vietnam war our streets were full of demonstrators, and many campuses had their riots and sit-ins. Similarly, in recent years there have been protest marches against the sending of fifty-five military advisers to El Salvador. But there have been very few demonstrations by Americans (or others) against the sending of more than 100,000 Soviet troops to Afghanistan.

Why hasn't the Afghan liberation struggle excited the interest and support of the American public, at least of those who habitually champion the underdog? For people seeking a worthy cause these days it would be hard to find a better one than the cause of the Afghan resistance fighters. Their cause is almost perfect; telling the good guys from the bad guys is easy. Yet neither the Afghan rebels nor the more than 3 million refugees have aroused much sympathy around the world.

A handful of French doctors have been doing their best to care for the wounded guerrillas and civilians in Afghanistan, but apparently there are no American doctors serving either the rebels or the refugees in Pakistan. Except for a few journalists, Americans generally have ignored Afghanistan. Movie star Kirk Douglas visited Afghan refugee camps in Pakistan, but he seems to be the only celebrity who has championed the Afghan cause. One wonders, where are the Joan Baezes and Jane Fondas demanding that the Russians get out of Afghanistan? Where are the congressional committees examining the plight of the refugees? Where are the Hemingways writing novels about the heroic struggles of the Afghans for freedom? And where are the young idealists, volunteering to fight and die on the side of the poor, oppressed peasants?

STRENGTHEN THE U.S. POSITION IN THE GULF

If the biggest danger to the United States from the Soviet occupation of Afghanistan is the potential threat to the Gulf, then the most important thing for us to do is to strengthen our position in that area. This is no simple task, particularly since the Gulf is so close to the USSR and so far from the United States. It requires the simultaneous pursuit of several interrelated policies:

1. Increase the strength of the American navy in the Gulf and the Indian Ocean.
2. Establish and/or expand bases and other military facilities in Diego Garcia, Oman, Kenya, Somalia, Egypt, Turkey, and elsewhere. Preposition large quantities of arms and supplies in the Middle East. Practice military exercises with these states.
3. Speed up the development of the Rapid Deployment Force. Build the cargo planes and ships necessary to transport these forces quickly around the world.[28]
4. Exert every effort to improve relations with Iran, the most important state on the Gulf. If that is impossible with the present regime, support pro-American forces trying to overthrow that regime.
5. Demonstrate to the states of the Gulf, especially Saudi Arabia, that the United States has the will and the power to protect them from Soviet encroachments. Sell them the military equipment they need to defend themselves.
6. Provide economic and military support to Turkey, which lies on the flank of Soviet invasion routes from Transcaucasia to the Gulf and which has serious economic and political difficulties.
7. Send more military and economic aid to Pakistan and thereby give it the strength to preserve its independence, aid the Afghan rebels, and help defend the Gulf.
8. Pressure our allies in Europe and Japan to contribute their fair share to the defense of Gulf oil, which is more vital to them than to us.
9. Do whatever we can (and that may not be much) to promote stability in the crisis-prone countries surrounding the Gulf.
10. Protect Oman and North Yemen from any aggression by South Yemen.

Accomplishing all these tasks will not be easy. They represent, in the words of Harold Brown, former secretary of defense, "the greatest current challenge to the United States' geostrategic and military plan, and to our international political skill."[29] But the energy that flows from the Gulf to the United States and its friends is so important, and the Soviet position so threatening, that these things must be done.

TRY TO PREVENT FUTURE COMMUNIST TAKEOVERS

What can the United States do to prevent more communist takeovers like the one in Afghanistan? In some cases it can do nothing. It could not prevent the communist coup in Afghanistan because that happened too far away and too suddenly.[30] Nor could the United States have sent troops there without risking war with Russia. In some cases the cost of intervening may be more than the American people are willing to pay, as in Vietnam. But we must rid ourselves of the widespread attitude that American military intervention in any country, under any circumstances, is both evil and doomed to failure. If the Soviets conclude that the United States is suffering from a permanent case of "Post-Vietnam Paralysis," they will feel that they can support communist takeovers anywhere and everywhere without fear of opposition. The United States must be prepared to intervene diplomatically, economically, and, if necessary, militarily. The development of a strong Rapid Deployment Force should help. If the United States can get troops to a trouble spot before the Soviets or Cubans or Vietnamese do, this would be a great advantage because then *they* would face the risks of attacking our forces, rather than vice versa.

The United States should promote and support progressive, democratic regimes wherever possible. It should try also to identify potential trouble spots before communist revolutions occur: upholding an existing government is more acceptable in terms of morality and world opinion than overthrowing one. Besides, it is much more difficult to oust a communist regime once it has seized power. Above all, the United States must not give Moscow the impression that it is unable and unwilling to act, as this might encourage the USSR to embark on more foreign adventures, thereby leading to an unexpected confrontation with the United States. A miscalculation by the Soviets that the West will continue to let them get away with more Afghanistans might well lead to World War III.

It is to be hoped that in the future the United States will demonstrate to the Soviets that in the long run they can gain more by living peacefully with the noncommunist world than by engaging in armed aggression or by promoting communist takeovers. Through the use of the carrot-and-stick approach, perhaps we can show them that actions such as the invasion of Afghanistan bring losses to them: the killing of SALT II; the intensification of the arms race; the curtailment of trade with the United States, including trade in high technology; and above all—the increased threat of war. Maybe we can convince the Soviets that in a world of two giant superpowers, both armed with globe-destroying weapons, the most important objective of all— much more important than control of Afghanistan—is the establishment of peaceful relations between the United States and Russia.

NOTES

1. A Reuters dispatch in the *Washington Post* on June 18, 1981, p. 24A, reported as follows: "Afghan rebels attacked the Soviet air base at Bagram, 36 miles north of Kabul, on June 9 and caused large-scale fires in ammunition and gasoline stores." The rebels are quite active in the vicinity of Qandahar and Shindand.

2. *U.S. News and World Report*, July 7, 1980, p. 27.

3. Ibid.

4. Francis Fukuyama, *The Security of Pakistan: A Trip Report* (Santa Monica, Calif.: Rand Corporation, September 1980), pp. v, 17; interview with State Department official; Edward Girardet, "With the Resistance in Afghanistan," *Christian Science Monitor,* September 26, 1981, p. 3.

5. Fukuyama, *The Security of Pakistan,* pp. 17–19.

6. *Washington Post,* March 8, 1981, p. A15; March 17, 1981, pp. A1, A14; and April 26, 1981, p. A24; *Time,* March 30, 1981, pp. 32–33. The hijackers ordered the plane to Kabul, where it remained for seven days. During that time they were greeted by Murtaza Bhutto, the former prime minister's eldest son. Despite appeals by the U.S. State Department to the Soviet Union to use its influence to end the hijacking, the Soviets did nothing. While in Kabul, all of the hijackers were out of the plane at one time, within rifle range of Soviet and Afghan troops, but no effort was made to detain or shoot them. The State Department later accused the Soviet government of failing to try to end the hijacking and strongly suggested complicity by the Soviet government.

7. For similar views see Fukuyama, *The Security of Pakistan,* pp. v, 19.

8. *New York Times,* July 20, 1980, p. 12. Professor Leon B. Poullada, in a letter to me, presented his views on the sending of military aid to the Afghan rebels:

> The argument that it is too difficult to send arms to the Afghan resistance through Pakistan is an excuse for a cop-out. It can be done in at least three ways if the will is really there to arm the mujahidin: (1) Use air drops from Turkish bases or aircraft carriers on the Indian Ocean. (2) Channel the weapons through the Islamic Conference; Pakistan would find it impossible to deny access to that group. (3) Use the well-worn path of arms smuggling through the Makran Coast. For over a century arms smugglers have operated on the coast of Baluchistan. They are organized better than the Mafia and will deliver anything anywhere for a price.

9. *New York Times,* July 20, 1980, p. 12.

10. *New York Times,* July 16, 1980, p. A3. Zbigniew Brzezinski, who went to Pakistan to discuss the aid offer, admits that Zia was justified in complaining that $400 million was not enough. But he argues that it was a tactical error on Zia's part to make the "peanuts" remark in public because it undercut support in Congress and made any efforts to increase the aid offer impossible at that time. The remark received a great deal of publicity, partly because of President Carter's well-known agricultural activities. Interview with Brzezinski.

11. *New York Times,* January 16, 1980, cited in Vernon V. Aspaturian, "The Afghan Gamble: Soviet Quagmire or Springboard?" in Vernon V. Aspaturian, Alexander Dallin, and Jiri Valenta, *The Soviet Invasion of Afghanistan: Three Perspectives* (Los Angeles: Center for International and Strategic Affairs, University of California, 1980), p. 54, footnote 24.

12. *Washington Post,* January 17, 1980, p. A1. The quoted words are those of the military governor of the Northwest Frontier Province.

13. Fukuyama, *The Security of Pakistan,* pp. 24–25.

14. Ibid., p. 24.

15. *New York Times,* December 8, 1982, pp. A1, A6.

16. See, for example, the editorial in the *Washington Post,* "Slow on Pakistan," March 25, 1981, p. A18; Jack Anderson, "Pakistan's Zia: 'Shah Syndrome' Revived," *Washington Post,* May 6, 1981, p. E19; and *U.S. News and World Report,* June 30, 1980, p. 31.

17. Fukuyama, *The Security of Pakistan,* pp. 33–34.

18. *Washington Post,* June 16, 1981, pp. A1, A12.

19. *New York Times,* July 21, 1981, p. A11.

20. Selig S. Harrison, "India, and Reagan's Tilt Toward Pakistan," *New York Times,* July 15, 1981, p. A23. Reagan's failure to give such assurances to India contrasts with the pledge President Eisenhower gave to India when he sent arms to Pakistan. Selig S. Harrison, "Fanning Flames in South Asia," *Foreign Policy,* no. 45 (Winter 1981–1982), p. 95.

For a defense of the Reagan aid program to Pakistan see the letter by James L. Buckley in the *New York Times,* August 5, 1981, p. A22. As under secretary of state, Buckley negotiated the aid package. See also "The Case for Pakistan" by Niaz A. Naik, Pakistan's chief delegate to the UN, in the *New York Times,* August 5, 1981, p. A23.

21. Robert H. Donaldson, "Soviet Involvement in South Asia and the Indian Ocean Region," in *Soviet Foreign Policy in the 1980s,* ed. by Roger E. Kanet (New York: Praeger, 1982), pp. 347–348.

22. Amaury de Riencourt, "India and Pakistan in the Shadow of Afghanistan," *Foreign Affairs,* vol. 61, no. 2 (Winter 1982/1983), p. 433.

23. Ibid., p. 434.

24. Harrison, "Fanning Flames in South Asia," p. 101.

25. Drew Middleton in the *New York Times,* July 21, 1981, p. A11.

26. Leslie Gelb in the *New York Times,* August 7, 1981, p. 4A. His sources were U.S. administration officials.

27. *New York Times,* May 4, 1981, p. A22. President Reagan has also been criticized for canceling the grain embargo on the grounds that he is bailing out Soviet agriculture and the Soviet economy generally, instead of forcing the regime to suffer the consequences of its economic inefficiency. It has been pointed out also that as long as the United States continues to sell large quantities of grain to the USSR, it is difficult for Reagan to tell West European countries that they should not support the Soviet gas pipeline project, sell Russia high technology goods, grant credits, and so on.

Alexander Haig, after his resignation as secretary of state, said that the lifting of the grain embargo was "the greatest foreign policy mistake" of the Reagan administration. *New York Times,* June 28, 1982, p. A15.

28. On the deficiencies of the Rapid Deployment Force as of the fall of 1980, see the *New York Times,* September 26, 1980, pp. A1, A24.

29. "U.S. Security Policy in Southwest Asia: A Case Study in Complexity," a speech delivered at The Johns Hopkins School of Advanced International Studies, Washington, D.C., April 30, 1981, p. 27.

30. The United States could have prevented the communist takeover in Afghanistan if it had responded to Afghan requests for military and economic assistance

back in the 1950s when the Soviets were making concerted efforts to establish their predominance in Afghanistan. The communist coup of April 1978 was carried out by military officers trained in the USSR. For a strong statement on this point see Leon B. Poullada, "Afghanistan and the United States: The Crucial Years," *The Middle East Journal,* vol. 35, no. 2 (Spring 1981), pp. 178–190.

Constitution of the People's Democratic Party of Afghanistan

The original of this document was given to Theodore L. Eliot, Jr., the American ambassador to Afghanistan, in June 1978 by someone he trusted. It was translated from Dari into English by the embassy, and a report about it was cabled to the State Department on June 19, 1978 (confidential telegram no. 4946 from Kabul). In the cable, Bruce Amstutz, deputy chief of mission, said: "We believe that the 'constitution' is a genuine party document, but we are unsure of its date. We are fairly certain the document predates the coup two months ago, and conceivably it is the PDPA's founding document dating from 1965. Whatever the case, it constitutes one further indication that the organization wielding political power in this country is a pro-Soviet type political party."

James E. Taylor, an officer in the embassy at that time, cleared the document for transmission to the State Department. He said in an interview that there was no doubt in his mind at the time—or now—that the document was genuine. I obtained the constitution under the Freedom of Information Act. At the time of this writing it has not, as far as I know, been publicly available in any language.

It is interesting to note how similar the constitution is to the Rules of the Communist Party of the Soviet Union (CPSU). This is perhaps most striking in the organizational structure of the Afghan party, which apes its Soviet counterpart with a general secretary, Politburo, Secretariat, Party Control Commission, Central Revision (Supervisory) Commission, Central Committee, Congress, cell, and so on. The similarities are also noticeable in the section describing the duties and rights of party members and in the section on "democratic centralism," where the wording of the two documents is almost identical. They are alike from beginning to end, but this is not to say that the Afghan constitution is little more than a translation of the Soviet party rules. Rather, one gets the impression that an educated, articulate Afghan (perhaps Taraki) studied the CPSU rules carefully and then proceeded to adapt them, in his own words, to Afghan conditions.

Those wishing to compare this document with the rules of the CPSU can consult any of the English translations, such as: Robert H. McNeal (ed.), *Resolutions and Decisions of the Communist Party of the Soviet Union,* vol. 4, *The Khrushchev Years, 1953–1964* (Toronto: University of Toronto Press, 1974), pp. 264–280. These pages contain the rules adopted at the 22nd Party Congress on October 31, 1961.

Anyone in the American Embassy in Kabul or in the State Department who was familiar with the Soviet Communist party should have been able immediately to see that the People's Democratic Party of Afghanistan was organized along traditional communist party lines. He or she would also have been tipped off by the statement that the ideology of the PDPA is Marxism-Leninism and by the requirement that party members strengthen "the friendly relations between Afghans and Soviets."

The translation by the embassy was not a finished product; it contained many awkward sentences and other mistakes in English. I did not have the original document in Dari and thus was unable to have it translated again; the best I could do was to try to put this translation into reasonably good English, without changing the meaning. For some unknown reason there is no Article 13. I cannot say whether this is because Afghans consider 13 an unlucky number, the translator skipped it, or there was a mistake in the numbering.

This version of the constitution was sent to the State Department as an attachment to airgram no. 60 on July 3, 1978.

Constitution of the People's Democratic Party of Afghanistan
(the party of the working class of Afghanistan)

The People's Democratic Party of Afghanistan:

Article 1. The PDPA is the highest political organ and the vanguard of the working class and all laborers in Afghanistan. The PDPA, whose ideology is the practical experience of Marxism-Leninism, is founded on the voluntary union of the progressive and informed people of Afghanistan: the workers, peasants, artisans, and intellectuals of the country.

MEMBERSHIP

Conditions of Membership

Article 2. Any Afghan subject who has reached the age of 18 and has not acted against the interests and freedom of the people; who accepts the ideological objectives and constitution of the Party and struggles for its realization; who participates and works in one of the active Party organizations; who observes and executes the resolutions and decisions of the Party and accepts the terms of membership can become a member of the Party.

Acceptance of Membership in the Party

Article 3. The conditions of acceptance for membership in the Party are as follows:

a. Acceptance of membership can only take place on an individual basis through the cell. The Central Committee in exceptional cases can accept the group membership of candidates.
b. Confirmation of membership is granted by the Central Committee or an official authorized by it to do so.
c. A candidate for membership must be introduced by two full members of the Party who have served a minimum of one year in the Party. The sponsors must be thoroughly acquainted with the candidate's former political, social, and moral connections and be able to guarantee his character, competence, and performance to the Party.
d. The candidate must present his own written application to the relevant Party organization.
e. The candidate will spend a probationary period furthering his Party education, raising the level of political and ideological awareness and broadening his outlook of the party's objectives and constitution. The candidate, depending on his class, will spend between 4 months and 1 year on probation and after completing his probation, can be accepted as a full member of the Party.
f. Party probationers, with the exception of the right to be elected and electing, have equal rights and duties with full members of the Party, and in Party sessions are given a consultative vote.

g. The necessity of a probationer participating in a cell and his role in the Party is subject to the view of the relevant Party organization.

h. The Party record of a member is held in abeyance until the competent authority approves his full membership.

i. If a probationer during his probationary period does not show his worth to the full membership, the official or relevant organization shall either reject his application for membership or extend his period of probation.

j. The procedure of acceptance for probationers and full-members shall be the same.

Membership Cards

Article 4. The regulation and distribution of membership cards is the responsibiliry of a member of the Central Committee or an official authorized by them. The distribution of membership cards is subject to conditions and circumstances.

Duties of Party Members

Article 5. Every Party member is responsible for:

a. raising his own ideological awareness and learning the political theories of Marxism-Leninism; endeavoring to strengthen ideological solidarity, party organization and unity; combatting any action that, either within or outside the Party, harms the interests of the Party; rejecting enemies of the workers, the People's Party, and the nation; and struggling against colonialism and all social and national difficulties.

b. observing the Party constitution, regulations, and discipline; disseminating and propagating the general and current party objectives and policies among the people and striving for their realization.

c. participating regularly in the activities of the relevant organizations; acting sincerely, decisively, forcefully, and without deviation for the party's aims, objectives, goals, and in accord with instructions; paying membership fees regularly; holding comradely Party functions among members; and creating within the Party a spirit of comradeship, cooperation, and brotherhood.

d. propagating the thoughts of scientific socialism, the ideas of proletarian rationalism and internationalism among the masses.

e. struggling to strengthen the unity of the masses, toilers, and brothers resident in our unique country of Afghanistan in the cause of complete equality of rights, the brotherly cooperation of all the people, tribes, and ethnic groups of Afghanistan, both large and small, and for their solidarity within the organizations of the laborers, both political organizations (the Party of the entire proletariat of Afghanistan) and workers, peasants, cooperatives, cultural, women's, youth, and student's unions.

f. expanding and strengthening Afghan/Soviet friendly relations and such relations between Afghanistan and the socialist fraternity, international workers' movements, peoples' liberation movements of Asia, Africa, and Latin America; and fulfilling Afghanistan's nationalist and internationalist duties.

g. setting an example in encounters with people of being sincere, humble, diligent, and accomplished, and in one's own personal and social life of being progressive in speech and deed; knowing the wishes of the people and striving for the influence and esteem of the party among the people.

h. attracting the informed and active elements of all classes and the laborers to the Party and giving them instruction about the Party's structure and organization.

i. protecting the Party's secrets stringently and at all times being vigilant and firm against infiltrators; and defending the Party against the influence of anti-populist elements and deviationists.

j. developing and expanding criticism (in general) and self-criticism and correcting and pursuing mistakes that veer from the path of true criticism.

k. combating from within the Party all manifestations and inclinations toward factionalism, splinter groups, regionalism, chauvinism, local nationalism, revisionism, demagogy, any kind of rightist or leftist opportunism, liberalism, and subjectivism. Giving priority to the interests of the Party and the people. Being honest and correct toward the Party and the people. In choosing an individual for Party duties and responsibilities, taking into consideration their ability, honesty, quality, awareness, and class background.

Rights of Party Members

Article 6. Every Party member has the right to:

a. participate in elections of Party officials as an elector or electee.

b. participate in debates and resolution of problems concerning the policies and scientific activities of the Party, in party sessions and publications. Until the relevant Party organizations and officials take a decision on a matter under discussion, active participation and free expression will be allowed.

c. have their suggestions, criticisms, and questions passed to Party authorities including the Central Committee. Inside the sessions of the organizations a member, whatever his position, may criticize the actions of party officials.

d. participate in all sessions where actions or deeds or methods are under scrutiny. Whenever the aims of the Party authorities are not deemed wise or methodical and are subject to protest, a member can present his complaints to the higher Party authorities including the Congress.

Note 1: Under certain conditions it is possible for a Party member to investigate actions or deeds.

Note 2: Under certain conditions it is possible for a Party member to be denied permission to attend a meeting at which his own actions are being investigated.

THE STRUCTURE OF PARTY ORGANIZATIONS

Article 7. The main principle and guideline of the structure of the PDPA is democratic centralism, whose basic features are as follows:

a. Party leaders from the highest to the lowest levels are elected through an open ballot or a closed ballot when necessary.

b. the presentation of a report by Party officials to relevant organizations and to a higher Party authority.

c. adherence of the minority to the majority on Party decisions and instructions and the strict observance of Party discipline by all individuals in all positions.

d. adherence of lower officials to the decisions of higher officials.

e. enforcement of collective basic leadership and individual responsibility.

Article 8. Party leaders from the highest to the lowest level must avoid individualistic and bureaucratic methods. A logical proportion between Party centralism and democracy is to be preserved, based on the difficulty of Party activities and the spread of criticism against the Party. Incorrect methods of action are to be eliminated. In the performance of duties, initiative, creativity, and informed discipline are to be shown among Party members. Any manifestation of liberalism, troublemaking, personality cults, splinter groups, or internal Party factions that in any shape or form appear within the Party are to be prevented, and centralism, linked to democracy, is to be established and strengthened.

Article 9. The competence and responsibility of the Party leadership may be expanded as required by the necessity of furthering the Party's affairs and protecting Party organizations. The appointment to a position of senior officials or individuals at all levels who, in principle, have been elected, can be made. The relevant authorities may take the following points into consideration:

   a. The correct method or procedure for utilizing the cadres and Party officials should be based on basic performance, ability, and awareness in relevant matters and political reliance on these—not on personal considerations and inclinations.
   b. The organization responsible for Party vigilance can in no way permit destructive elements to influence the party.
   c. Complete precision in regard to the views and suggestions of Party members.
   d. Precise and correct implementation of the decisions of Party authorities.

Article 10. The organizational divisions of the Party are as follows: Provincial, city, woluswali,* and district organizations. Under certain circumstances, on the recommendation of the provincial committee and the agreement of the Central Committee, other organizations can also be established. Any one of these organizations can make decisions on local problems provided that they do not defy general Party policies and the decisions of their superior authorities. The limits of the actions of any one of these groups is set by higher authorities.

THE HIGHEST PARTY AUTHORITY

The Party Congress

Article 11. The highest Party authority of the PDPA is the Party Congress, which is comprised of representatives elected by provincial conferences. In normal circumstances, the Party Congress will meet once every four years. If necessary or in unusual circumstances, it is possible for the Central Committee to decide to invite the Congress to assemble earlier or later than the appointed time. An Extraordinary Party Congress may take place on the decision of the Central Committee or on the basis of a proposal by two-thirds of the Party members. The Congress is officially competent only when a majority of elected members, that is to say more than one-half of the Party representatives, are present at a session. A number of Congress representatives, proportional to the number of Party members and relevant organizations, are appointed to the Central Committee.

Article 12. The duties and jurisdiction of the Party Congress consist of:

   a. hearing the report of the Central Committee and the Central Supervisory Commission, debating and assessing their findings, and ratifying them.
   b. revising, reforming, changing, and ratifying the Party's objectives and constitution.
   c. setting Party policy.
   d. electing full and alternate members to the Central Committee and Central Supervisory Commission.

---

*A woluswali is a subprovince.

e. establishing the number of full and alternate members of the Central Committee and Central Supervisory Commission.

[There is no Article 13.]

The Central Committee

Article 14. The Central Committee of the Party is the highest authority after the Party Congress.

The Central Committee during the period between two Congress meetings is responsible for relations with other parties and political organizations. The Central Committee, while accountable to the Congress, leads and administers the political establishment and activity and organization of the Party; and is responsible for the financial administration, overseeing the publication of Party publications, and Party participation in the Parliament.

The Central Committee is responsible for organizing subordinate organizations, Party committees, and Party members in setting up relevant organizations, that is, mass organizations such as workers' unions, peasants, artisans, cooperatives, unions for low-ranking officials, teachers, lecturers, doctors, students, youth and women, cultural and sports clubs, etc. If any such organizations are founded by other organizations it is essentially in line with Party policy to actively participate in the former.

Article 15. If for any reason the place of some full member of the Central Committee is vacated or if it becomes necessary for the number of Central Committee members to be increased by a fixed number, then the Central Committee can by a two-thirds majority vote appoint to full membership any of its substitute members.

However, if necessary or in extraordinary cases the Central Committee is empowered to appoint outstanding individuals in the Party Membership to full membership in the Central Committee or alternate membership. The basic condition in appointing or electing full or alternate members of the Central Committee is that they have at least two years of previous Party service.

Article 16. The Central Committee can choose from its own members the members of the Political Bureau of the Central Committee and members of the Secretariat of the Central Committee and the General Secretary of the Central Committee, who is also a member of the Political Bureau.

Article 17. The Plenum of the Central Committee, in order to form the Second Congress of the PDPA and to elect the Central Supervisory Commission, elects from the Congress as full and alternate members the Supervisory and Control Commission and its officials.

Article 18. The Central Committee as necessary sets up branch organizations for propaganda, theory and education, finance, international affairs, and mass organizations. The Central Committee can also as necessary set up other branches and commissions, either permanent or temporary. The officials of these commissions elect the Political Bureau from the full members of the Central Committee.

Article 19. The Plenum of the Central Committee will, under normal circumstances, meet at least three times a year. Alternate members will participate in the Plenum of the Central Committee and will have the right to a consultative vote.

Article 20. The Central Committee can raise for free discussion and Party advice some of the Party's problems.

Article 21. The Political Bureau in the period between Central Committee meetings administers and heads the Party's activities and affairs, and is responsible to the Central Committee.

Article 22. The Secretariat of the Central Committee during the period between the meetings of the Political Bureau conducts the current affairs of the Central Committee. The Secretariat prepares the ways and means of carrying out the decisions of the supreme authorities of the Party leadership and supervises and researches their precise execution. The Secretariat is responsible to the Political Bureau. The Commissions and Departments of the Central Committee operate, execute, and serve under the supervision of the Secretariat.

The Central Supervisory and Control Commission

Article 23. The Central Supervisory and Control Commission has the following duties:

    a. supervision of the current affairs of the Central organs.
    b. supervision over the Central Committee's financial affairs
    c. ensuring the observance by Party members and probationary members of Party discipline and unity and correct execution of Central Committee decisions; and taking action against those Party members who infringe the Party's objectives, constitution, regulations or code.
    d. investigation into the general complaints of Party members from Party organizations sentenced to be punished and seeking litigation.

Party Conferences

Article 24. During the period between two Congresses, the Central Committee can invite Party conferences formed of representatives of the committees of provincial, urban, woluswali, and district organizations, to debate and discuss problems relating to practical policies and other essential problems. The Central Committee appoints a number of its representatives.

Provincial, Urban, Woluswali, and District Organizations

Article 25. Provincial, urban, woluswali, and district organizations are to be guided in their actions by the objectives and constitution of the Party. They are to propagate Party policies and execute all decisions and instructions of the Central Committee and their own superior authorities, be it provincial, urban, woluswali, or regional. The basic duties of the provincial, urban, woluswali, and regional organizations and their leading officials consist of:

    a. organizational and political work among the masses.
    b. striving to realize the objectives and goals of the Party and raising the level of political and class awareness of the workers and actively participating in the organization of the masses.
    c. regulating ideological work, propagating practical socialism, and distributing Party publications and pamphlets.
    d. conforming to the constitution, selecting and spotting outstanding individuals and adjusting them to progressive, honest and true thoughts and beliefs, and feelings of loyalty and responsibility to the people's nation and Party.
    e. the circulation and propagation of the Party's objectives, publications, and pamphlets in the language of the people of the region.

THE SUPREME AUTHORITIES OF THE PROVINCIAL, URBAN, WOLUSWALI, AND DISTRICT ORGANIZATIONS

Conferences

Article 26. The highest authority of the provincial, urban, woluswali, and district organizations is the conference. Provincial conferences under favorable conditions are invited by their respective committees to take place once every two years and urban, woluswali, and regional conferences, under favorable conditions, are held annually. Extraordinary conferences are formed on the decision of the superior committee or the majority of members of the relevant organization.

Article 27. The conferences of the provincial, urban, woluswali, and district organizations invite the elected representatives of every organization based on a proportion of those who have been appointed or the recommendation of the organization's committee and the approval of the superior authorities.

Article 28. The competence and duties of the provincial, urban, woluswali, and district conferences consists of:

   a. hearing, discussing, assessing, and ratifying the report of the relevant committee or supervisory commission.
   b. adopting a decision on the problems and affairs of the relevant organization and its future course of action.
   c. electing representatives for the conferences of superior organizations and electing members to the relevant organization's committees and supervisory commission.

   Note: A provincial conference elects a representative to the Party Congress.

Committees

Article 29. Provincial, urban, woluswali, and district committees are the highest authority of the relevant organizations during the period between the two conferences.

Article 30. The provincial, urban, woluswali, and district committees elect their secretaries and assistant secretaries from among their own members.

Article 31. The provincial, urban, woluswali, and district committees establish branches for organization, propaganda, theory, and financial instruction and any other necessary branches. The officials of these branches are appointed by the members of the committee. The secretaries and assistant secretaries of the committee supervise these branches.

Article 32. The provincial, urban, woluswali, and district committees form their subordinate organizations, leadership, and new organizations. The committees carry out the decisions of the conference according to the instructions of superior authorities and they are responsible to the latter.

Article 33. The secretaries and assistant secretaries undertake the duties of carrying out the current business of the relevant committees and are responsible to the committee. They investigate and supervise the ways and means of executing the decisions of the leadership as well as preparing and correctly putting into practice such decisions.

   Provincial, urban, woluswali, and district committees assemble at least once a month.

Supervisory and Control Commission

Article 34. Members of the Supervisory and Control Commission are elected at general meetings of the relevant organizations at the provincial, urban, woluswali, and district levels to form a relevant conference from the members of the appropriate committees. The Supervisory and Control Commissions carry out the duties of the Central Supervisory and Control Commission with, of course, the difference that every Supervisory and Control Commission has competence and responsibility for its own organization's and committee's activities.

Primary Organization of the Party (or cell)

Article 35. The primary organization of the Party consists of the cell, which is to be considered the essential foundation of the Party. Cells are founded by local action and local residence. A Party cell is formed with the approval of the provincial, urban, woluswali, or district committee or of higher authorities. Depending on the circumstances, the maximum number of individuals in a cell will be determined by higher authorities.

Article 36. Whenever the number of cells is increased as a result of local action or residence at the district level, subsidiary committees for local action and residence can, with the agreement of superior authorities, be formed and are subject to the district organization. Members of these committees are elected in public meetings of the cells or in meetings of the district representatives.

Article 37. The cell will meet at least twice a month. At a cell meeting, the secretary and assistant secretary will be appointed for a term of one year.

Article 38. The cell will be guided in its work by the Party objectives and constitution, will propagate the Party's policies, and execute all the decisions and instructions of the superior authorities. The cell forges the link between the leadership and Party members, the Party with the people, and establishes close relations with the masses. The cell, mindful of Article 26, has responsibility for:

a. recruiting new members to the Party membership and investigating all aspects of the background of Party members, strengthening Party discipline among all cell members, distributing Party publications and pamphlets, and regulating the education of cell members.
b. paying constant attention to the feelings and wishes of the people and reporting them to the superior Party authorities. Paying complete attention to the economic, social, political, and cultural living conditions of the masses and relating them to the Party instructions or struggling for the people's desires.

DESTINY AND PUNISHMENT

Destiny

Article 39. Party members through their actions, testimony, loyalty, and sacrifice are destined to achieve observance of the regulations, discipline, original action, ethics, objectives, and policies of the Party, and the decisions of the superior Party organizations and Central Committee for the sake of the goals of the Party.

Punishment

Article 40. Party organizations from top to bottom can, according to circumstances and conditions, take the following legal decisions concerning an infringement of the decisions of superior Party authorities, the aims of the Central Committee, a violation of the objectives and constitution or discipline of the Party, a transgression of the party regulations, or not carrying out one's Party duties. Punishments may be the following: private verbal reprimand or public written reprimand; demotion by one or several ranks of a responsible Party member; change a full member into a probationary member; suspension of Party membership or expel the member from the Party.

Article 41. If a full or probationary member of the Party does not pay his membership dues for three months without presenting an acceptable excuse or does not attend Party meetings on three successive occasions without a reasonable excuse and after a reprimand and warning does not heed Party regulations, he can be expelled from the Party on the recommendation of relevant authorities.

Article 42. Any Party organization at any level or position can, bearing in mind the difficulty of the struggle, act under Article 41 against any member violating Party regulations and report him to higher authorities. The higher authorities are entitled to specify the punishment appropriate to the infringement. They may also acquit, reduce, or increase the punishment.

Article 43. In cases where a violation by a Party member has seriously damaged the unity, dependence, prestige, or existence of the Party, the guilty individual will be expelled from the Party. Every Party entity is entitled to expel a particular Party member, although the ultimate competence lies with the Central Committee or the authorities that are given such discretion by the Central Committee.

Article 44. Expulsion from the Party is considered the maximum and most severe judgement of the Party. All Party organizations when adopting a decision to approve an expulsion will take careful note of all brotherly remarks and observations; witnesses and relevant documents will be carefully studied and investigated. The accused's complaints will be given careful attention, and his mental inclinations, personal motives, and abuse of position will be seriously studied.

Article 45. A convicted member must be informed of the reasons for conviction and if he thinks the sentence unjust, he may protest and demand a retrial of the relevant authorities or complain to higher authorities.

Article 46. In expelling a full or alternate member of the Central Committee from the Central Committee or the Party, the Plenum of the Central Committee must take the decision, and this decision must be reached by a two-thirds vote of the full membership of the Central Committee.

Resignation of Party Membership

Article 47. Whenever a full or probationary member of the Party wishes to resign, he must tender his resignation letter to the relevant organization. Whenever a Party member is the perpetrator of a clear violation of the Party's constitution, regulations, or discipline and wishes to resign, acceptance of his resignation is equal to expulsion from the Party.

Financial Matters of the Party

Article 48. The Party's funds will come from membership dues, the sale of Party publications and pamphlets, and the contributions of Party members or the people.

Article 49. The extent of full and probationary membership and the inclusion of members in the Party will be determined by the Central Committee.

Article 50. The Central Committee has the right to determine how the Party's funds will be used.

Relations of the Party and the Electoral Organizations of the Country

Article 51. Participation in the elections for organizations and electoral organizations is subject to the agreement of provincial, urban, woluswali and district committees. The activities of Party members in electoral organizations is subject to the practical policies of the Party.

Bibliography

INTERVIEWS

Archer K. Blood, former chargé d'affaires, American Embassy, Kabul. (December 16, 1981)

Henry Bradsher, former correspondent in Afghanistan for the *Washington Star*. (September 1980 through May 1981)

Zbigniew Brzezinski, national security adviser in the Carter administration. (November 3, 1981; November 12, 1981; December 4, 1981; January 4, 1982)

Warren Christopher, deputy secretary of state in the Carter administration. (April 14, 1982)

Confidential interview with former U.S. intelligence officer. (1981)

Confidential interview with State Department official. (1980)

Alvin J. Cottrell, Center for Strategic and International Studies, Georgetown University. (December 12, 1980)

Gary Crocker, expert on military affairs in Afghanistan, Department of State. (Spring and summer 1981)

Louis Dupree, leading scholar on Afghanistan; representative of Universities Field Staff International in South Asia. (December 1980)

Colonel James Edgar, military attaché in Kabul from 1977 to 1979. (September 17, 1980)

Theodore L. Eliot, Jr., former American ambassador to Afghanistan. (August 13, 1980)

Bruce Flatin, former political counselor in the American Embassy, Kabul. (September 3, 1980; January 12, 1981)

Melvin Goodman, specialist on Afghanistan for Central Intelligence Agency. (September 22, 1980)

Ernestine Heck, Afghan desk officer, Department of State. (November 1980 through February 1982)

Paul Henze, specialist on the Middle East for the National Security Council during the Carter administration. (November 24, 1981)

Alan Hetmanek, specialist on Central Asia, formerly with the Library of Congress. (May 29, 1981)

Rear Admiral Robert P. Hilton, vice-director, operations, U.S. Joint Chiefs of Staff; specialist on Soviet military affairs. (December 5, 1981)

Zalmay Kalilzad, assistant professor of political science, Columbia University. (December 4, 1980)

Habibullah Karzai, high-ranking member of the Popolzai tribe, now in exile. (November 30, 1980)

Malcolm Mackintosh, Soviet specialist in the British Cabinet Office. (November 5, 1980)

John M. Maury, chief of Soviet operations at Central Intelligence Agency for eight years. (1980–1981)

James Arnold Miller, specialist on world mineral supplies. (June 18, 1981)

Eden Naby, associate of the Center for Middle Eastern Studies, Harvard University. (August 14, 1980)

Robert G. Neumann, former American ambassador to Afghanistan. (September 4, 1980)

Richard Newell, professor of history, University of Northern Iowa, specialist on Afghanistan. (Fall 1981)

Rouhollah K. Ramazani, professor of government and foreign affairs, University of Virginia, specialist on the Middle East. (1980–1983)

Karen Eide Rawling, director of the International Affairs Program, University of Maryland, specialist on Afghanistan. (November 29, 1980)

Dana Adams Schmidt, former foreign correspondent covering the Middle East. (September 25, 1980)

Marshall Shulman, formerly chief adviser on Soviet affairs for Secretary of State Vance; director of the Russian Institute, Columbia University. (August 6, 1981; November 15, 1981)

Gaston Sigur, director of the Institute for Sino-Soviet Studies, George Washington University; formerly representative of the Asia Foundation in Afghanistan. (September 2, 1980; December 2, 1980; May 27, 1981)

James E. Taylor, Department of State, formerly stationed in the American Embassy in Kabul. (October 27, 1981)

Cyrus R. Vance, secretary of state in the Carter administration. (January 6, 1982)

Eliza Van Hollen, specialist on Afghanistan for the State Department. (January through October 1981)

Robert G. Weinland, specialist on Soviet military affairs, Center for Naval Analyses. (November 24, 1980)

Malcolm Yapp, School of Oriental and African Studies, University of London. (November 5, 1980)

UNPUBLISHED DOCUMENTS

The author obtained many unpublished State Department documents under the Freedom of Information Act. These documents were formerly classified—many of them "secret"—and consist mainly of cables from the American Embassy in Kabul to the Department of State. They deal with developments inside Afghanistan and with Afghan-American relations for the years 1971–1979.

PRINCIPAL PUBLISHED SOURCES

Federal Broadcast Information Service (FBIS).

This gold mine of data, published daily by the U.S. government, consists of translations of radio broadcasts, newspaper stories, press-agency reports, and miscellaneous other sources. Afghanistan is now covered in the South Asia Series, but formerly was included in the Middle East and North Africa Series. The Soviet Union has its own separate series. *FBIS* is especially valuable for obtaining the texts of speeches by important Afghan officials and other official governmental pronouncements. However, it also includes reports from sources outside of Afghanistan.

Kabul Times.

Published daily in English by the Afghan government, it contains a wealth of details about goings-on in the country. Written from the government point of view, it is nevertheless a very valuable source, although difficult to find in the United States. After the Soviet invasion, the name was changed to *Kabul New Times.*

BOOKS AND PAMPHLETS

Adamec, Ludwig W. *Afghanistan's Foreign Affairs to the Mid-Twentieth Century; Relations with the USSR, Germany, and Britain.* Tucson: University of Arizona Press, 1974.

Agabekov, Georges [Grigorii S.], *OGPU: The Russian Secret Terror.* New York: Brentano's, 1931.

Akademiia Nauk SSSR, Institut Vostokovedeniia. *Sovremennyi Afganistan.* Edited by N. A. Dvoriankov. Moscow. Izdatelstvo vostochnoi literatury, 1960.

Akhramovich, R. T., ed. *Nezavisimyi Afganistan; 40 let nezavisimosti; sbornik statei.* Moscow: Izdatelstvo vostochnoi literatury, 1958.

Arnold, Anthony. *Afghanistan: The Soviet Invasion in Perspective.* Stanford, Calif.: Hoover Institution Press, 1981.

Aspaturian, Vernon; Dallin, Alexander; and Valenta, Jiri. *The Soviet Invasion of Afghanistan: Three Perspectives.* Los Angeles: Center for International and Strategic Affairs, University of California at Los Angeles, 1980.

Barmine, Alexander. *One Who Survived: The Life Story of a Russian Under the Soviets.* New York: Putnam's, 1945.

Becker, Seymour. *Russia's Protectorates in Central Asia: Bukhara and Khiva, 1865–1924.* Cambridge: Harvard University Press, 1968.

Bradsher, Henry S. *Afghanistan and the Soviet Union.* Durham, N.C.: Duke University Press, 1983.

Brzezinski, Zbigniew. *Power and Principle: Memoirs of the National Security Adviser, 1977–1981.* New York: Farrar, Straus, Giroux, 1983.

Carter, Jimmy. *Keeping Faith.* New York: Bantam Books, 1982.

Chaliand, Gérard. *Report from Afghanistan.* Translated by Tamar Jacoby. New York: Viking, 1982.

Cottrell, Alvin J., ed. *The Persian Gulf States.* Baltimore, Md.: Johns Hopkins University Press, 1980.

Cronin, Richard P. *Afghanistan: Soviet Invasion and U.S. Response.* Washington, D.C.: Library of Congress, Congressional Research Service, Issue Brief No. IB80006, 1981.

Democratic Republic of Afghanistan Annual, 1979. Kabul: Government Printing Press, 1979.

Dubinskii, Ilia V. *Primakov.* Moscow: "Molodaia Gvardiia," 1968.

Dupree, Louis. *Afghanistan.* Princeton, N.J.: Princeton University Press, 1980.

_____ . *Afghanistan: 1980.* Hanover, N.H.: American Universities Field Staff Reports, 1980/no. 37, Asia.

_____ . *Afghanistan 1977: Does Trade Plus Aid Guarantee Development?* Hanover, N.H.: American Universities Field Staff Reports, vol. 21, no. 3 (August 1977), South Asia.

_____ . *The Democratic Republic of Afghanistan, 1979.* Hanover, N.H.: American Universities Field Staff Reports, 1979/no. 32, Asia.

_____ . *Militant Islam and Traditional Warfare in Islamic South Asia.* Hanover, N.H.: American Universities Field Staff Reports, 1980/no. 21, Asia.

_____ . *Red Flag Over the Hindu Kush.* Part I: *Leftist Movements in Afghanistan.* Hanover, N.H.: American Universities Field Staff Reports, 1979/no. 44, Asia.

_____ . *Red Flag Over the Hindu Kush.* Part II: *The Accidental Coup, or Taraki in Blunderland.* Hanover, N.H.: American Universities Field Staff Reports, 1979/no. 45, Asia.

_____ . *Red Flag Over the Hindu Kush.* Part III: *Rhetoric and Reforms, or Promises! Promises!* Hanover, N.H.: American Universities Field Staff Reports, 1980/no. 23, Asia.

_____ . *Red Flag Over the Hindu Kush.* Part IV: *Foreign Policy and the Economy.* Hanover, N.H.: American Universities Field Staff Reports, 1980/no. 27, Asia.

_____ . *Red Flag Over the Hindu Kush.* Part V: *Repressions, or Security Through Terror Purges.* Hanover, N.H.: American Universities Field Staff Reports, 1980/no. 28, Asia.

_____ . *Towards Representative Government in Afghanistan.* Part II. Hanover, N.H.: American Universities Field Staff Reports, 1978/no. 14, Asia.

Dupree, Louis, and Albert, Linette, eds. *Afghanistan in the 1970s.* New York: Praeger, 1974.

Eudin, Xenia Joukoff, and North, Robert C. *Soviet Russia and the East, 1920–1927; A Documentary Survey.* Stanford, Calif.: Stanford University Press, 1957.

Fischer, Louis. *Men and Politics; An Autobiography.* New York: Duell, Sloan and Pearce, 1941.

_____ . *The Soviets in World Affairs.* 2 vols. London: Jonathan Cape, 1930.

Fraser-Tyler, Sir William Kerr. *Afghanistan: A Study of Political Developments in Central and Southern Asia.* 3d ed. New York: Oxford University Press, 1967.

Fukuyama, Francis. *The Future of the Soviet Role in Afghanistan: A Trip Report.* Santa Monica, Calif.: Rand Corporation, September 1980.

_____ . *The Security of Pakistan: A Trip Report.* Santa Monica, Calif.: Rand Corporation, September 1980.

Great Britain, House of Commons, Foreign Affairs Committee. *Afghanistan: The Soviet Invasion and Its Consequences for British Policy.* London: Her Majesty's Stationery Office, 1980.

Gregorian, Vartan. *The Emergence of Modern Afghanistan.* Stanford, Calif.: Stanford University Press, 1969.

Hammond, Thomas T., ed. *The Anatomy of Communist Takeovers.* Hew Haven, Conn.: Yale University Press, 1975.

Hetmanek, Allen, and Whelan, Joseph G. *Afghanistan Invasion: The Soviet Muslim Factor.* Washington, D.C.: Library of Congress, Congressional Research Service, Major Issues System, Issue Brief No. IB80019, March 20, 1980.

Kaplan, Stephen S. *Diplomacy of Power: Soviet Armed Forces as a Political Instrument.* Washington, D.C.: Brookings Institution, 1981.

Kapur, Harish. *Soviet Russia and Asia, 1917–1927: A Study of Soviet Policy Towards Turkey, Iran and Afghanistan.* Geneva: Michael Joseph, 1966.

Khrushchev, Nikita. *Khrushchev Remembers.* Boston: Little, Brown, 1970.

————. *Khrushchev Remembers: The Last Testament.* Boston: Little, Brown, 1974.

Kline, David. *Afghanistan: David Kline's Reports from Behind Rebel Lines on the Resistance to Moscow's Aggression.* Chicago: Call Publications, 1980.

Laqueur, Walter Z. *The Soviet Union and the Middle East.* New York: Praeger, 1959.

Monks, Alfred L. *The Soviet Intervention in Afghanistan.* Washington, D.C.: American Enterprise Institute, 1981.

Newell, Nancy Peabody, and Newell, Richard S. *The Struggle for Afghanistan.* Ithaca, N.Y.: Cornell University Press, 1981.

Newell, Richard S. *The Politics of Afghanistan.* Ithaca, N.Y.: Cornell University Press, 1972.

Nollau, Gunther, and Wiehe, Hans Jurgen. *Russia's South Flank; Soviet Operations in Iran, Turkey and Afghanistan.* New York: Praeger, 1963.

Park, Alexander. *Bolshevism in Turkestan, 1917–1927.* New York: Columbia University Press, 1957.

Pipes, Richard. *The Formation of the Soviet Union; Communism and Nationalism, 1917–1923.* Rev. ed. Cambridge: Harvard University Press, 1964.

Political Department of the People's Armed Forces of Afghanistan. *On the Saur Revolution.* Kabul: Government Printing Press, May 22, 1978.

Poullada, Leon B. *Reform and Rebellion in Afghanistan, 1919–1929; King Amanullah's Failure to Modernize a Tribal Society.* Ithaca, N.Y.: Cornell University Press, 1973.

Ramazani, Rouhollah K. *The Foreign Policy of Iran, A Developing Nation in World Affairs, 1500–1941.* Charlottesville: University Press of Virginia, 1966.

————. *Iran's Foreign Policy, 1941–1973: A Study of Foreign Policy in Modernizing Nations.* Charlottesville: University Press of Virginia, 1975.

————. *The Northern Tier: Afghanistan, Iran, and Turkey.* New York: Van Nostrand, 1966.

————. *The Persian Gulf and the Strait of Hormuz.* Alphen Aan den Rijn, Holland: Sijthoff & Nordhoff, 1979.

Seagrave, Sterling. *Yellow Rain: A Journey Through the Terror of Chemical Warfare.* New York: M. Evans, 1981.

Sontag, Raymond J., and Beddie, James S., eds. *Nazi-Soviet Relations, 1939–41; Documents from the Archives of the German Foreign Office.* Washington, D.C.: Department of State, 1948.

Sovetsko-afganskie otnoshenii, 1919–1969 gg. Dokumenty i materialy. Edited by V. M. Vinogradov and others. Moscow: Politizdat, 1971.

Tang, Peter S.H. *Russian and Soviet Policy in Manchuria and Outer Mongolia, 1911–1931.* Durham, N.C.: Duke University Press, 1959.

Teplinskii, Leonid B. *50 let sovetsko-afganskikh otnoshenii, 1919–1969.* Moscow: "Nauka," 1971.

The Truth About Afghanistan—Documents, Facts, Eyewitness Reports. Moscow: Novosti Press Agency Publishing House, 1980.

U.S. Congress, House of Representatives, Committee on Foreign Affairs, Subcommittee on Europe and the Middle East. *An Assessment of the Afghanistan Sanctions: Implications for Trade and Diplomacy in the 1980s.* Report prepared by Dr. John P. Hardt, Congressional Research Service. Washington, D.C.: Government Printing Office, April 1981.

————. *East-West Relations in the Aftermath of Soviet Invasion of Afghanistan.* Washington, D.C.: Government Printing Office, January 30, 1980.

————. *United States Policy and United States–Soviet Relations, 1979.* Washington, D.C.: Government Printing Office, 1979.

U.S. Department of Defense. *Soviet Military Power.* 2d ed. Washington, D.C.: Government Printing Office, March 1983.

U.S. Department of State. *Afghanistan: Soviet Invasion Attacked in U.N.* Washington, D.C.: Department of State, Current Policy No. 124, January 6, 1980.

————. *Background Notes: Afghanistan.* Washington, D.C.: Department of State, April 1980.

————. *Chemical Warfare in Southeast Asia and Afghanistan: Report to the Congress from Secretary of State Alexander M. Haig, Jr., March 22, 1982.* Washington, D.C.: Department of State, March 22, 1982.

————. *Soviet Invasion of Afghanistan.* Washington, D.C.: Department of State, Special Report No. 70, April 1980.

Valenta, Jiri. *Soviet Intervention in Czechoslovakia, 1968: Anatomy of a Decision.* Baltimore, Md.: Johns Hopkins University Press, 1979.

Vance, Cyrus. *Hard Choices: Critical Years in America's Foreign Policy.* New York: Simon and Schuster, 1983.

Van Hollen, Eliza. *Afghanistan: Three Years of Occupation.* Washington, D.C.: Department of State, Special Report No. 106, December 1982.

————. *Afghanistan: 2 Years of Occupation.* Washington, D.C.: Department of State, Special Report No. 91, December 1981.

————. *Afghanistan: A Year of Occupation.* Washington, D.C.: Department of State, Special Report No. 79, February 1981.

————. *Soviet Dilemmas in Afghanistan.* Washington, D.C.: Department of State, Special Report No. 72, June 1980.

Violations of Human Rights and Fundamental Freedoms in the Democratic Republic of Afghanistan. London: Amnesty International, 1979.

Weinland, Robert G. *An (The?) Explanation of the Soviet Invasion of Afghanistan.* Alexandria, Va.: Center for Naval Analyses, Professional Paper 309, May 1981.

————. *The Soviet Invasion of Afghanistan: Why Did They Do It? To What Extent Does It Represent a Harbinger of Things to Come in Southwest Asia?* Alexandria, Va.: Center for Naval Analyses, June 3, 1980.

Wilber, Donald N., ed. *Annotated Bibliography of Afghanistan.* 3d ed. New Haven, Conn.: Human Relations Area Files, 1968.

Wilber, Donald N., and others. *Afghanistan, Its People, Its Society, Its Culture.* New Haven, Conn.: Human Relations Area Files, 1962.

Wimbush, S. Enders, and Alexiev, Alex. *Soviet Central Asian Soldiers in Afghanistan.* Santa Monica, Calif.: Rand Corporation, January 1981.

ARTICLES, CHAPTERS IN BOOKS, AND UNPUBLISHED PAPERS

ABC, "20/20." "Afghanistan—The Secret War." Transcript of television program, June 18, 1981.

Arnett, Peter. "Report from a War Zone." *Parade Magazine* (February 20, 1983):12, 16, 19.

Aspaturian, Vernon V. "Superpower Maneuvers—Moscow's Afghan Gamble." *The New Leader* 63 (January 28, 1980):7–13.

Bennigsen, Alexandre. "Islam in the Soviet Union, the Religious Factor and the Nationality Problem in the Soviet Union." In *Religion and Atheism in the USSR and Eastern Europe*, edited by Bohdan Bociurkiw and John W. Strong, pp. 91–100. Toronto: University of Toronto Press, 1975.

————. "Soviet Muslims and the World of Islam." *Problems of Communism* 29 (March-April 1980):38–51.

Bernstein, Carl. "Arms for Afghanistan." *The New Republic* 185 (July 18, 1981):8–10.

Blechman, Barry M. "The Afghan Angle: Where Detente?" *Washington Quarterly* 3 (Autumn 1980):100–108.

Brown, Harold. "U.S. Security Policy in Southwest Asia: A Case Study in Complexity." Text of speech delivered at The Johns Hopkins School of Advanced International Studies, Washington, D.C., April 30, 1981.

Chaliand, Gérard. "Bargain War." *New York Review of Books* 28 (April 2, 1981):31–32.

————. "With the Afghan Rebels." *New York Review of Books* 27 (October 9, 1980):21–23.

Charters, David. "Coup and Consolidation: The Soviet Seizure of Power in Afghanistan." *Conflict Quarterly* 282 (Spring 1981):41–48.

Chubin, Shahram. "Leftist Forces in Iran." *Problems of Communism* 29 (July-August 1980):1–25.

————. "The Northern Tier in Disarray." *World Today* 35 (December 1979):474–482.

Critchlow, James. "Soviet Prospects: Minarets and Marx." *The Washington Quarterly* 3 (Spring 1980):47–57.

Dawisha, Karen. "The U.S.S.R. in the Middle East: Superpower in Eclipse?" *Foreign Affairs* 61 (Winter 1982/1983):438–452.

de Riencourt, Amaury. "India and Pakistan in the Shadow of Afghanistan." *Foreign Affairs* 61 (Winter 1982/1983):416–437.

Dil, Shaheen F. "The Cabal in Kabul: Great-Power Interaction in Afghanistan." *American Political Science Review* 71 (June 1977):468–476.

Donaldson, Robert H. "Soviet Involvement in South Asia and the Indian Ocean Region." In *Soviet Foreign Policy in the 1980s*, edited by Roger E. Kanet, pp. 330–349. New York: Praeger, 1982.

Dupree, Louis. "Afghanistan Under the *Khalq*." *Problems of Communism* 28 (July-August 1979):34–50.

————. "Inside Afghanistan: Yesterday and Today: A Strategic Appraisal." *Strategic Studies* (Islamabad) 2 (Spring 1979):64–83.

Eliot, Theodore L., Jr. "Afghanistan After the 1978 Revolution." *Strategic Review* 7 (Spring 1979):57–62.

————. "The 1978 Afghan Revolution: Some Internal Aspects." *The Fletcher Forum* 3 (Spring 1979):82–87.

Feshbach, Murray, and Rapawy, Stephen. "Soviet Population and Manpower Trends and Policies." In *The Soviet Economy in a New Perspective*. U.S. Congress, Joint Economic Committee, pp. 113–154. Washington, D.C.: Government Printing Office, 1976.

Furlong, R.D.M., and Winkler, Theodor. "The Soviet Invasion of Afghanistan." *International Defense Review* 13, no. 2 (March 1980):168–169.

Goldman, Minton F. "Carter Administration Policies and the Soviet Decision to Intervene in Afghanistan." Paper presented at the Southern Conference on Slavic Studies, Lexington, Kentucky, October 23, 1981.

Greenway, H.D.S. "Tales from the Land of the Pathans." *The Boston Globe Magazine* (June 28, 1981):8–9, 22–24.

Griffith, William E. "The Implications of Afghanistan." *Survival* (July-August 1980):146–151.

Haggerty, Jerome J. "Afghanistan—The Great Game." *Military Review* 60 (August 1980):37–44.

Halliday, Fred. "Afghanistan—A Revolution Consumes Itself." *The Nation* 229 (November 17, 1979):492–495.

————. "Revolution in Afghanistan." *New Left Review*, no. 112 (November-December, 1978):3–44.

————. "War and Revolution in Afghanistan." *New Left Review*, no. 119 (January-February 1980):20–41.

Harrison, Selig S. "Dateline Afghanistan: Exit Through Finland?" *Foreign Policy*, no. 41 (Winter 1980–1981):163–187.

————. "Fanning Flames in South Asia." *Foreign Policy*, no. 45 (Winter 1981–1982):84–102.

————. "Nightmare in Baluchistan." *Foreign Policy*, no. 32 (Fall 1978):136–160.

————. "Rough Plan Emerging for Afghan Peace." *New York Times*, July 12, 1982, p. A15.

Heller, Mark. "The Soviet Invasion of Afghanistan." *Washington Quarterly* 3 (Summer 1980):36–59.

Hopkins, Mark. "As Leaders Change: Arms and the Men in Moscow and Washington." *The New Leader* 63 (December 29, 1980):3–6.

Hough, Jerry F. "Why the Russians Invaded." *The Nation* 230 (March 1, 1980):225, 232–234.

Hyman, Anthony. "Afghanistan's Unpopular Revolution." *The Round Table*, no. 275 (July 1979):222–226.

Ignatov, Alexander. "Three Months of the Revolution." *New Times*, no. 35 (1978):27–30.

Kakar, Hasan. "The Fall of the Afghan Monarchy in 1973." *International Journal of Middle Eastern Studies* 9 (May 1978):195–214.

Kalilzad, Zalmay. "Soviet-Occupied Afghanistan." *Problems of Communism* 29 (November-December 1980):23–40.

––––––––. "The Struggle for Afghanistan." *Survey* 25 (Spring 1980):189–216.

Kazemzadeh, Firuz. "Afghanistan: The Imperial Dream." *New York Review of Books* 27 (February 21, 1980):10–14.

Keiser, R. Lincoln. "The Rebellion in Darra-i-Nur." Paper presented at the meeting of the American Anthropological Association, Washington, D.C., December 5, 1980.

Kenez, Peter. "Mobilizing the Public: What Russia is Reading About Afghanistan." *The New Leader* 63 (February 11, 1980):8–9.

Khan, Afzal. "With the Afghan Rebels." *The New York Times Magazine*, January 13, 1980, pp. 29–37, 48.

Kimura, Hiroshi. "The Impact of the Afghanistan Invasion on Japanese-Soviet Relations." In *Soviet Foreign Policy and East-West Relations*, edited by Roger E. Kanet, pp. 144–165. New York: Pergamon Press, 1982.

Klass, R. T. "The Great Game Revisited." *National Review* 31 (October 26, 1979):1366–1368.

Luttwak, Edward N. "After Afghanistan, What?" *Commentary* 69 (April 1980):40–49.

Medvedev, Roy. "The Afghan Crisis." *New Left Review*, no. 121 (May-June 1980):91–96.

Mehta, Jagat S. "A Neutral Solution." *Foreign Policy*, no. 47 (Summer 1982):139–153.

Mironov, L., and Polyakov, Genrikh. "Afghanistan: The Beginning of a New Life." *International Affairs* (Moscow) (March 1979):46–54.

Moss, Robert. "Reaching for Oil: The Soviets' Bold Mideast Strategy." *Saturday Review*, April 12, 1980, pp. 14–22.

Naby, Eden. "The Ethnic Factor in Soviet-Afghan Relations." *Asian Survey* 20 (March 1980):237–256.

Negaran, Hannah [pseud.]. "The Afghan Coup of April 1978: Revolution and International Security." *Orbis* 23 (Spring 1979):93–113.

––––––––. "Afghanistan: A Marxist Regime in a Muslim Society." *Current History* 76 (April 1979):172–175.

Neumann, Robert G. "Afghanistan." *Washington Review of Strategic and International Studies* 1 (July 1978):115–118.

––––––––. "Afghanistan Under the Red Flag." In *The Impact of the Iranian Events Upon Persian Gulf and U.S. Security*, edited by Z. Michael Szaz, pp. 128–148. Washington, D.C.: American Foreign Policy Institute, 1979.

Newell, Richard S. "Revolution and Revolt in Afghanistan." *The World Today* 35 (November 1979):432–442.

––––––––. "Soviet Intervention in Afghanistan." *The World Today* 36 (July 1980):250–258.

O'Ballance, Edgar. "Soviet Tactics in Afghanistan." *Military Review* 60 (August 1980):45–52.

Oren, Stephen. "The Afghani Coup and the Peace of the Northern Tier." *The World Today* 30 (January 1974):26–32.

Philips, James. "Afghanistan: Islam Versus Marxism." *Journal of Social and Political Studies* 4 (Winter 1979):305–320.

————. "Pakistan: The Rising Soviet Threat and Declining U.S. Credibility." The Heritage Foundation *Backgrounder* No. 122 (June 4, 1980): 23 pp.

Pipes, Richard, and Kennan, George. "How Real Is the Soviet Threat?" *U.S. News and World Report* (March 10, 1980):33.

Poullada, Leon B. "Afghanistan and the United States: The Crucial Years." *The Middle East Journal* 35 (Spring 1981):178–190.

————. "The Failure of American Diplomacy in Afghanistan." Mimeographed.

Press Release. "The President's State of the Union Address." January 23, 1980.

Public Broadcasting System. "MacNeil-Lehrer Report." "Afghanistan: War Continues." Transcript of television program, October 16, 1981.

Ramazani, R. K. "Security in the Perisan Gulf." *Foreign Affairs* 57 (Spring 1979):821–835.

————. "Weapons Can't Replace Words." *Newsweek*, September 22, 1980, p. 17.

Rubinstein, Alvin Z. "Afghanistan: Embraced by the Bear." *Orbis* 26 (Spring 1982):135–153.

————. "The Last Years of Peaceful Coexistence: Soviet-Afghan Relations, 1963–1978." *Middle East Journal* 36 (Spring 1982):1–13.

————. "Soviet Imperialism in Afghanistan." *Current History* 79 (October 1980):80–83, 103–104.

Rywkin, Michael. "Central Asia and Soviet Manpower." *Problems of Communism* 28 (January-February 1979):1–13.

Shabad, Theodore. "The Soviet Union and Afghanistan: Some Economic Aspects." Paper presented at the annual meeting of the American Association for the Advancement of Slavic Studies, Monterey, California, September 20, 1981.

Shahrani, Nazif. "Ethnic Relations Under Closed Frontier Conditions: Northeast Badakhshan." In *Soviet Asian Ethnic Frontiers*, edited by William O. McCagg, Jr., and Brian D. Silver, pp. 174–192. New York: Pergamon Press, 1979.

Shireff, David. "Afghanistan Keeps Its Plan Under Wraps." *Middle East Economic Digest* 20 (August 27, 1976):3–5.

Simons, Lewis M. "Standoff in Afghanistan." *The New Republic* 187 (August 16 and 23, 1982):23–25.

Smith, Hedrick. "Russia's Power Strategy." *The New York Times Magazine*, January 27, 1980, pp. 27–29, 42–47.

Sonnenfeldt, Helmut. "Afghanistan: Hard Choices for the U.S." *Worldview* 23 (June 1980):5–7.

————. "Implications of the Soviet Invasion of Afghanistan for East-West Relations." *NATO Review* 28 (April 1980):1–5.

"Soviet Military Involvement in Afghanistan." *Radio Liberty Research*, no. 365/79 (December 7, 1979).

Stockwin, Harvey. "A New Great Game? Consequences of the Coup in Kabul." *Round Table*, no. 271 (July 1978):242–252.

Teplinsky, Leonid. "The People Defend Their Revolution." *New Times*, no. 14 (April 1979):10–11.

"Top State Soviet Expert Sees Limited Reason for Invasion." *Defense/Space Daily* (February 12, 1980), p. 223.

Trofimenko, Henry (Genrikh Alexandrovich). "The Third World and the U.S.-Soviet Competition: A Soviet View." *Foreign Affairs* 59 (Summer 1981):1021–1040.

U.S. Department of State. "Reports of the Use of Chemical Weapons in Afghanistan, Laos and Kampuchea." Mimeographed. Washington, D.C.: Department of State, 1980.

————. "Update to the Compendium on the Reports of the Use of Chemical Weapons." Mimeographed. Washington, D.C.: Department of State, March 1981.

"U.S. Intervention in Afghanistan." *CounterSpy* 4 (October 1979):8–19.

Valenta, Jiri. "From Prague to Kabul; the Soviet Style of Invasion." *International Security* 5 (Fall 1980):114–141.

————. "The Soviet Invasion of Afghanistan: The Difficulty of Knowing Where to Stop." *Orbis* 24 (Summer 1980):201–218.

Van Praagh, David. "The Greater Game: Implications of the Afghan Coup." *International Perspectives* (March-April 1979):12–16.

Vertzberger, Yaacov. "Afghanistan in China's Policy." *Problems of Communism* 31 (May-June 1982):1–23.

Volsky, Dmitry. "The Target: Afghanistan's Revolution." *New Times*, no. 24 (1979):12–13.

Whitney, Craig. "The View From the Kremlin." *The New York Times Magazine*, April 20, 1980, pp. 30–33, 91–92.

Wimbush, S. Enders. "Afghanistan and the Muslims of the USSR." Paper delivered at the annual meeting of the American Association for the Advancement of Slavic Studies, Monterey, California, September 20, 1981.

"World Communist Solidarity With the Afghan Revolution." *New Times*, no. 3 (January 1980):8–10.

Zeray, Saleh M. "Afghanistan: The Beginning of a New Era." *World Marxist Review* 22 (January 1979):103–109.

NEWSPAPERS AND PERIODICALS USED

Aside from newspapers, the following list includes periodicals that publish anonymous articles and that are not cited above in the section "Articles, Chapters in Books, and Unpublished Papers."

Afghanistan Newsletter

Alarm: Alert Letter on the Availability of Raw Materials

Aviation Week and Space Technology

The *Boston Globe*

Charlottesville Daily Progress

The *Christian Science Monitor*

The *Economist*

Events: News Magazine of the Middle East
The *Far Eastern Economic Review*
FBIS Trends in Communist Media
The *International Herald Tribune*
Izvestiia
Komsomol'skaia pravda
Krasnaia zvezda
Literaturnaia gazeta
The *Los Angeles Times*
Middle East Research and Information Project Reports
The *New York Times*
News Leads: Afghanistan
Newsweek
Pravda
Soviet Analyst
Time
U.S. News and World Report
The *Wall Street Journal*
The *Washington Post*
The *Washington Star*

Index

Other Works by Thomas T. Hammond

Witnesses to the Origins of the Cold War

The Anatomy of Communist Takeovers

Soviet Foreign Relations and World Communism: A Selected, Annotated Bibliography of 7,000 Books in 30 Languages

Lenin on Trade Unions and Revolution, 1893–1917

Yugoslavia Between East and West